THE OTHER EVEREST

Navigating the Pathway
to Authentic Leadership

By David Irvine

GONDOLIER

THE OTHER EVEREST

Publication: July 2018

Published in Canada by
Gondolier, an imprint of Bayeux Arts Digital - Traditional Publishing
2403, 510 6th Avenue, S.E.
Calgary, Canada T2G 1L7
www.bayeux.com

Author: David Irvine
Email: david@davidirvine.com
www.davidirvine.com

Distributed by:
Literary Press Group of Canada
University of Chicago Press Distribution

Cover design by Fine Method Studios

Library and Archives Canada Cataloguing in Publication
Irvine, David, 1956-, author
     The other Everest : navigating the pathway to authentic leadership / David Irvine.

Issued in print and electronic formats.
ISBN 978-1-988440-28-6 (hardcover).—ISBN 978-1-988440-29-3 (softcover).—
ISBN 978-1-988440-30-9 (HTML)

     1. Leadership. 2. Business. 3. Organizational effectiveness. I. Title.
HD57.7.I78 2018   658.4'092   C2018-903344-4
                                                                  C2018-903345-2

The ongoing publishing activities of Bayeux Arts Digital - Traditional Publishing under its varied imprints are supported by the Government of Alberta, Alberta Multimedia Development Fund, and the Government of Canada through the Book Publishing Industry Development Program.

Alberta Culture   LIVRES CANADA BOOKS   Canadian Heritage   Patrimoine canadien

Printed in Canada

Praise for
David Irvine

"'Know thyself' is the most ancient and wise tenant of human psychology and an essential element of true authentic leadership. In "The Other Everest" David Irvine has provided the most complete and comprehensive roadmap for life and leadership that I have ever read in over fifty years on my own personal growth journey. Highly, highly recommended!"

— Jim Reger, Past President, The David Foster Foundation
(providing financial and emotional support across Canada
for families of children who require organ transplants)

"Join David Irvine on his travels through life toward authenticity. Take a journey toward your true self by accompanying others on their journeys. Their experiences will hearten and inform you."

— Geoff Bellman, Consultant and Author of *Your Signature Path* and
Getting Things Done When You Are Not in Charge

"The true essence of leadership is service and moral courage. Both service and moral courage are enhanced by authenticity. David Irvine has greatly facilitated our understanding of how to empower and synergize our collective productivity with The Authentic Leader."

— Dr. Len Marrella, Founder and President, Center for Leadership
and Ethics, and Author of *In Search of Ethics*

"David's works have meant a tremendous amount to me, both professionally and personally, as I manage my way through life as a father, husband, and leader in one of the most incredible and diverse industries imaginable. I recommend David highly to anyone who believes they are a student of life and career."

— Sean Durfy, Former President and CEO, WestJet

"When I heard David Irvine say that leadership is a personal choice, I had a hunch that his messages would resonate with Farm Credit Canada's leadership team. I was right... David's messages about authenticity, accountability, and balance are both practical and profound. In today's world where change is the norm and leaders are needed at every level in organizations, David's messages are powerful."

— Greg Stewart, Board of Directors
of the Bank of Canada

"You can do all you want in an organization about team building and training, but accountability and authenticity can only start with the individual. An individual's values, knowing who you are, need to be in sync with the values of their organization. This is David's strength—helping us get the internal alignment."

— Ed Rodenburg, Former President &
CEO, Lilydale Inc.

"David helps illuminate the difference between capriciously floating along and intentionally navigating a more satisfying course through life."

— Vincent Deberry, Executive Director,
University of Oklahoma,
Center for Public Management

"David's work has always resonated with me, particularly his insights into authentic leadership. Leadership starts with knowing deeply who we are; our beliefs, strengths, and talents, as well as our weaknesses and shortcomings. It's only through deep self-awareness that we can begin the journey to true leadership and be the kind of leader that people are willing to follow. David has impacted my life through his work and through his friendship."

— Tim O'Connor, CEO,
Results Canada Inc.

"The concepts underpinning 'The Other Everest' are simple, practical, actionable, and will provide immense support to an emerging breed of leaders who want to deliver incredible outcomes for their staff, shareholders, consumers, and the greater community. Those prepared to go deep and explore their authentic selves will scale their own Everest and can look forward to supporting and celebrating the successes that will come!"

— Adam Siegel, Executive Director, Visage Invest
Active Investment and Scaling Up Advisory,
Melbourne, Australia

"Organizations are at the forefront of our efforts to manage the resources available to us and the life-supporting environment that sustains them. And never before have we so desperately needed the authentic organizational leadership that David describes to make sure management succeeds in this effort. This book couldn't have come at a better time."

— Allan Savory, Founder and President, Savory Institute,
African Centre for Holistic Management

"*The Other Everest* is a very thoughtful and delightful read. Dave's a highly experienced coach helping readers find and energize their authentic self toward deeper and more lasting leadership. His unique blend of stories, frameworks, and practical how-to tips make this a highly inspiring and useful guide to finding your pathway."

— Jim Clemmer, Leadership Author, Speaker,
and Workshop/Retreat Leader

"This book will make you actually do what it advises: slow down, reflect, and reach inside yourself to clarify what you were put on this earth to do. As you move through its pages, you cannot help but reflect David's many stories back on yourself to draw insights from your own experience, to light the path ahead."

— Dr. Lauryn Oates, Professor, School of Humanitarian
Studies, Royal Roads University and Programs Director,
Canadian Women for Women in Afghanistan

To all those who have the courage to take the inner journey.

*"If we knew what was there we wouldn't have to go,
so we need to go to find out what's there."*

JACQUES COUSTEAU

*"You can sail around and around on the ocean for years,
But it is only when you dive in that you know the beauty of the sea."*

R. SHARATH JOIS

Contents

"The Core of Leadership Lies Within"

It's not the mountain we conquer but ourselves.
EDMUND HILLARY

Preface

Author's Note

In today's fast-paced, rapidly evolving business and professional environment, a high value is placed on looking outward and striving for the next summit. But there is also an inner journey that each of us must take if we are to reach our full potential with our lives and careers, families, communities, businesses, and organizations.

After more than thirty years of experience and research in the leadership development field, I have come to the conclusion that the world is in need of leaders who are committed to _substance_ over _superficial_, _character_ over _charisma_, and _service_ over _self-interest_. In short, we need leaders who are authentic—people whose inner compass guides their daily actions and inspire trust by being honest and real.

To come to this place of impact and influence requires slowing down, going inside, and developing a relationship with an interior self. It's about finding one's voice—away from the voices of the world. To attain the capacity to influence in today's changing and demanding world, along with the depth to lead with a strong, authentic presence, requires an _inner_ journey, a journey to one's heart, a journey to what I call the _"Other Everest."_

The Other Everest is as vast and formidable as any physical peak. It is just as important to our personal development and to the attainment of our own definitions of success as any outward pathway we may wish to pursue.

It's a journey that requires leaving our comfort zone at the surface and diving far within ourselves, often facing up to difficult questions and hard truths. But ultimately, it is an adventure that is rich in rewards, providing us with invaluable insights and guideposts toward becoming real, developing our leadership presence, and amplifying our impact—three key components to harnessing the power of authentic leadership.

Over my long career of connecting and communicating with CEOs, senior executives, entrepreneurs, companies, and organizations, I have come to the conclusion that the process of developing authentic leadership—of aligning who you are with how you lead—has never been more relevant to sustained success, growth, and continual improvement than it is today. The more we explore and develop our capacity for authentic leadership, the better we are as people for our families and communities, and the better equipped we are as leaders to help ourselves and our organizations adapt, innovate, and thrive in the face of ongoing change and new challenges.

Whether you are a CEO entrusted with an entire company, a supervisor committed to building a great team, a middle manager who oversees a division, a front-line healthcare professional, an entrepreneur, a parent, a coach, a teacher, a community volunteer, or a citizen dedicated to making a difference, we all have the potential to lead in our own unique ways and to develop our authentic leadership capacity. Along my own journey, I have come to know that true leadership is about *presence*, not position. It's about character, and it's about authenticity. Ultimately, authentic leadership is synonymous with being oneself. It's that simple, and it's also that difficult.

I have dedicated my professional life to helping people and teams navigate the pathway of authentic leadership. *The Other Everest* is a milestone book in my career for business leaders and anyone committed to their own personal growth, providing a synopsis of what I have learned. It draws upon the concepts, insights, and stories from all of my previous books, supplemented with fresh learnings and perspectives. It is designed as a down-to-earth, usable guide to help you develop and improve your authentic leadership approach. While I hope you find inspiration and opportunities for valuable self-reflection, this book also features a wealth of practical insights and approaches for business leaders and others committed to shaping better organizations, building better teams, developing better people, and getting better results.

The teachings and examples in this book will help you learn the essentials of authentic leadership, including insights and tools to assess and strengthen your authentic leadership approach. It will also help you develop ways to strengthen your presence and influence, by tapping into deeper levels of learning and self-awareness beyond mere methodology. Finally, it will help you maximize your potential by understanding and learning how to master six core accountabilities as a leader.

Perhaps most important, *The Other Everest* recognizes that the pathway to authentic leadership is a journey, not a destination. This book will provide you with a framework and the tools for lifelong improvement that you can come back to time and again ... to help you reach continually greater summits of success.

I hope you enjoy reading this book as much as I enjoyed writing it, often reminiscing with warmth and gratitude on the many people, experiences, and learnings that have immeasurably enriched my own journey over the years.

– DAVID IRVINE

Dualities

To reach our greatest outward potential,
we must first look deep within...

One of the profound mysteries of the world is the inherent duality of nature found both in the physical world and within ourselves.

The Earth's highest peak is Mount Everest, rising 8,848 meters above sea level.

Far lesser known, the Earth's deepest point is found in the Mariana Trench, a crescent-shaped scar in the Earth's crust located in the western Pacific Ocean, which virtually equals an inverted Everest at more than 8,000 meters below sea level.

The deepest part of the trench, a small slot-shaped valley in its floor known as the Challenger Deep, reaches a depth of 11,034 meters below sea level. At this point, if Mount Everest were dropped into the trench, its peak would still be over 1.6 km underwater.

As people, we tend to look outward and upward to the achievements we hope to realize.

But success isn't just about height. It's about depth.

The journey down ... the journey within ... is equally important.

By looking within ourselves to identify our authentic values, passions, and strengths, we open the door to our greatest potential for meaning, fulfillment, and true success.

By diving down to the bottom, we learn the fundamental truths to help us reach our greatest heights.

Are you ready to take the journey?

Compass

*David's key concepts for navigating
the pathway to authentic leadership.*

The journey toward authentic leadership is a process that involves
continually strengthening the core elements of leadership *presence*
(center of the compass) and utilizing this as the foundation of leadership *practices* (middle layer).

Achieving alignment between presence and practices, while striving for
continual improvement in all areas, is the key to advancing as an authentic
leader and driving a high-performance organization (outer layer).

Core Elements of Authentic Leadership *Presence*

1. **Clarity:** Living in Alignment with Your Values
2. **Character:** The Courage to Face the Demands of Reality
3. **Centering:** Knowing Your Worth Away from Your Work
4. **Calling:** Where the World's Need Meets the Soul's Desire
5. **Creativity:** Awakening the Artist Within
6. **Community:** Connecting with Your Tribe

Core Objectives of Authentic Leadership *Practices*

1. **Build Trust:** The Power of Assurance
2. **Create Clarity:** The Power of Focus
3. **Engage Talent:** The Power of Internal Alignment
4. **Embrace Change:** The Power of Possibility
5. **Ensure Results:** The Power of Accountability

PART I

Finding Your Pathway

Introduction

"Mountains are not stadiums where I satisfy my ambition to achieve, they are the cathedrals where I practice my religion."

Anatoli Boukreev, mountaineer

I have enjoyed hiking and climbing in the mountains all my life. On this day, at the summit of Mount Yamnuska, in Banff National Park, about an hour's drive from my home in the Rocky Mountain foothills, I am looking out onto the broad horizon, reflecting on many things.

I am thinking about the adventurer and writer Allan Hobson. At the age of 29, he set out to realize his greatest childhood dream, to reach the highest point in the world. It took him ten grueling self-guided and self-organized expeditions to high altitudes, including three expeditions to Mount Everest, to achieve his dream at age 39 by standing on the summit and taking in the view from the top of the world.

Allan had a parallel dream—to one day also reach the deepest point of the ocean. It's a remarkable fact that both the highest and lowest points on Earth are almost the same distance from sea level. No person has ever touched both. Allan wanted to be the first. At the age of 42, he was diagnosed with leukemia and found himself at a new bottom. Cancer became his new challenge and depth to explore.

As I sit on this mountain, reflecting further, I am thinking about my brother, who, a year ago died peacefully in his living room. A successful and dedicated rural physician and anesthetist, Hal had just flown to Vancouver, joining his colleagues across the country to receive the Canada Family Physician of the Year Award for the province of Alberta, when he had a seizure in his hotel room. A few days later, the diagnosis was delivered—a grade III anaplastic astrocytoma—an aggressive, inoperable tumor intersecting three lobes of his brain. The ensuing months led me through a journey with Hal he called his "Adventure with Astrocytoma"—providing a renewed awakening to the power of caring.

Hal's dying changed my living. Spending time with him during the last months of his life not only provided moments of deep intimacy and self-reflection but had the effect of s-l-o-w-i-n-g me down—deepening my relationship, not only with Hal but with the present moment, providing a rest note of peace and wisdom in the allegro of my life. This time with Hal heightened my profound and precious realization that the life we have today won't last forever. And as such, paradoxically enables us to appreciate it and to live it more deeply. Embracing our challenges, and more importantly, the wisdom and teachings they provide, allows us to better know our true selves and what is important to us—opening up our potential to lead lives of meaning and fulfillment.

As I rest on the summit of this 2,200-meter limestone mountain, looking down the sheer 500-foot face, I think of my father. A picture of him sits on my desk at home doing a one-handed handstand near this very spot, at the top of Mt. Yamnuska (as a young man he was a nationally ranked gymnast). He loved coming up here and hiking in the area over much of his youth. From here I can see the next valley over, where Hal and I used to climb ice falls with a pick and ropes. As I think of my family and the early experiences that shaped my life, my mother also comes to mind, as I reflect upon the sacrifices she made in her life for the sake of her children and the wisdom I gleaned from her. My thoughts also turn to my wife, Val, and my daughters and grandchildren who have been an endless source of enrichment and learning, fueling my development as a husband, father, grandfather, and human being.

The milestones of my professional life also enter my thoughts. Over a progression that began with marriage and family therapy, then shifting to providing counsel for leadership and organizational development, including speaking engagements to many hundreds of people every year, I have come to not only appreciate, but truly cherish the openness of thousands of individuals from all walks of life, who have shown the courage to share with me their struggles and desire for improvement.

My thoughts linger over one recent experience, representative of many hundreds I have encountered over the years, when an executive in one of my leadership development programs called to ask me if I would take him on as a coaching client. The presenting problem was that his 360-degree feedback came back with low scores in how he was relating to people. "I've always gotten by with an ability to deliver results, but interpersonal skills have never been my strength," he said.

"So, why work this now?" I asked. There were several moments of silence, followed by an awkward inarticulate expression of a man in some discomfort. "I suppose it started with my son," he responded, leading into the story of how his son ended up on a psychiatric ward of a local hospital after a suicide attempt. This man was certainly not the cause of his son's choices. However, the ordeal exposed a failure he had long ignored in relating to and truly being there for the people who mattered most in his life—including his own son and family. As he learned to understand and acknowledge this through subsequent counseling with his son, this issue was rooted in the experience of growing up with a father who, though he built a successful business, was likewise absent and emotionally unavailable. "After working with my son, I have gained a new perspective on my life, and I want to change."

Many catalysts drive our collective desire for positive change. Often, they begin as challenges. As we overcome them, they transform into fresh opportunities for enlightenment and personal growth. I have seen this time and again in the experiences of hundreds of leaders I have coached and counseled over the years. They may have endured the challenges of addiction, divorce, illness, a job or business failure, death of a close family member, or many other challenges both personal or professional.

By learning to go through the hard stuff, with courageous acceptance, honesty, curiosity, and support, these horrific experiences can be, in the long view, transformative. It is from here, in the bottom of the chaos, that we can discover the truth, wisdom, gifts, and love that are sustaining and indestructible. It is from our lowest points that we can emerge as better people and better leaders.

I know this also from my own experience. As I reflect on many formative experiences and defining moments that have shaped me into the person I now am, I consider the triumphs and the failures, the challenges and the suffering, the victories and the defeats. While the successes have been, without a doubt, life-changing, it is in the healing of the traumas and the wounds, the facing of the illnesses, the grieving in the losses, and ultimately the reconciliation of all these, that have ultimately made me who I am today.

Taking this time for respite and mindfulness here in the mountains, during an important time of reflection, renewed awakening and balance in my life. I am more aware than ever of a powerful common thread that ties together many of the stories I have both listened to and experienced throughout the years.

There is a universal truth I have come to see very clearly: our greatest capabilities lie not so much in being able to control the outcomes of our life, but rather to tap into the power of our own authenticity to help us meet challenges, become better people, and make a mark on the world that has meaning and impact.

For those of us committed to personal development, including strengthening our leadership capacity, dedicating ourselves to better understanding and developing this power of authenticity is essential work. While we must all find our own pathway, we can gain inspiration and insights from others, to provide us with guideposts along the journey.

The culmination of three decades of connecting and communicating with people from all walks of life has led me to the conclusion that there is a certain kind of inner work necessary in the development of a leader.

It starts with your life story ... knowing where you came from, who you are, and the experiences that have shaped you along the way. It continues with learning and reflection, taking time to understand and connect with your true nature, as your life is shaped by new experiences, connections, and opportunities.

Often our greatest periods of development come in the course of dealing with adversity—for example, facing up to ordeals such as a job loss, an illness, death of a loved one, a failure, or a business going under. I have come to learn that whatever the experience, when we face these challenges honestly, without blame or becoming a victim, we can use these moments as opportunities for positive transformation—to gain insight on what we truly value, and ultimately, help bring us closer to identifying and embracing our life's true work. When we ask ourselves, "How has this experience—along with my response to the experience—helped shape me into the person I am meant to be?" we come to see this value more clearly.

Through strengthening our connection with the innermost part of ourselves, we are able to connect with and lead in accord with our true nature. This journey into the depths of self-discovery, it turns out, isn't just a personal adventure. It's a transformational voyage that will amplify your impact in the world through a stronger leadership presence.

As I stand here on the mountain, I have never been more convinced that while many search externally for opportunities and answers in our lives, the "journey within" is the essential pathway we must embark upon if we are to truly reach our full potential. It is a journey that provides us with the opportunity to see life from a new perspective and unlock the hidden potential that lies within each of us, at the source of our authentic selves.

As I look back on my own journey, and those of the people who have touched my life, I am struck with the profound awareness that all forms of achievement and leadership development are realized with much deeper impact when they come from a place of authenticity. Our tendency is often to look outward when striving to achieve more—to climb the metaphorical corporate ladder or mountain of success. But the moment we realize the most important journey is within is the moment our journey truly begins ...

Traveling Tips

While there is no one formula for developing authenticity, just as there is no one right way to lead, the intent of this book is to offer learnings and insights that can serve as guideposts to help you on the journey.

First, a few "traveling tips" are in order.

- **Respect and Trust Yourself.** Your journey to authentic leadership requires that it be uniquely your own. No one can prescribe the shape your leadership is meant to take. The paths to growth and expression of the authentic self are as unique and numerous as the human expression itself. Everyone is unique, and our needs change over time. You may not relate to some of my experiences, or you may be in a different life stage. Each of us has to do the work of discovering and awakening authenticity in our own unique way. The value of another's experience is to share and shine a light, not to tell us how or whether to proceed. Relax and enjoy the learning process, even in the moments when you might be uncomfortable with the new insights. Take what fits and leave the rest.
- **Festina Lente.** This advice from the Roman emperor Augustus means "make haste slowly." Be patient with yourself and those around you. Living life authentically requires perseverance and persistence. The journey of authenticity requires remembering that anything worth doing is worth doing slowly, and

that *direction* is more important than *velocity*. Aim for progress rather than perfection. Expect to succeed, but over the long haul. There are no quick fixes here. Be gentle with yourself. Small, steady, incremental steps are more important than huge leaps, especially when the leaps are followed by colossal crashes and disappointment.

- **Be a Student, but Not a Follower.** Socrates said, "Wisdom begins with wonder." Choose curiosity over the familiarity of certainty. Give yourself permission to explore those areas that you find uncomfortable. It's the terrain outside your comfort zone where growth lies. One of the qualities of authenticity is the willingness to be open and receptive. *Openness,* however, is not necessarily the same as *agreement.* Everything you read here needs to be weighed and debated in your own conscience, matched against your own experience and perceptions, then integrated with your own being before calling it your truth.

- **Sit While the Credits Roll.** Many people seem to be in a hurry to get out of a theater after a touching movie. Maybe it is the discomfort of being in another world and coming back to reality, or maybe they were not touched at all, or perhaps they just had an appointment to get to. Regardless, deepening your presence means allowing life to touch you as you sit with the credits and the subsequent stirrings. Give life the opportunity to move you and shape you. We all need to be moved before we get moving. If something stirs you or even irritates you as you read, sit with it. Write about it. Talk about it. Meditate about it. Resist the tendency to shift too quickly to your next experience. The journey to authentic living is through the heart. Learning to be still when discomfort surfaces can be a vital way to access your authentic self.

- **Make it Real by Reaching Out.** Find an ally, a trusted confidant, to share the insights that come to you. Get feedback from people who will help you see your blind spots and be honest with you. Be honest with yourself and with others as you share your reflections, reactions, and learnings. Authenticity is a lonely journey, but it can't be done alone. Growth requires a combination of self-awareness and risk-taking. Sharing your awareness with others as you practice new ways of being, beyond what is familiar to you, is what makes it real.

- **Become Attuned to Your Inner Compass.** Above all, follow the mantra: "To thine own self be true." The more honest and aligned you are with your true self, that you will come to know more deeply in this book, your essential self that resides below the surface of the impulse of immediate emotions, the more you will become attuned to your 'inner compass' that without fail, will point in the direction you are meant to follow. Your inner self—your true nature—is what holds all the secrets to making your journey to develop authentic leadership a positive and successful one. With this compass as your guide ... let the adventure begin!

Awakenings

"As human beings, our greatness lies not so much in being able to remake the world ... as in being able to remake ourselves."

Mahatma Gandhi

In the 1970s, scotch and cocaine supplied Jerry Chamales' highest moments. In 1977, at the age of twenty-seven, after a period of homelessness and hospitalization due to drug and alcohol abuse, he realized that being an alcoholic and drug addict was no longer his life's authentic destiny. Resolved, he sobered up and straightened his life out. In 1980, Jerry founded what is now known as Rhinotek Computer Products and by 1998, the company then known as Omni Computer Products, had 250 employees and $25.5 million in sales. Four years later, the company earned more than $45 million in sales. One-third of Jerry's employees were, like him, formerly unemployed or homeless drug addicts or alcoholics, whom he also assisted with addiction counseling and mentorship programs. A keen conservationist, Mr. Chamales donated a percentage of Omni's proceeds to the Save the Rhino Foundation and the Lewa Wildlife Conservancy in Kenya.

A key guidepost for expressing our own authenticity and recognizing the power of authentic leadership is observing and recognizing this in others. We have all known people with a remarkable ability to reach and rouse others with a particular kind of presence, a gift to influence those around them with seeming ease. Through their compelling authenticity, combined with their values, vision, cause, and passion, they inspire and bring out the best in others.

There are many ways to describe these people, but a common thread is they are "real." And each in their own way is a true leader, making a difference in the world through their own unique contribution.

You will find these people in all walks of life, across professions, companies, organizations, and communities. You'll find them among teachers, engineers, police officers, physicians, farmers, firefighters, community volunteers, accountants, ecologists, parents, soldiers, lawyers, nurses, clergy, civil servants, and customer service representatives. You'll find them waiting on tables, organizing community efforts, fixing your car, filling your teeth, and renovating your house. They may be CEOs, middle managers, professionals, administrative assistants, front-line supervisors, or laborers.

They are living proof that leadership is about *presence*, not position. It's about character, and it's about authenticity.

The Inner Path of Leadership

The journey toward authentic leadership—including navigating *The Other Everest*—is ultimately a process of becoming real that starts with a better understanding and connection with ourselves.

We all have an authenticity—a powerful realness at the core of our being—but often our alignment with it becomes lost as we travel through life, bending ourselves to false perceptions of what the world wants us to be or what we think we ought to be, rather than who we truly are. This authenticity is a living, evolving element of our nature, an internal compass that shifts throughout our years based on new learnings and experiences that shape our values and choices.

Becoming more fully attuned and aligned to our authenticity is a process that requires looking beyond the shallow surface and delving deep within ourselves. It requires a dedication to continually seek, discern, and move toward the evolving truth about who we are, what we stand for, and what impact we wish to make in the world around us.

It requires honesty and gradual removal of the facades we tend to create—ones that uphold a false front, masking our true selves and protecting us from our fears and vulnerabilities. Perhaps most of all, it requires trusting ourselves by listening to our inner voice and learning from what it has to say.

Insights Toward Authenticity

By becoming more attuned to our authentic selves, we nurture a process of continual strengthening toward becoming who we truly want to be. The destiny of the mighty oak tree is inscribed in the tiny acorn, and like that acorn, we are all born as a seed of possibilities to fulfill in our lifetime. Life is a journey that awakens us to who we are uniquely destined to be, to a voice we are meant to bring to life. All of our life experiences are necessary for this awakening to occur. The call of authenticity is to be a gardener, cultivating and nourishing the soil of our soul, creating an environment that supports the unfolding of our unique potential.

Through authenticity, we become conscious contributors in our lives as we transform our experiences into a portal toward our life's most vital work.

The great Sufi master Hazrat Inayat Khan, who introduced many important teachings to the West in the early twentieth century, offers an excellent metaphor for the development of the authentic self. He compares the light of our spirit, of our authentic self, to the light reflected brilliantly within a perfectly cut diamond. Just as a diamond requires careful curating to achieve a perfect shape and fully capture the light, our authentic selves must be nurtured and cultivated to express our full beauty.

Embracing the Rewards of Facing up to Challenges

As a child on the farm, I remember watching our neighbor's chicken eggs hatch. The chicks were pecking their way out of their shells, and in an effort to help them, I cracked their eggs. To my astonishment, the chicks died. That day, I learned a hard and important lesson: help isn't always helpful. We all have the capability to struggle, learn, and overcome—to take our first steps in a new direction without the expectation of others to rescue us from our unhappiness—or the expectation that we must rescue those we care about from their unhappiness.

Those chicks needed the struggle of hatching to learn to survive and thrive. They needed to crack their own dependency eggs; they didn't need me to do it for them. I believe the same is true for human beings. If we are to embrace change, if we are to connect with our passions and become more of our true selves, if we are to live a life of meaning, vitality, and eventual contentment—based on our own definitions of success—then we will need to identify our dependency eggs and crack them ourselves. In many ways, the struggle itself is a necessary ingredient to break free from what holds us back and move down the pathway to grow as a leader.

Creating Time and Space for Self-Reflection

For many people, the process of understanding and aligning with our realness, our core authenticity, starts with building time into our lives to step away and reflect—to connect with our inner feelings and thoughts, to remind ourselves of where we came from and what is important to us.

A good friend, Don Campbell, reminds me often that you never want to be so busy *doing* that you do not have time to *think* about what you're doing. As a leader, taking this time is arguably the most important thing you can do for yourself and for the people around you who depend on your sound judgment.

Making time and space to reflect also provides us with opportunities to open ourselves up and see the world in new ways. There is powerful truth, also originating from Don, reflected in the saying, "If you want to make small changes in your life, change the way you *do* things. If you want to make big changes in your life, change the way you *see* things."

First Steps

"Two roads diverged in a wood. I took the one less traveled by, and that has made all the difference."

Robert Frost

Don Calveley, a successful entrepreneur on Vancouver Island, grew up hunting and fishing every weekend with his father. They usually hunted for pheasant, grouse, and duck. He recalls doing that until about age 15. One day, on the first day of the new duck-hunting season, the two, as part of a hunting team, were up in the highlands preparing to "scare a lake." This is when one person goes to the opposite side of the lake to scare the ducks, which sends them up in the air in the direction of the other people who are waiting with their shotguns in hand.

On this particular morning, it was Don's turn to scare the ducks. But when he arrived at the other side of the lake, he came across an entire family of ducks—actually numerous families of ducks—waddling around and playing with their young. The sun was shining. It was an idyllic moment of natural beauty. Though he started to move, Don realized he could not bring himself to scare those ducks.

"It was the first time in my life that the thought had registered with me that 'I have a mind and I have a choice, and I don't want to do this,'" says Don. Even with the ribbing of all the other hunters on the other side of the lake, he wouldn't do it. At that time, Don had been a bravado-driven youngster who rode motorcycles and did all sorts of things to show off. But this was a moment of reflection and a moment of choice—and he had made his choice. "I put down my gun that day, and I have never hunted again," says Don. "It's just one of those things that a person makes a decision about."

Discovering Authenticity

Discovering your authentic self is often a process marked by defining moments like these, times when we experience an epiphany about our true values and make a conscious decision to not just recognize those values—but live them.

The easy choice, like the easy path, is often not the most rewarding.

When we take the path less traveled, when we commit to creating our own journey, we break free of what is holding us back to becoming our true selves. We open the door to realizing our full potential not just as people, but also as leaders.

A children's book I have long admired is *The Velveteen Rabbit*, by Margery Williams. It tells the story of a stuffed rabbit and his desire to become real, through the love of his owner. I have always found remarkable wisdom in the following passage:

> "What is real?" asked the Rabbit.
> "Real isn't how you are made," replied the Skin Horse.
> "It's a thing that happens to you ... It doesn't happen all at once ... You become ... It takes a long time."
> "Does it hurt?" asked the Rabbit.
> "Sometimes," replied the Skin Horse. "When you become Real you don't mind the hurt ... Becoming Real doesn't often happen to people who break easily, or who have sharp edges, or who have to be carefully kept. Generally, by the time you are Real, most of your hair has been loved off, and your eyes drop out and you get loose in the joints and very shabby. But these things don't matter at all, because once you are Real, you can't be ugly, except to people who don't understand."

Over my career, I have interviewed and listened to thousands of people from a wide variety of organizations. When asked what they expect from their leaders, I have found that the vast majority of their statements can be boiled down to essentially one response: "What we want from our leaders is to get past the gimmicks, the fads, the flavors of the month. We want our leaders to be honest. We want our leaders to be *real*."

As I began to write about leadership, I discovered that before you can be a real leader, you first have to be a real human being. Your leadership, your capacity to impact others, comes from the strength of that realness.

Listening to Life's Quiet Messages

Before his death, I spent a day with a longtime friend and colleague who had been facing cancer with a grinding mix of chemotherapy and radiation for more than eighteen months. In our time together, Bernie articulated what the whole experience meant to him:

> Ambitions for achievement in my business, my drive for financial success ... well, let's just say they have been 'radiated' out of me. The only thing that seems to matter these days is love— for my life partner who has been beside me every step of this journey, for the beauty that surrounds me every waking moment, and for the people who matter most in my life.
>
> I have also learned to value deeply the very small things in my life: being able to put my feet on the floor in the morning, to go for a walk in the sunlight, to be able to swallow. I am somehow strangely grateful for this experience of cancer. Not just grateful that I am alive today, but grateful for the deepening that this whole experience has given to the quality of my life. I'm a different person today. Although I would never wish this hell on anyone, today I feel more profoundly, I suffer more deeply, and I love more intensely.
>
> I have no idea how long I have left: two years or twenty years. I live each moment with a presence of mind that I have never had in my life. Coming so close to death, I have been awakened to life. I have become less tolerant of the stupid, trivial things people get upset with in our culture. The frivolous things

of my life have been percolated out of me. I have been boiled down to a deep awareness of what really matters in this existence we call human.

Bernie recognized that the cancer and the enormous pain he experienced did not simply need to be eradicated; it actually needed to be *listened* to. His illness was not the enemy but a *messenger* that he had the courage to learn from and pass on to others. By examining the message and facing death, he deepened his connection to life. Everyone who spent time with Bernie in his last days was impacted by this awareness in their own life.

Embracing Our Scars Humbly

Ultimately, all experiences, especially the most difficult ones, provide us with opportunities for personal development and strengthening our capacity for authentic leadership.

I have seen the examples time and again in countless people and experiences: A respected executive who, in his upbringing, had to face ridicule from his school classmates for having type I diabetes. A teacher who lost a spouse all too soon in a car accident. A struggling middle manager coming to grips with an addiction. A young couple grappling with unimaginable pain in the aftermath of the death of a child. A long-time employee facing a job layoff.

While we wouldn't wish any of these experiences on anyone, I have witnessed over and over how even the most challenging times can become defining moments that transform people to attain a new level of presence, of character, and subsequent credibility in their leadership. By connecting more deeply with our authentic selves, we were better able to connect more deeply with those around us.

Positive experiences that challenge us and make us look at life in a brand new light are also rich opportunities for defining moments. Finding your life partner, entering a new career, becoming a parent, traveling to a distant land … all of this and more can awaken us to new perspectives and give us strength and wisdom to become better people and thus better leaders.

Having the Courage to Break Away

Discovering your authentic self is often described by those who climb their inner mountain, as a process of breaking away from conforming to the cultural norms and expectations that others have placed upon them and finding their own voice.

Those who succeed in breaking away often find they also break through fears, including those associated with revealing oneself to others or living up to the expectations of others.

The duck hunting example with Don Calveley illustrates both the challenge of facing these fears and the rewards of overcoming them:

> When I came back to the group, a couple of jokes were made, but I just said, "I'm over it, guys. I'm not interested in hunting anymore … Clay pigeons, skeet shooting, fine, that's no problem. But that's a sport. These are animals, and they're happy …" I don't have an issue with hunting per se if you're eating what you're hunting. I'm just choosing not to do it anymore.
>
> My father was at an age and a time in his life when hunting was a way to stay connected to me. By us spending time together, he thought he was doing it for me because I was a teenager and he wanted us to have a close relationship. That was important to him. So we discussed it, and he agreed with me. He thought my decision was fine.

Finding Your Element

When we live a life that we are born to live—in alignment with our authentic self—we discover meaning, purpose, and fulfillment.

Living authentically means living with less stress, greater contentment, and more peace. We are comfortable with ourselves. Our worth and security come from within. We aren't threatened by the opinions of others. We are secure within ourselves.

The process takes some work and attention. It requires breaking through many barriers, often of our own creation. However, discovering and living your authentic self is a journey that is a reward unto itself—both daring as well as deeply and profoundly gratifying.

I think of Michelangelo, who was asked once how he carved and created such magnificence and beauty from a slab of cold marble. Michelangelo reportedly replied, *"I didn't do anything. God put Pietà and David in the marble. They were already there. I only had to carve away the parts that kept you from seeing them!"*

Carving away the parts that no longer fit, that block you from your truest self, usually comes through a series of life-changing events, significant turning points in your life. Like a chisel striking marble, these stages were initiated by the hammer of "instructional moments of disillusionment."

Although the experiences may have been painful or traumatic at the time, they were actually necessary and profound teaching moments providing a passage to a deeper connection to your authentic self. At the time they seemed to be random occurrences that you cope with the best way you know how, without knowing that they actually lead you to your destiny.

Heeding the Call Toward Who We Are Meant to Be

As we reach new milestones on the pathway, often we become more aware of a guiding, compelling force calling us to our authentic selves. Below the surface of our challenges and traumas, we may actually better hear an inner voice, our great internal sculptor, calling and preparing us to connect with a deeper essence that addresses the fundamental questions: "What is it, in my heart, in my soul, that I must do and be? Who am I, really?"

There is no prescribed way to carve away the parts of your life that keep you from your destiny. The beauty of the authentic journey lies in finding your own unique pathway to fully realizing who you are meant to be.

For anyone who aspires to strengthen their leadership potential, this process of moving along the authentic journey offers countless opportunities for improvement toward becoming a more impactful, influential leader.

As my friend and colleague, John Scherer, puts it, "You are a leader second. First, you are a human being." Developing the leader as a human being is the hardest and most enduring and rewarding work that can be done.

Leaders who are more aligned with their true selves, who are more authentic and real, are more trusted and better able to influence others. We are drawn to people who are honest, sincere, and real. We all have the potential to better embody those qualities to improve our lives and our impact on the world.

Heeding the Call

"Authenticity is the daily practice of letting go of who we think we're supposed to be and embracing who we are."

Brené Brown

Measuring authenticity gets difficult. Articulating how someone is authentic is like trying to explain beauty. Trying to describe *why* or *how* a work of art exhibits beauty to someone who has not experienced the artistic expression can actually diminish the experience. If we stop and pay attention, we simply *know* when something is beautiful, just like we *know* when someone is authentic.

Here are some easily recognizable traits of authenticity—both in yourself as well as those around you.

Personal Responsibility

One of the most persistent falsehoods of modern life is that we are *entitled* to a good job, a good boss, a good relationship, and a good life. Entitlement—the belief that you deserve something just because you want it—means that someone else is responsible for our happiness.

The truth is that there is only one person responsible for the quality of your workplace and the quality of your life. That person is the only person you can change. That person is *you.*

Accountability precedes authenticity and, as such, personal responsibility is an early recognizable trait of being an authentic human being. Accountability—the ability to be counted on—means taking 100 percent ownership for your life. It means taking 100 percent personal responsibility. It means deciding, once and for all, that all blame is a waste of time. Once you take personal responsibility for everything that happens to you, your life will change forever.

The life stories of authentic leaders cover the entire range of defining moments that end up shaping a person's ability to impact others with presence, including both the positive and negative impact of parents, teachers, coaches, and mentors, as well as the inspiration that came from difficult and painful experiences in their lives. They describe the transformative effects of healing from abuse, the loss of a job, the untimely death of a loved one, or finding a way to respond to discrimination or marginalization. Authentic leaders understand that circumstances don't determine a person. Instead, they *reveal* a person.

Personal responsibility, expressed another way by Chris Lowney, in his book, *Heroic Leadership*, says: "Leaders imagine an inspiring future and strive to shape it rather than passively watching the future happen around them. Leaders extract gold from the opportunities at hand rather than waiting for golden opportunities to be handed to them."

When it comes to leadership and life, you will soon discover that *waiting* is not a very effective strategy. It starts, instead, with courageous action in the world around us—however small that might be.

Another colleague and mentor, Peter Block, said that we expect and thus project onto our leaders that which we are unwilling to create for ourselves. Far too often we expect our leaders to offer us perfect certainty, predictability, and consistency. Authenticity requires that we be mindful that we don't put such high expectations on our leaders that they have to create an illusion of perfection to be called a leader, and then they lose our respect when they are not perfect. Never take what people say they want from their leader at face value. Sometimes it has more to do with the sender than it does the receiver.

Identity and Security that Comes from Within

If you've been around as long as I have, you'll remember the children's story of *Br'er Rabbit and the Tar Baby*. Br'er Rabbit, in the famous Joel Chandler Harris story of the old south, walks along the road of life, whistling and happy, until he encounters a tar baby on the side of the road he believes is insulting him. Br'er Rabbit strikes out at the tar baby because he thinks he would not be true to himself if he were to let someone say nasty things about him. But by kicking and hitting the tar baby, he ends up getting completely embroiled in the tar. He actually loses his sense of self by reacting to someone else's evaluation of him.

Just because you are upset with someone doesn't mean you have to confront them in order to prove your authenticity. You can be honest with yourself, quietly walk away from a situation that diminishes who you are, and through your actions show what you stand for, without necessarily showing your "true self" indiscriminately to the world and potentially getting enmeshed in tar.

Br'er Rabbit loses his way by reacting to someone else's opinion of him. The more we react to other people's evaluation of us, the more we demonstrate a lack of self-assurance. We all have thoughts and feelings and tendencies and impulses in our lives that are better left unspoken, or at best spoken only with trusted friends or confidants.

People who are overly dependent on others for a sense of worth spend their time and energy seeking approval, rather than pursuing their own values and goals. They also spend time proving themselves rather than expressing themselves. Subsequently, they fall short of their potential. They are obsessed with getting recognition from others instead of relaxing and bringing to the world who they are meant to be. Authenticity, by definition, means that you are committed to making the shift away from dependence on the views or opinions of others to define you. Being authentic means being comfortable with who you are, which opens a space for humility. Authentic people are humble enough to bring curiosity rather than rigidity to their relationships. They can set their own limits while also considering the views of others. Rather than needing to defend themselves or criticizing, they respect differing opinions and are open to learning.

Fueled by a Sense of Purpose

Dr. Martin Luther King, Jr.'s unwavering persistence in fighting for civil rights, justice, anti-discrimination, and peace inspired a broken nation. An athlete training for the Olympics will persevere through the pain of getting up early, endure the hours of brutal workouts, and see it all the way to the end. A mother will stay up all hours of the night to care for a sick child. Why? Because of the power of purpose, a vision beyond their own self-interest. It's a compelling vision, along with a profound and sustaining commitment to that vision that inspires and awakens the human spirit. Leaders may not know how. They may not know when. And they may not know where or what or who. But one thing they are clear about. They are clear about *why*. They have a clear reason for getting up in the morning.

Those on the authentic journey, regardless of their title or lack of title, have a deep and profound awareness that they aren't just laying bricks; they are building a cathedral.

In simplest terms, authenticity is "what you see is what you get." You may have a role in what you are doing, but what's underneath that role is still authentic. You may decide, for example, to wear a suit and tie to work because, given the nature of your job, it shows respect to your colleagues and customers, even though you would prefer to wear blue jeans. This is not necessarily compromising your authenticity. Authenticity, at times, may mean having the mental toughness to do the right thing for your team, even when it is not what's comfortable or easy for you. Authenticity is not self-serving. It lies instead below the surface emotions of approval, pleasure, and immediate gratification. At the bottom of it all, authenticity is coming to know who you are and what you stand for—and then deciding the right action based on a commitment to the betterment of all who are impacted by your choices. It's stopping to align your deepest values with your choices.

My life is consumed with a sense of purpose, and that gives me energy. This sense of purpose doesn't come instantly for most of us. For me, excavating my reason for being came through a series of events, significant turning points in my life, coaching experiences, and defining moments. It has taken, and will take, years to fully realize and express. Ultimately this brought me to the realization that my life's work is to inspire and guide difference-makers to connect with their authentic self so that they may amplify their impact on the world. This purpose has fueled my career as a speaker, counselor, facilitator, and advisor to leaders.

Strengthening Your Footing

"Too often we underestimate the power of a touch, a smile, a kind word, a listening ear, an honest compliment, or the smallest act of caring, all of which have the potential to turn a life around."

Leo Buscaglia

The CEO of a financial services firm contacted me some time ago to coach his vice-president of sales. "Darryl is just not getting the results from his sales team that we need. I want him to grow into his role. He was one of our top senior salespeople, but I don't know if he's got what it takes to lead a team. I'd like you to help me assess this and, if he is willing and capable, help him develop his leadership skills."

In my initial assessment interview, the executive was noticeably frustrated with his sales team. He unashamedly blamed them for their lack of effort and weak results.

"It's the millennial generation," Darryl ranted. "They just don't have the work ethic needed to get the job done. In my day, we worked seventy hours a week. It was about the numbers, and we made sure we got the numbers. Today, these young kids just don't have the commitment. They only want to work thirty-five hours a week, and they still expect the big commissions." He went on to quote some of the "lame excuses" his team members had for their failure to achieve his targets.

After listening to Darryl for several minutes and trying to understand and empathize with his irritation and annoyance with virtually every member of his sales team, I interrupted him. "Before you go further, I have a question for you. I want you to think very carefully about your answer to this question: 'Darryl, do you care?'"

"What do you mean? Of course, I care. I care about sales results. I've put a lot of years into this company, and my reputation is in jeopardy. The lack of production on this team is evidence that they aren't stepping up and getting the job done. What are we paying them salaries for anyway? I think we should go back to the old days when people worked on straight commission. We've made things too easy for them. They just don't have the drive that's needed for the job. There has to be more accountability here."

I sat quietly while Darryl ranted on for a few more minutes. When he ran out of steam, he sat gathering his thoughts, seeming to be building an even stronger case to explain why his team wasn't producing. "You didn't answer my question, Darryl. Do you care about the salespeople on your team?"

"What do you mean?" he repeated. His frustration, which was obvious before, heightened even more.

"Do you care about what matters to each member of your team? Do you care about their families and their kids and the relationships in their lives? Do you care about what working here is like for them? Do you care about why they come to work? Do you care about how they feel about you as their boss? Do you care about them as human beings with values, feelings, and needs? Do you care?"

There was a long pause ... a very long pause ... and Darryl finally shrugged. "Not really. When you put it that way, I don't really care."

I expressed my respect for his honesty, and we went on to explore what was blocking him from caring. Good leadership is largely a matter of caring. If you honestly don't care, you would do yourself and your organization well by getting out of management.

Capturing the Power of Caring

My career has been about guiding leaders—in all walks of life—to their authentic self. It is a challenging and rewarding journey. A good part of the voyage has been about introspection, self-awareness, and soul-searching. I've learned that self-reflection is necessary to discover my authentic self, but going within won't take me all the way. What's also required for living authentically is *caring*. Caring is a powerful tool that reveals new guideposts to authenticity.

Intentionally learning to care—whether for a dying parent, a troubled employee, a cause beyond our own self-interest, or perhaps even learning to care about ourselves, makes us a little more real. The two—authenticity and caring—are inseparable. Learning to care deepens the connection to your authentic self, just as learning to be authentic deepens your caring capacity. You can tell when a leader is worth following, in part by how much they care—about the work they do, about the people they serve, and about the results they achieve.

The late Dr. Lois Hole was a co-founder of Hole's Greenhouses, a well-known horticultural business in Alberta. Lois was a successful businesswoman, philanthropist, social activist, author of 14 best-selling books on gardening, a school trustee, a member of the Order of Canada, and Chancellor of the University of Alberta. In 1999, the Prime Minister of Canada appointed Lois as Lieutenant Governor of Alberta. Yet with all her titles, her leadership was not a result of her positions. Her leadership was a result of her presence. Like beauty, words cannot describe this essence. Lois was described by the strength—and impact—of her presence.

Lois's son, Jim, once said: "Mom was famous for her hugs. You sometimes get hugs from people when you know it's a formality or something, but with Mom, it was genuine. I think she hugged many dignitaries that maybe she shouldn't have because of protocol, but she just kind of ignored protocol at times."

Her older son, Bill, also described his mother's genius about human nature: "She understood that there was a 'cylinder' that people have and that she could invade it and then capture a person's focus by getting inside of that cylinder—and her hugs did that."

Lois said, "I have faith in a better future because I have faith that most human beings want to do the right thing. If we can put aside differences of ideology, if we can learn to love one another, then one day we will enjoy a world where no one needs to live in fear, where no one needs to go hungry, and where everyone can enjoy a good education, the fellowship of friendly neighbors, and the security of a world at peace with itself at long last."

Lois had an authenticity that was manifested in her sense of compassion, her humanity, and her courage to stand by her principles, which she used in her leadership role. Yet her role did not make her powerful. Her role was merely a tool for expressing her presence. Lois probably did not view herself as authentic, or even as a leader. She simply did what she loved to do and, in the process, had an amazing impact on thousands of people because she cared.

"Caring," I write in my book, *Caring is Everything*, "makes schools worth learning in, workplaces worth working in, relationships worth being in, and lives worth living in. Caring is everything."

Adventure of a Lifetime

"We shall not cease from exploration. And the end of all our exploring will be to arrive where we started and know the place for the first time."

T.S. Eliot

When the seventy-five members of the Stanford Graduate School of Business Advisory Council were asked to recommend the most important capability for leaders to develop, their answer was almost unanimous: self-awareness. Yet so many leaders, particularly those early in their careers, are so driven by external rewards of financial success, status, power, public recognition, and material accomplishments, they leave little time for reflection or self-evaluation.

The drive for outer success pushes meaning and connection aside, diminishing the ability to sustain the success. As they age, they discover that something is missing. They realize how they have inadvertently been holding back from being the person they are meant to be. Knowing their authentic selves requires courage, honesty, and often the support of a trusted guide in order to take a careful look at their experiences and choices. As they step into the authentic journey, not only do they begin to be at peace with themselves, they also amplify their impact on those around them through the strength of a stronger presence.

Take the Inner Journey

Authentic people seek to know themselves. The authentic journey begins when we start examining what drives our lives and shifts from the external validation of productivity, financial rewards, and achievements; the necessity of appointments, schedules, goals, productivity, and activities; toward an internal orientation in our lives, where values, dreams, passion, purpose, legacy, and meaning replace the outer definitions of success.

Moving from the external validation of personal achievement toward authentic expression requires both clarity and courage. But at some point, authentic leaders begin to respond to an inner urging leading them to pursue a more meaningful success. Alice Woodwark, former Associate Principal of McKinsey & Company, had the wisdom and clarity to begin her authentic journey at the age of twenty-nine. Already having achieved notable success, she reflected, "My version of achievement was pretty naïve, born of things I learned early in life about praise and being valued. But if you are just chasing the rabbit around the course, you're not running toward anything meaningful."

Seek Alignment and Integration

Authentic people don't show up as one person one day and another person the next. Integrating their lives is one of the greatest challenges leaders face. Integration takes discipline, particularly during stressful times when it is easy to become reactive and slip back into bad habits. As John Donahue, former president of eBay Marketplaces stressed, "Being authentic means maintaining a sense of self no matter where you are." He warned, "The world can shape you if you let it. To have a sense of yourself as you live you must make conscious choices. Sometimes the choices are really hard, and you make a lot of mistakes … There is no nirvana, as the trade-offs don't get any easier as you get older … I have no doubt today that my children have made me a far better leader … Having a strong personal life has made the difference."

The ability to clarify and pursue what you genuinely want for yourself while also maintaining close relationships with others—and respecting them to also be themselves—is one of the major attributes of an authentic person. Most of us are able to do only one of these at a time. We either conform to the culture in order to be accepted or cut ourselves off from others in order to be ourselves. It's a sign of authenticity if you are able to walk the line between seeking both independence *and* connection.

Pursue Real Success, Rather Than an Illusion

Authenticity pursues destiny over comfort, curiosity over certainty, and honesty over an illusion of perfection.

> *"Each person has only one genuine vocation: to find the way to themselves... Their task is to discover their own destiny—not an arbitrary one—and live it out wholly and resolutely within themselves. Everything else is only a would-be existence, an attempt at evasion, a flight back to the ideals of the masses, conformity and fear of one's own inwardness."*
>
> Hermann Hesse in *Demian*

Until Joseph Jaworski found his genuine vocation, he lived a life in the fast lane, what he described as Hesse's "would-be" existence as a top corporate international lawyer. Making loads of money, earning a supposedly great reputation, having girlfriends in every city, and gambling, Jaworski blindly believed that he was making his contribution. The day his wife asked him for a divorce was the beginning of his long journey down into what he described as "darkness."

Authenticity entered the day he quit his law firm to follow his heart and a dream to start the American Leadership Forum (ALF). The fascinating part of Jaworski's destiny is that when he finally decided to leave law and begin the ALF, he knew nothing about leadership curriculum and development. He had much fear and uncertainty. Yet he forged onward. And things began to happen that assisted him in actualizing his dream. When we have a hint of our own destiny, synchronicity (an unseen force, an energy that moves us toward that goal) enters our journey and assists us in realizing our mission.

Lao Tzu, the ancient Chinese philosopher and writer, said over twenty-five hundred years ago, "*The way to do is to be.*" Being is a kind of aliveness and authentic way of relating in the world that calls us to service, to leave what we have and move forward, not without fear, yet not succumbing to the fear. It is a call to define what is possible, to see a vision of a new world and to be willing to undertake, step-by-step, what is necessary in concrete terms to achieve that vision.

The Courage to Serve

A lightening rod attracts power by its mere presence. In the same way, great leaders must seek substance, depth, and strength of character.

"Our lives begin to end," said Dr. Martin Luther King, Jr. "the day we become silent about things that matter." Authenticity is not only hard work; authenticity can be dangerous. Abraham Lincoln, Mahatma Gandhi, John F. Kennedy, and Dr. Martin Luther King, Jr. are prime examples. Political leaders, however, are not the only leaders that get assassinated. When you courageously take a stand for something or when you dedicate yourself to making a difference, you become a lightning rod that attracts both positive and negative power by your mere presence. But authenticity and the leadership that emerges from it requires the realization of a cause beyond comfort.

How do we know our daily actions are aimed towards fulfilling our destiny? Robert Greenleaf, in his landmark book, *Servant Leadership*, provides two key questions: "Do those served grow as persons? Do they, while being served, become healthier, wiser, freer, more autonomous, more likely themselves to become servants?"

Authenticity calls us to the realization that all the problems and conflicts of the world are reflected in each of us, and the world is a reflection of ourselves. Therefore, we must seek the key to their solutions from within. If we can come from the self first, we find within us the seeds of possibility to realize our destiny as the servant leaders that Greenleaf inspired us to be.

Embrace Devotion to Life-Long Learning

Authentic leaders are committed to life-long learning. They understand that you can't grow amidst certainty, and, as such, are committed to stepping into the discomfort of ambiguity that opens the door to new vistas. If you have a desire to grow and learn for the benefit of the world around you, you are already on your way to becoming an authentic leader.

Seek Personal Transformation

When I went to my first yoga class, after more than three decades of competitive running, I was so tight I couldn't touch my lower shins without bending my knees. When I looked around the room, it felt like I was sitting in the middle of a bunch of Cirque du Soleil performers. It wasn't until I kept going to yoga classes for years that I learned that yoga has nothing to do with what you see when you look around the room. Yoga is what's going on inside you.

When was the last time you embarked on an adventure that put you in the place of being a "novice?" Where have you given yourself the opportunity to be an imperfect beginner? Learning to be vulnerable, to be imperfect, to admit your inadequacies, are crucial for developing a leadership presence. Jumping into something that puts you in the place of being a beginner is a great way to develop this. You cannot guide others where you have not been. You earn credibility as a transformational leader by investing and engaging in your own transformational journey. Where have you traveled to unfamiliar territory? When have you embarked on some kind of personal adventure?

Set Your Sail by Living Your Philosophy

"The pessimist complains about the wind. The optimist expects it to change. The leader adjusts the sails."

John Maxwell

On September 28, 1962, in Birmingham, Alabama, the gales of racism, inequality, segregation, and violence against African Americans were blowing fiercely when Dr. Martin Luther King, Jr. firmly set the sail for the civil rights movement. Dr. King was a man of principle and lived what he preached—nonviolence.

On that hot Friday afternoon, Dr. King was giving the closing speech at the annual meeting of the Southern Christian Leadership Conference (SCLC). The auditorium was packed with three-hundred black religious and civil rights leaders who had organized and participated in numerous boycotts, protests, rallies, and marches, all conducted peacefully, following the guidance of Dr. King.

On the sixth row sat Roy James, a 6-foot 2-inch, 200-pound white man, who stood out because of his skin color and white T-shirt. The SCLC meeting was open to all; however, its members didn't know that James was known to the FBI as a member of the American Nazi Party. James came to this speech with a mission, and his anger mounted as Dr. King spoke.

Finally, James could take no more. He sprung from his seat, bolted onto the stage and slammed his fist into Dr. King's cheek, hitting the 5-foot 7-inch civil rights leader so hard it made a loud noise. The audience shrieked as James pummeled Dr. King. As people rushed to the stage, there was an instant when Dr. King was able to stand and face James. As James got ready to hit him again, King dropped his hands and looked his assailant in the eyes.

Dr. King was bleeding profusely from the punches. His lips and face were swelling, but the crowd watched in awe as Dr. King did as Jesus and Gandhi had advised all of humanity, "to turn the other cheek." James expected the black men to beat him to a pulp. But immediately Dr. King's voice rang out, "Don't touch him. We have to pray for him." And no one harmed James. Instead, they prayed for him. As they prayed, Dr. King assured James he wouldn't be harmed. Then he took James to a private room and even after James revealed that he was a Nazi, King refused to press charges.

The reason that those three-hundred delegates were inspired to renew their commitment to a nonviolent civil rights movement wasn't because King had given an inspiring speech extolling nonviolence. It was because they witnessed King himself turning the other cheek. They looked to him for leadership because he actually *lived* his philosophy of nonviolence and demonstrated by his actions that it worked. This is the power of being a principled leader who knows clearly the philosophy with which to set his sails.

Ten Guideposts

"One ship drives east and another drives west
With the self-same winds that blow.
'Tis the set of the sails
And not the gales
That tells us the way to go."

Ella Wheeler Wilcox

While there are many puzzle pieces for leadership success, without developing a sound philosophy, the other pieces are of little value. Your philosophy is the set of the sail that will determine your destiny. Authentic leaders work at identifying their own philosophy and living in alignment with what they believe. I have found there are a number of principles commonly held by strong, authentic leaders that serve as pillars we can all rely upon.

What follows are ten of the top examples of these principles—ones that I continually lean on to inform my own fundamental philosophy of leadership.

1. Leadership Starts with a Decision to Serve

In 1996, a young woman became enraged after reading a newspaper article about the Taliban's treatment of women in Afghanistan. Waging a one-woman anti-Taliban movement from her parent's home in West Vancouver, she gathered 400 signatures on a petition and fired it off to Canadian cabinet ministers, human rights groups, and the United Nations. She found a fax number on the internet for the Taliban and sent them a copy overseas.

Two years later, she called up the national organization, Canadian Women for Women in Afghanistan, and offered to start a Vancouver chapter. Its president, Janice Eisenhower, gratefully accepted. At the time, Eisenhower had no idea she was speaking to a sixteen-year-old. And when Lauryn Oates, who is my niece, was an undergraduate at McGill University, she opened another chapter in Montreal.

Currently, Lauryn runs a Canadian aid program that also trains Afghan teachers. It's a mammoth undertaking in a country where most teachers are barely literate themselves. Aid delivery in Afghanistan can be fraught and dangerous. It involves driving for hours on dusty, treacherous roads, confronting hostile bureaucrats, avoiding suicide bombers, and returning to the program's service regions, month after month, to ensure donor-funded programs really are delivering the services they set out to provide.

It isn't a job for the faint of heart. While most aid workers hunker down in Kabul compounds, Lauryn has traveled to every region of the country from Jalalabad to Herat—mainly by car—making contacts with locals who can smooth the path of aid delivery. She has been in hotel lockdowns when the embassy next door was under siege, had known colleagues who were shot soon after sharing a meal with them, and has been nearby when a restaurant she often frequented was blown up by a suicide bomber. These horrific and dramatic events, to name only a few, have not once dampened her dedication to the cause of advocating for the universality of human rights, making public education accessible in a developing region of the world, and protecting liberties, like freedom of thought and expression, that are being denied by groups such as the Taliban.

Despite the modest funding provided to her aid group, Lauryn's Afghan staff includes more than a dozen instructors who, to date, have trained thousands of teachers. Education is what gives them the most leverage, she tells me. "You can come in here and fund reconstruction by building roads and buildings. Or you can spend less money teaching Afghans to do this work for themselves."

Lauryn has been "commuting" to Afghanistan regularly from Vancouver, yet her commitment remains strong. "I believe in this place. For all its flaws, it still has a soul. Besides, it isn't a sacrifice. I'm totally, madly in love with this place, and I'd be happy to do what I'm doing here forever."

William Blake, in the poem "A Memorable Fancy," enters into an imaginary conversation with the prophet Isaiah: "Does a firm persuasion that a thing is so, make it so?" the questioner asks. Isaiah replies, "All poets believe that it does, and in ages of imagination this firm persuasion removed mountains." And so, my niece, in her conviction that she can shift mountains in Kabul, is doing just that. And it all started with a decision.

The root of the word courage is *cor*—the Latin word for heart. Leadership means the courage to decide to follow our heart and make a difference. It means, at times, the courage to stand alone as we stand up for something or someone we care about.

You don't need a title to be a leader. All it takes is a decision to make the world a better place. Most great leaders I have met don't even necessarily seek to be a leader. What they seek—and decide—is to make a difference. This makes every person in your organization a potential leader.

I have come to believe that a very small minority of the people actually run the world. They don't run the world because the world anointed them to do it. They run the world because they thought they had something to say and something to contribute. They stood up and took a stand, "This is how I want my world to be."

Leadership starts with a decision. The moment you decide to do your part to make the world a better place is the moment you step into leadership.

The decision most common to authentic leaders is the decision to serve. Although there are many good books on leadership, one of the best for serious students is Robert K. Greenleaf's book on *Servant Leadership*. Whenever you hear the question, *"How can I help?"* you know you are in the presence of a leader. Leaders bring a generous spirit to what they do. The decision to serve comes largely from caring. Without serving and caring, you aren't leading. You are manipulating and controlling. Turn your organization chart upside down. Take care of your people so they can take care of the people your organization serves. Do you treat your employees the way you want them to treat your best customers? The customer experience will never exceed the employee experience. Serving doesn't mean you have to give people what they want so they'll be happy. Serving means having their back. Serving means being committed to giving people what they need to help them do their job and grow as people.

Leadership goes beyond "getting a job done." Leadership is about the release of human possibilities. Leadership, in its truest form, goes beyond control to the unleashing of potential. To inspire, support, and guide people to growth and be all they can be requires a desire and commitment to serve.

Does every person on your team know you are committed to doing everything in your power to help them find the resources and support to do their job? Do they know you are there to help them grow and be all they can be? Leadership isn't about you. It's not about how great you are, how noble you are, or how profound you are. Leadership is about others and what you do to give credit to others. If you are going to earn the credibility to influence others in the long term, you better have a strong enough ego that you can leave it at the door. Credibility comes from giving credit, not taking it. People don't remember what you said; they remember how you made them feel. Serving breeds commitment.

The late motivational guru, Zig Ziglar once expressed service this way: "You can have everything in life you want if you will just help other people get what they want." Success, it has been said, belongs to the group; failure belongs to leadership. Perhaps Harry Truman said it best: "It is amazing what you can accomplish if you do not care who gets the credit." Leadership is an ego reduction activity. As you move up in the organization, don't think you'll get more power. What you get is more accountability. It's never about you. It's about the people around you that you serve.

Leadership is about making a difference in people's lives. The late Ray Nelson, co-founder of Nelson Homes, a successful building and lumber company in Western Canada and long-time client and friend, used to say, *"It's easy to make a buck; it's harder to make a difference."* Leaders are committed to adding value through service. It's about what you give, not what you get. You find yourself when you serve others. You respect yourself when you choose service over self-interest.

2. Leadership Must Be Earned

Raised in Port Coquitlam, British Columbia, Canada, Terry Fox was an active teenager who participated in many sports. In 1977, when he was only 18 years old, he was diagnosed with Osteogenic Sarcoma (bone cancer). His right leg was amputated six inches above the knee. While in the hospital, Terry was so overcome by the plight of other cancer patients (many were young children) that he decided to run across Canada to raise money for cancer research. Terry said: "Somewhere the hurting must stop." He called his journey the Marathon of Hope.

After 18 months and running over 5,000 kilometers in preparation for the run, Terry started his run in St. John's, Newfoundland on April 12, 1980, with little fanfare. Although it was difficult to garner attention in the beginning, enthusiasm soon grew, and the money collected along his route began to grow. He ran 42 kilometers a day through Canada's Atlantic Provinces, Quebec, and Ontario. It was a journey that Canadians will never forget.

On September 1, 1981, after 143 days and 5,373 kilometers, outside of Thunder Bay, Ontario, Terry was forced to stop running before he collapsed from exhaustion. Cancer had reappeared in his lungs. An entire nation was stunned and saddened.

This heroic Canadian was forced to stop running, but his legacy was just beginning. On February 1, 1981, only five months before his death on June 28, Terry's "unimaginable dream" of raising $1 from every Canadian to fight cancer was realized. The population of Canada at that time was 24.1 million people. Terry Fox's Marathon of Hope fund totaled $24.17 million.

At the time of this writing, more than $700 million has been raised in over 400 countries for cancer research in Terry's name through the annual Terry Fox Run.

If Terry were alive today and I asked him if he would consider himself a leader by the influence of his actions, I believe he would respond the same way so many other great leaders would respond. Most of the best leaders don't perceive themselves as leaders, they are simply doing what they love and are committed to making a difference. Terry would, in all likelihood, not see himself as a leader but as an ordinary person with a vision to make the world better.

While you may get promoted to being a boss, you don't get promoted to being a leader. You have to earn the right to be called a leader. Leadership is not a designation you can bestow upon yourself. Leadership is in the eyes of the people that are around you. You aren't a leader until someone says you are. Leadership is defined by how others perceive you. Leadership is not self-declared. Leadership must be earned.

3. Leadership is About *Presence*, Not Position

The perception of people as leaders has little or nothing to do with having a title. In fact, many people who are acknowledged as leaders have no title at all. While a title undoubtedly gives you a greater scope of influence and accountability, good leadership isn't about your position. Good leadership, instead, comes from the identity and integrity of the leader. Leadership is about how you live your life. Authentic leaders demonstrate such qualities as the ability to bring out the best in others and collaborate with a team. They live their lives with a sense of ownership, a commitment to excellence. They strive for strong character. They care. They demonstrate a commitment to serve. They are oriented toward service. Their lives are fueled by a sense of purpose, vision, and passion. Authentic leaders have a strong sense of personal identity that infuses their work. While far from perfect, authentic leaders are human beings who devote their lives to the simple and worthy cause of making the world a better place.

Some typical responses of how people define the leaders around them include:

- They are comfortable with themselves.
- They don't have to prove themselves.
- They don't have a huge ego, so they can make their work about inspiring and encouraging others instead of making themselves look good. It's about others, not them.
- Their life is about service rather than self-interest.
- When you are around them, you feel better about yourself.
- When you are with them, you feel that you are the only person on the planet that matters to them at this moment. They are fully present in the present.

One person I met said she could not describe the leaders in her life because they differed so greatly from one another. What she could describe was her bad leaders: disconnected, self-serving, egotistical, unethical, uncaring, controlling, and "a bully." Far too many people have not experienced being around a true authentic leader.

Foundational to leadership, independent of your title, is the ability to influence others, characterized by having followers. Not followers in the conventional sense of being subservient, compliant, or submissive. Leaders have followers in the truest sense: they follow not because they have to but because they *want* to. True followers trust the leader and themselves. They are engaged and committed. True leadership development is about becoming a person that is worth following. It's about attraction rather than promotion.

The power of presence, however, is not developed by selfishly trying to develop the power of your presence. I met a woman once who, unmarried at the time and advancing in her years, sought my advice in finding a good husband. She said to me, "How can I find a husband?" She knew many eligible men, but nobody that she thought was suitable for her. I said, "Well, the only thing I can think of is make an intention to be the kind of person that the kind of person you want to be with, would want to be with. Don't try to find the right partner. Put your attention, instead, on being the person that will be attractive to the right partner."

While I never did find out if this strategy worked for her, what I do believe is that this approach can be useful in developing one's authentic leadership presence. Start by asking yourself what it would be like to be an employee that worked for you. Then go about becoming the kind of person you would like for a boss. Work at becoming a person worth following.

You don't become an artist by putting on a beret and sitting in cafes, just because you see artists doing that. There's a lot more to it than that. You just have to work on the art of being yourself. When you do, some people find it attractive and other people are repelled. That's a good thing. Authentic leaders don't get too hung up on wasting their time on people who don't want to be led in the directions they want to go. Rather than dragging people around, it's about facilitating common vision and values and action. When you are conscious and focus on getting better at being yourself, you'll find enough people who will believe in you. Regardless, presence has to come from your inner self. Otherwise, it isn't authentic, and it won't be sustainable.

Authentic leaders understand the true nature of power. Because their security comes from within, authentic leaders have no interest in tearing others down to build themselves up. They are humble because they know themselves. They have a sense of their own identity and true nature. They feel comfortable with themselves and know that trust must be earned. Because they are at peace with themselves, they have no need to use their positional power to control, manipulate, bully, or abuse anyone. They understand that power must be earned, and the ultimate source of power comes from giving it to others. In the words of the late Margaret Thatcher, "Being powerful is like being a lady. If you have to tell people you are, you aren't."

Authentic leaders know that moving into positions of leadership in an organization doesn't give you more power. They know that with positions comes increased accountability. Holding a position of leadership is like having a driver's license. Just because you have one doesn't make you a good one. With added titles and designations comes added responsibility to serve. Rather than power, authentic leaders think of *influence*.

4. Leadership Means Going Where No One Else Has Gone Before

Leadership is about taking people into unfamiliar territory. It's about realizing a shared vision of something we haven't yet seen. It's about initiating a future where we haven't yet been. If you aren't inspiring and engaging people in embarking on a vision of new frontiers, you aren't leading; you are merely managing. If you are traveling familiar paths, you haven't gone far enough into the wilderness. How have you embarked in new and unfamiliar territory with those you lead and serve? One of the most powerful ways to go where no one else has gone is to give your power to others. Be honest with people. Delegate authority. Once you have made your expectations clear, trust others. Relinquish control wherever you can. Only secure leaders can do that.

Another way to take people into unfamiliar territory is through a powerful vision. A vision precedes a plan. The vision of the future is a powerful force. In his "I Have Dream" speech, Dr. Martin Luther King, Jr. did not proclaim a strategic plan. While plans may be necessary, it is dreams that inspire, uplift, and engage us. Whatever your vision, live it well and you will inspire others to engage with you.

5. Leadership is Largely a Matter of Love

Guideposts contributor JoAnn C. Jones relates an experience in which her university professor taught her about the importance of caring:

> During my second month of nursing school, our professor gave us a pop quiz. I was a conscientious student and had breezed through the questions until I read the last one: What is the first name of the woman who cleans the school?
>
> Surely this was some kind of joke. I had seen the cleaning woman several times. She was tall, dark-haired and in her fifties, but how would I know her name? I handed in my paper, leaving the last question blank. Before the class ended, one student asked if the last question would count toward our quiz grade. "Absolutely," replied the professor. "In our careers, you will meet

many people. All are significant. They deserve your attention and care, even if all you do is smile, say hello, and find out their name."

Leadership is ultimately about love. If you are uncomfortable with that word, call it caring, because leadership involves caring for people, not manipulating people. As the leadership expert John Maxwell expresses, "You have to get to people's heart before you ask them for a hand." "People don't care how much you know," my father used to say, "until they know how much you care." Leadership means caring about the *person* as much as you care about the task you have given the person. Leadership is about seeking to be interest*ed*, instead of attempting to be interest*ing*. People buy in to the leader before they buy in to the vision. With no connection, you can have no influence.

In this age of social media and hand-held devices, everyone communicates, but very few connect. If you want to lead, you will need to connect. You connect when you care enough to bring value and effort and energy to those you depend on and those who depend on you. You connect when you care enough to turn off your cell phone and give another person your full attention and presence. You connect when you care enough to call people by their name, when you sincerely show interest, when you treat people as people, not as a number or a role. You connect when you care enough to catch people doing things right, when you see the gifts and unique talents in others, when you create a safe place to take risks.

"Our offices and direct level managers, 60 to 70 people, get together quarterly to review results, discuss plans, and examine ideas and directions," writes Max De Pree, former CEO of Herman Miller, the world-renowned office furniture company. "Shortly before one of these meetings, I had received a wonderful letter from the mother of one of our disabled employees. It was a touching letter of gratitude for the efforts of many people at Herman Miller to make life meaningful and rich for a person who is seriously disadvantaged. Because we have a strong, albeit quiet, effort going on in the company to empower the disadvantaged and to recognize the authenticity of everyone in the group, it seemed to be a good idea to read this letter to the officers and directors."

"I almost got through this letter but could not finish. There I stood in front of this group of people—some of them pretty hard-driving—tongue-tied and embarrassed, unable to continue. At that point, one of our senior vice presidents, Joe Schwartz—urbane, elegant, mature—strode up the center aisle, put his arm around my shoulder, kissed me on the cheek, and adjourned the meeting. That is the kind of weeping we need more of."

Intentionally learning to care—whether for a dying parent, a troubled employee, a cause beyond our own self-interest, or perhaps even learning to care about ourselves—makes us a little more real. The two—authenticity and caring—are inseparable. Learning to care deepens the connection to your authentic self, just as learning to be authentic deepens your caring capacity. You can tell when a leader is worth following, in part by how much they care about the work they do, about the people they serve, and about the results they achieve.

6. The Best Leaders are Committed to People's Growth

"Thank you for doing all the things I never told you to do." Those words capture the leadership philosophy of the former LEGO CEO, Jorgen Vig Knudstorp. Knudstorp believed you don't "control" people to innovation and success. The leader's job is to provide the supporting environment and the permission for people to offer their best. As my friend, Corey Olynik, taught me to ask leaders: "Do your team members feel empowered to do stuff, to try things you've not told them to do? Or … are they cautious, reluctant, even scared to make an un-approved move?"

Authentic leading involves compassionately and courageously creating environments that inspire and guide others to be all they can be. It's about focusing on people's unique gifts rather than their limitations. It's about strengthening people's strengths rather than trying to strengthen their weaknesses. Authentic leadership is about a commitment to get the right employees on the bus, and then to *fit* people, rather than *fix* people. Ray Taillefer, founder of Alta-Fab Structures Ltd., with more than 250 employees and annual sales over $50 million, communicated this clearly when he talked about his commitment to building his company based on growing *people*. "I try not to focus on the sins of people or concentrate on their weaknesses. I prefer to see their talents and their potential ... If measured, my success would be in terms of our people and how they have grown."

Authentic leaders guide people to their authentic self. Everyone is talented, original, and has something to contribute. There is an innate desire in all of us to make a difference that is aligned with our values, unique gifts, vision, and passion. While great leaders may be able to create results through others, authentic leaders are also committed to inspiring and guiding others to find and express their voice, their unique gifts, their passion, and help them find a way to make a meaningful contribution.

As a founder of a family ranching operation, Don Campbell spoke of his commitment to building a strong future by having strong successors in his family business. "That is vital. My goal is to create an opportunity for young people to grow, to develop their talents, improve their skills, and to hopefully become more successful than I am." Don defined leadership as "letting people grow."

7. The Best Leaders are Oriented Toward Results and Have High Standards

Although he reportedly sent out 30,000 hand-written thank you notes in his ten-year transformational journey at Campbell Soup, Doug Conant is not a touchy-feely guy. Leaders, he says, need to be tough-minded and set high expectations. Three years into his tenure at Campbell, he replaced 300 out of 350 senior managers. "They either didn't have the skills to lead their organization," he said, "or they weren't engaged in the culture-building we needed to do."

Leaders understand that activity is not the same as results. Results are the name of the game. Without results, you can't call yourself a leader. Just because you are busy, and you can get others busy, doesn't make you a leader. You have to hold up high standards for yourself and others, model the way, and ensure accountability.

The great coaches, bosses, teachers, and mentors in my life were all people who held me to high standards of excellence—beyond what was popular or easy. And they fostered these high standards not through control but through caring. Norris, a hired hand on our farm, cared enough to work alongside me while he was, at times, tough on me. His standards were modeled by how he lived his life. The two of us built a barn, and I watched him get to work early, measure twice, cut carefully, assemble the lumber into place with pride, meticulously attend to detail, and thoroughly clean up afterward. He would remind me of the importance of *giving* more than you get paid for, showing up on time, and bringing a high standard of quality to everything you do. By supporting me through some difficult jobs, by believing in and encouraging me when I didn't believe in myself, Norris taught me that you don't take pride in doing something easy. He insisted that "If you are going to spend your time doing something, do it well and do it right. If you don't have time to do it right, when will you have time to do it over?" A true and rare craftsman, Norris would remind me, "It takes less time to do a thing right than it does to explain why you did it wrong."

While oriented toward high standards of excellence, the leaders I respect are also oriented toward results. They don't need to be supervised, and they finish a job once they start it. It's more than merely "working hard" or "doing your best." While leadership is about building and empowering people, it's ultimately about ensuring that the job gets done. Leadership is measured by results, not effort.

8. A Leader is More than Just a 'Boss'

Several years ago, I was pulled over by a police officer for rolling through a stop sign. Before handing me the ticket, he paused. When I looked up at him, I could see he was actually fighting back tears. "Before I give you this ticket," he said, "I want to tell you *why* I am I doing so … I just came from a fatal collision in which three young children were killed. They died because someone went through a stop sign … I'm issuing you a ticket because I wouldn't want that to happen to you."

Through my work with the Royal Canadian Mounted Police (RCMP), years later I was able to find this officer and I sent him an email:

> ... I want to thank you for stopping me that night and telling me that story before you ticketed me ... Now when I approach stop signs, I often think of the story you told me that night, and it helps remind me to come to a complete stop as I take the time to look both ways. Because of your actions, I am a safer driver. But it not only made *me* a safer driver. For the past several years I have been telling this story to corporate audiences across the continent and several people over the years have told me that my story has helped change their driving habits and made them safer drivers.
>
> So ... your service in our community has changed lives and likely saved lives. I just wanted to write and express my sincere appreciation to you. You and your colleagues in the RCMP do incredible work that is far too often unacknowledged and unappreciated.

There are two aspects to every job. First, there is a *transactional* component. Police officers, for example, write tickets, arrest criminals, and fill out paperwork. A cashier at a grocery store scans items, answers inquiries, processes money, and bags groceries. A manager in an organization sets goals for the group, decides what work needs to be done to meet these goals, divides the work into manageable activities, selects people to accomplish necessary tasks, and tells people what to do. A parent insists that their teenager can't get screen time on their device until they get their homework done.

But there's another aspect to every job, and that is the *transformational* component. Police officers have an opportunity, through caring actions, to inspire a driver to drive more safely. Cashiers, through their attitude and actions, can create a remarkable customer experience and transform someone's day. A manager, if they care enough, can inspire people around them by taking time to listen, encourage, and mentor. A parent takes time to connect before they attempt to control. Transformational action, even in small and caring ways, is possible for everyone. This makes every person a potential leader.

The difference between transaction and transformation is what separates a "boss" from a "leader." Many people have a role as a "boss" that comes with specific responsibilities, a title, and accountability. But being a leader is something more.

The distinction between the transactional and transformational aspects of leadership is found in the following examples:

- While bosses *drive* others, leaders also *coach and mentor*.
- A boss is about a *position*, while a leader is also about a *presence*.
- Bosses are about *strategy*, while leaders are also about *vision*.
- While bosses *supervise*, leaders also *serve*.
- Bosses *enforce*, while leaders also *inspire*.
- While bosses focus on *policies and procedure*, leaders also focus on *values and principles*.
- Bosses are about "*knowing*," while leaders also focus on "*learning*."
- Bosses *transact*, while leaders *transform*.
- While bosses *control*, leaders also *unleash*.

Imagine that you met a remarkable person who could look at the stars and amazingly tell the time. Wouldn't it be even more amazing if, instead of telling the time, that person could help you build a clock that would tell the time even after you are gone? Bosses, in the words of Jim Collins and Jerry Porras, are time tellers, and their direct reports set their watches accordingly. Leaders, on the other hand, are also clock builders. While the accomplishments of a boss are about the execution of a great idea, the accomplishment of a task, or the achievement of an outcome, leaders also build organizations and teams that last—beyond the leader. While time tellers may get results in the short term, those who are also clock builders take the long view.

The characteristics of both bosses and leaders are needed to run any organization, whether a family or school or fortune 500 corporation. The problem comes when an organization gets out of balance when you get over-bossed and under-led.

Experienced bosses and leaders eventually discover that you can't really separate these two functions. The best bosses are actually the best leaders, while the best leaders are the best bosses. Both are vital.

Both are necessary. Both are needed to build a great organization and great life. Being both a great boss and a great leader requires being an integrated person—clear and caring, courageous and compassionate, tough and soft, strategic and visionary, confident and vulnerable, competent and imperfect. It's about knowing your strengths and weaknesses, knowing who you need around you to do what you can't do, and being able to discern when a boss is required and when a leader is required.

9. Authentic Leaders Never Forget the Importance of Humility

Beverly Suek, Former CEO of the Women's Enterprise Centre, and associate of TLS Enterprises, a Canadian consulting firm, expressed the importance for humility in her work as a leader:

> "To lead, you have to recognize that humility is an important part of what you do. You are not as smart as you sometimes think you are. A CEO or a person who is surrounded by CEOs will have a really hard time not getting caught up in thinking that they are the most important person in the whole world. I really have to keep reminding myself that everybody has something to contribute.
>
> It's not just me …
>
> I started an organization years ago called Kali Shiva. Our son died of AIDS. He inspired us to eventually start an organization to help others who had AIDS. As an organization, we set up teams of volunteers to work with AIDS patients who wanted to stay at home as long as they could or wanted to die at home. June Menzies was one of our volunteers. June used to head up the Economic Council of Canada. I was always in awe of her. And now here she was, joining Kali Shiva as a volunteer. June's job was to pick up patients' laundry, wash it, and take it back to them. Everybody at Kali Shiva thought that June was the 'laundry lady.' She never corrected them. June never said, 'Really, I used to be head of the Economic Council of Canada …'

I've always aspired to be a 'laundry lady.' To me, that kind of humility is something leaders ought to strive for. They don't need recognition or acclamation from others because it's internal. It's part of who they are. They already feel good about themselves. That's always been my inspiration—to be the laundry lady and not have to tell people that I'm wonderful and great and important."

When I talk with leaders about the importance of humility in leadership, I ask them to describe the humble people they know. The characteristic that stands out is that they have self-respect. Their identity comes from within rather than from the approval of others. They are secure, so they don't have to try to prove that they are something other than who they are. Humble people have enough self-acceptance that they can be honest without having to put on airs. Humble people realize that their flaws are not pathologies to be hidden, but are part of the human condition to be expressed in beneficial, constructive ways.

Abusive, arrogant, demeaning behavior, as well as acting with a pretense of perfection, all come from low self-regard with no secure identity, and thus an unwillingness to be honest. Productive behavior, on the other hand, flows naturally from humility. Rather than self-deprecating, humility is a truthful assessment of yourself, knowing that everyone has something to teach you, that you have something to learn from everyone. Humility is gratitude in action. All great leaders—authentic leaders—are willing to give credit when and where it is due. Out of their inner security, competent action flows and results happen.

10. Authentic Leaders are Gardeners

I learned a great deal of leading from my wife, Val, who is an avid gardener. Plants won't grow because you demand that they do so or because you threaten them. Plants grow only when they have the right conditions and are given proper care. Creating the space and providing the proper nourishment for plants—and people as well— is a matter of continual investigation and vigilance. Virginia Satir, a former mentor and world renowned family therapist, planted the awareness around another reality about gardening: you really don't have much control over the harvest. Despite your best efforts, for a myriad of reasons, some plants simply won't turn out as we expect. You can't engage, inspire, or get results from everyone. Not everyone will follow you, and not everyone wants to be influenced by you. It's a reality we all live with.

Field Notes

Opportunities for reflection from Part I: Finding Your Pathway ...

1. *What does authentic leadership mean to you?*
2. *What awakenings have you experienced that provide insights toward your authentic self?*
3. *What first steps have you already accomplished?*
4. *Are you heeding the siren call? (Where do you feel the 'pull' to bring your life into greater alignment with your internal compass?)*
5. *How can you apply the power of caring to strengthen your footing?*
6. *What guideposts most resonate with you, as learnings or principles you most need to keep at the top of your mind as you move toward finding your pathway?*
7. *Who are five people from your own life who stand out as authentic leaders and what can you learn from their examples?*
8. *What are the top three 'notes to self' you can take away from this section of The Other Everest?*

Those using the companion Workbook: The Other Everest can find additional teachings and exercises in the workbook to help absorb and utilize the information from Part I.

PART II

Journey to Authenticity

Base Camp: Preparing for the Journey

"Everybody wants to reach the peak, but there is no growth on the top of a mountain. It is in the valley that we slog through the lush grass and rich soil, learning and becoming what enables us to summit life's next peak."

Andy Andrews

As aspiring leaders move further down the pathway of "becoming real" and strengthening their personal authenticity, they nurture within themselves a new depth of character and clarity of purpose. This dramatically expands their potential as impactful, authentic leaders.

However, even as you become better connected with yourself and what you stand for, as you develop your authenticity, you must also hone your ability to project that authenticity to others in a way that positively influences and inspires them. This ability to influence others is ultimately a true measure of a leader. To do that, you have to get to leadership presence.

The pathway to get there is unique to every individual. The world is teeming with tips on leadership practices, but great leadership cannot be reduced to technique. Great leadership comes from the identity and integrity of the leader. When you use those sources of power effectively to positively engage with others, you project a presence that is attractive and influential. This presence is what transforms you into a true authentic leader ... one that others recognize and follow naturally.

The Making of a Leader

"Often people attempt to live their lives backwards; they try to have more things, or more money, in order to do more of what they want, so they will be happier. The way it actually works is in reverse. You must first be who you really are, then do what you need to do, in order to have what you want."

Margaret Young, American singer

Just as Margaret Young describes how people can fall into the trap of living their lives backwards, the same can be said about traditional leadership development. So often we develop our leadership capacity backwards. There is a tendency to first learn new leadership skills, so we can be a more effective leader in order to make a greater impact on others, in order to get others to do what we want them to do and go where we want them to go. While tools and techniques are always helpful, the way it works is actually in reverse. When you make a choice to lead, you must first *be* who you really are, then do what you need to do in order to help create what matters most to those who are asking you for your support and guidance.

When we stop to think about the people who have had a strong positive impact on our lives—whether a parent or grandparent, a boss, a mentor, a friend or life-partner, a colleague, or even a child—typically we realize the impact they had was not just because of their skills, roles, or position. Something deeper, more substantive that lies below the surface of one's competence is at work. Ultimately, people make a difference in our lives by who they are and how they apply that identity to influence and benefit others. They exercise what we call authentic leadership through the very strength of their *presence*.

This presence is something that each one of us has the capacity to develop and strengthen, by becoming more attuned to our authentic selves.

Leadership—that decision to serve the world through the expression of your unique, authentic presence—begins with breaking away and remembering your identity—unearthing and evolving your soul—and then inspiring and guiding others to do the same. The privilege of a lifetime is being who you are. The privilege of authentic leadership is to support people to be who they are.

Six Compass Points

As you move along your own journey to authenticity, six compass points help guide the way: Clarity, Character, Centering, Calling, Creativity, and Community.

Clarity

"If you are guided by an internal compass that represents your character and values that guide your decisions, you're going to be fine. Let your values guide your actions and don't ever lose your internal compass, because everything isn't black or white. There are a lot of gray areas in business."

Brenda Barnes, Former President, Chairman,
and Chief Executive of Sara Lee

A rich industrialist from the north was horrified to find a southern fisherman lying lazily beside his boat, smoking a pipe.

"Why aren't you fishing?" asked the industrialist.

"Because I have already caught enough fish for the day," replied the fisherman.

"Why don't you catch some more?"

"What would I do then?"

"You could earn more money," responded the industrialist. "With that, you could have a motor added to your boat to go into deeper waters and catch more fish. Then you would make more money to buy more nylon nets. These would bring you more fish and more money. Soon you would have enough money to own two boats ... maybe even a fleet of boats. Then you would be rich like me."

"And what would I do then?" asked the fisherman.

"Then you could really enjoy life."

"What do you think I am doing right now?"

This southern fisherman demonstrates a vital quality of authenticity: the quality of clarity and the power of living your life in alignment with what matters most to you.

Rather than being controlled and manipulated by the expectations, pressures, and demands of others, he knew what was important to him, and lived in alignment with his own values. He was clear about the difference between a standard of living and a quality of life. He wasn't concerned about popularity or status or materialism or about how he "should" be or about living by anyone else's standards. Instead, he was secure enough within himself to know what was important to him and to live his life accordingly.

Too many people in today's fast-paced business environment complain of finding themselves stretched too thin or feel over-worked and under-focused, are busy but not productive, or feel like their time is continually being stolen by other people's agendas. All of them can learn from this example.

As I design and deliver leadership development programs for organizations across the continent, one word that forms a common thread amid every person I meet today, is the word *busy*. Everyone is busy. When I ask, "How are you today?" the reply is always, "I'm *busy!*" Busy has become a badge of honor. If, for some reason, you aren't "busy," it implies that, somehow, you are less than capable. You aren't in demand. There is something wrong with you.

My response is, "So ... is it a *good* busy?"

Then comes a pause. We intuitively know there is a difference between good busy and bad busy, but without time to stop and reflect on the question, it's not possible to answer it.

It's an old and ironic habit of human beings to run faster when we have lost our way.

I see conscious leaders today struggling between having confidence in their capacity to live a life of purpose and yielding to the daily demands of others. By too easily yielding to what is pressing, practical, and popular, we have sacrificed the pursuit of what is in our hearts.

Living with clarity is more than a time-management strategy or a way of juggling all the balls in your life. Clarity isn't about getting more done in less time. It's about getting *only the right things* done. We live in a world where there are far more expectations, demands, and opportunities than we have time and resources. Clarity involves learning to filter through all those options and selecting only those that are truly important. Although many of them may be worthwhile, the fact is that most are trivial, and few are vital. Clarity means living by design rather than by default. If you don't prioritize your life, someone else will.

Living with clarity is a systematic approach to personal leadership that will help you discern what is most important, then eliminate everything that is not, so you can make the highest possible contribution toward that which truly matters. It's what the leadership consultant and author, Greg McKeown, would call being an essentialist: the disciplined pursuit of less. By forcing us to apply more selective criteria for what is essential, clarity empowers us to reclaim control of our own choices about where to spend our priceless time and energy—instead of giving others power to choose for us.

Understand the Difference Between the Urgent and the Important

In 1967, in a little book about time management called *Tyranny of The Urgent,* Charles Hummel introduced his readers to the concept of the difference between the *urgent* and the *important.*

- *Urgent* is defined as expectations from others. The urgent acts on you, creating a sense of needing immediate attention.
- *Important* is defined as expectations that come from within you. The important contributes to your purpose, values, and goals.

While the urgent comes from outside of you, the important comes from inside of you.

Anytime anyone asks anything of you; it is defined as being urgent. A ringing cell phone or an incoming email is urgent. There are people who cannot stand the thought of not answering a ringing phone or replying immediately to an email or text message, just as there are people who cannot say no to a request.

The important demands are what you value. If, for example, you value your health or a relationship or spending time in your garden or reading an important book or getting adequate rest and renewal in your life, then these are important. They aren't necessarily urgent. They aren't pressing on you for instant action the way that demands from other people do. They come from an inner knowing that these are essential for a good life.

Hummel offered, more than fifty years ago, a concise reminder of how we so often allow the latest whim, or the most frequently repeated and loudest demand from the many "squeaky wheels" in our lives, to distract us from those things that matter most. The problem is that the important task rarely must be done today, or even this week. The urgent task, on the other hand, calls for instant action. The momentary appeal of these tasks seems irresistible and important, and they devour our energy. But in the light of times perspective, their deceptive prominence fades. With the sense of loss, we recall the vital task we pushed aside. We realize we have become slaves to the tyranny of the urgent.

Hummel's astute wisdom has been a guiding force in my life for many decades. While most of our time is spent doing what is necessary, attending to demands that are both urgent and important, it is the actions in the important realm that bring fulfillment. The best leaders are clear about what's important and focus their time there. Clarity is about ensuring that the things that matter most must never be at the mercy of things that matter least. If you neglect what's important in your life, be assured that they will eventually become urgent.

"Anything less than a conscious commitment to the important is an unconscious commitment to the unimportant."

Stephen Covey

Schedule the Big Rocks First

Years ago, Stephen Covey demonstrated a very powerful visual image of the difference between the urgent and the important. This demonstration has since been duplicated in various forms that can be found on YouTube. While standing in front of the group, Dr. Covey pulled out a one-gallon, wide-mouthed mason jar and set it on a table in front of him. Then he produced about a dozen fist-sized rocks and carefully placed them, one at a time, into the jar. When the jar was filled to the top, and no more rocks would fit inside, he asked, "Is this jar full?" Everyone in the class said, "Yes."

Then he said, "Really?" He reached under the table and pulled out a bucket of sand. Then he dumped some sand in and shook the jar causing pieces of sand to work down into the spaces between the big rocks. The rocks represent what's important in our life. The sand, on the other hand, represents what is urgent. If you don't have an intentional process for scheduling the big rocks in your life first, the urgency—the sand—will fill your life's jar, and there will be no room for what truly matters. On the other hand, by ensuring that the rocks are in place first, that you attend to the important, the urgency won't take over your life.

There are two vital times to clarify and schedule the big rocks: at the beginning of the year and the beginning of the week. An annual review will clarify things that are important to you and essential to what matters in your life. It is in this annual review that you will examine your core values—the big rocks—and what will be required during the next twelve months to ensure that you attend to the big rocks in your life. In the annual review, you will be considering things like how many days away from work you will schedule. How about learning opportunities? Courses you want to take? Time to travel or renew yourself? What really matters to you? What intentions do you have to improve—or sustain—your health? What attention is needed to your inner—spiritual—life and well-being? What friendships need fostering?

The second time to clarify and schedule the big rocks is at the beginning of each week. Set aside time before your week begins to schedule in your big rocks. If you only plan daily, you will find yourself merely managing the urgency. If you set aside 15-30 minutes at the beginning of each week to schedule in the big rocks—each of your top five values—you will ensure that you make the most important, most important.

What you are scheduling in are such things as building, repairing, or renewing relationships with family and friends, recommitting to deepen your spiritual connections or practices, restoring energy through rest and recreation, developing your unique gifts and passion or hobbies, or contributing through community service.

Scheduling in these values—both in your personal and professional life—is like giving the same self-respect and attention to yourself as you would to an important customer.

At the beginning or end of each day, it is also important to take 5-10 minutes to review your previous and upcoming day. Ask yourself, "What needs to be done today (or tomorrow) to ensure that the activities reflect my values and are taking me in the right direction?"

Years ago, I learned a fundamental lesson on financial planning that has stayed with me. I was under tremendous financial stress at the time, paying the mortgage, attending to household and living expenses, struggling to make my financial commitments, and was ending up month after month stretched with no money set aside for savings or investment in the future.

My financial advisor taught me to pay myself first: saving before you do anything else. Paying yourself first means putting a percentage of my income into investments at the beginning of each month, and then living on the rest—below your means. It's important, not urgent, to invest your money, but be assured if you don't invest—if you don't attend to the important—your financial situation, like your health or your relationships, will eventually become urgent.

Scheduling the big rocks first will ensure that the "essential few" do not take a back seat to the "trivial many." It will be a most important habit for living with clarity—in both leadership and in life.

When scheduling in the big rocks, it is important to remember ...

Prioritize Time and Space to Think, Learn, and Reflect

No matter how busy you think you are, one of the most important habits I have developed is making time and space to think, learn, and reflect—outside of the whirlwind of my workday. If people are too busy to think, they are too busy, period. And creating time and space for reflection, thinking, and learning requires at times being unavailable to others so that you can be fully available to yourself.

Jeff Weiner, the CEO of LinkedIn, schedules up to two hours of blank space on his calendar every day. He divides them into thirty-minute increments, yet he schedules nothing. In this space, he is able to think about the essential questions: What will the company look like in three to five years? What is the best way to improve an already popular product or address an unmet customer need? How will we widen a competitive advantage or close a competitive gap?

He also uses the space he creates to recharge himself emotionally. This allows him to shift between the problem-solving mode and the coaching-mode expected of him as a leader.

Another way to use thinking time is to reflect on what is essential: What is one area that if you did superbly well and consistently would have a significant impact on your personal life? What is one area that if you did superbly well and consistently would have a significant impact on your professional or work life? If you know this, what is stopping you from taking action now?

Since the 1980's, Bill Gates has regularly taken a "think week," a week off from his daily duties at Microsoft to simply think and read. Twice a year, during the busiest time in the company's history, he still created time and space to seclude himself for a week and do nothing but read articles (his record apparently is 112) and books, study technology, and think about the bigger picture. Today he still takes time away from his daily distractions of running his foundation to simply think.

I would not possibly have been able to write books without blocking off extended periods each week devoted strictly to writing.

Writing and thinking are big rocks for me and get scheduled in weekly. I learned from Greg McKeown the term "monk mode"—times of solitude when no one is able to reach me. I set aside time each week to read and learn. I personally like to devote an hour each evening to study. While I don't always achieve my goal, I generally like to read a book a week that will inspire me and stimulate my thinking.

Whether you invest two hours a day, two weeks a year, or even just five minutes every morning, it is important to make room to step back from the whirlwind of your life to think, to learn, to renew, and to listen to the voice inside you. If you don't go within, you'll go without.

Make Rest and Renewal Big Rocks

When my father coached me in high school track, his approach to training came from University of Oregon's track coach Bill Bowerman. The legendary running coach, Arthur Lydiard, who presided over New Zealand's golden era in world track and field during the 1960s, had mentored Bowerman. He introduced Bowerman to a philosophy of training that revolutionized American track and field in the 1960s.

Bowerman's approach to training had been the same as virtually every other American long-distance running coach at the time: progress through pushing. This philosophy was based on the belief that the harder you trained the more you would improve. The results revealed severe limitations. Prior to Bowerman, Americans were virtually absent in the world long-distance running realm.

After returning from New Zealand, Bowerman began exhorting his Oregon runners to finish workouts exhilarated rather than exhausted. His credo was that it was better to *underdo* than *overdo*. He had learned from Lydiard that *rest* was as important as *work* to both progress as well as to keep a runner from illness or injury. Bowerman realized that his runners' training was more effective when they allowed ample respite between hard workouts. He trained and raced his men to seasonal peaks but would back off before they crashed.

While commonly accepted now, the idea of alternating hard days in distance running training with rest days was revolutionary at the time. His new philosophy didn't go down so well with the coaching community. When Bowerman first articulated the hard-easy method, he was widely criticized. Kenny Moore, one of his legendary athletes and author of *Bowerman and the Men of Oregon*, wrote, "The anthem of most coaches then was '*the more you put in, the more you get out.*' In response to Bowerman, coaches were morally affronted. His easy days were derided … called coddling." Moore adds, "His commonsense approach is still resisted by a minority, and probably always will be."

Bowerman's response to his critics was to "crush their runners with his." Over his legendary career, he trained thirty-one Olympic athletes, fifty-one All-Americans, twelve American record-holders, twenty-two NCAA champions and sixteen sub-four-minute milers. During Bowerman's twenty-four years as coach at the University of Oregon, the Ducks track and field team had a winning record every season but one, attained four NCAA titles, and finished in the top ten in the Nation sixteen times.

As a side note, Bowerman also developed the first lightweight outsole that would revolutionize the running shoe. With some latex, leather, glue, and his wife's waffle iron, he created a durable, stable, and light waffle sole that set a new standard for shoe performance and helped him co-found the Nike Corporation. My dad bought me a pair of those original blue waffle running shoes with the yellow stripe. It was an amazing shoe at the time. Bowerman also ignited the jogging boom in America. How that happened is another great story.

Since Bowerman's successful days at the University of Oregon, the physiological foundation for the "hard-easy" system has been validated. In short, physiology has verified what Bowerman learned and applied. The trick is first to provide enough but not too much stress, and second, to allow enough recovery to replenish energy stores, heal, and adapt.

As in the outdated "no rest system" for training distance runners, I wonder if we aren't living our lives these days with an outdated belief that doesn't take into consideration the importance of rest and renewal. In today's world, with its unyielding emphasis on success, productivity, and efficiency, we have lost the rhythm of balancing between effort and recovery. Constantly striving, I see so many people exhausted and deprived in the midst of great abundance. How many of us long for time with friends, family, important relationships, even just a moment to ourselves, as we constantly look down at our devices and strive to achieve more? We now find ourselves compulsively checking for messages from work while in the midst of our vacations and at times when we need to be connected to who and what really matters.

My challenge for you is to create some structured time to rest, attend to what is important to you, and make room for whatever you would call renewal. Whether it's a two-week break a couple of times a year, a five-day break every quarter, one unproductive renewal day per week, or an hour a day to get some renewal, take the time to simply walk in nature, spend some time hanging out with kids, to think, or sit and read a novel. Carve out some time to rest your body and mind, restore your creativity, and regain your natural state of inner peace and well-being.

We are clever people, efficient, and high-powered, but in our fervor to get things done, we forget the simple art of living. Let us resolve that we will take a little time to relax, to be idle, to go more slowly, and be more attentive to the world around us. Let us take time to be still, to be present, to notice the beauty in this world, to watch the sun go down behind the hill.

Bill Bowerman knew the importance of rest in training Olympic athletes. We can all learn from the legacy he left us. Renewal and relaxation aren't a luxury. They, along with hard work, are a necessity to a life well lived.

Living in the Present

"Life is what happens to you while you're busy making other plans."

John Lennon

When we go for a walk with our dog, I imagine that he is not preoccupied with what he is going to do when he gets home. And I don't envision him feeling guilty about his inattentiveness to me yesterday or what he is going to have for supper tonight. No, Enzo is present. He is here now, in this moment. I'm not sure he smells the roses, but he does sniff the grass. He chases the grouse in front of him. He is alive and free and full of joy. Right here. Right now. I've decided that's one of the reasons why I love dogs so much. They are present in life. No judgment. No criticism. Simply pure presence.

Driving my Jeep east into the city this morning as the sun rises in front of me, I realize that I am thinking about the meeting I am going to be speaking at instead of noticing the magnificent sunrise in front of my eyes. I glance to the side and realize that the sun is beautifully reflected on the trees and the snow-covered crystallized field to my left. I recognize, at that moment, how much time I spend in the demands of life and miss the daily miracles going on around me. Instead of letting my eyes drink in the dawn, my mind is somewhere else. Such seems to be the nature of being human in a world filled with expectations and opportunities. Beauty, when I stop to notice it, surrounds me, in the people in our lives, in a creative expression, in a simple flower, in an honest human endeavor. Clarity is bringing myself back to this simple awareness.

Even while focusing on the importance of gaining clarity, it's essential to remember that planning isn't where life is lived. Having a structure for your life is like having a structure for the house you live in. You need a structure, but you don't live amidst the concrete and beams. The living room is contained within the structure, just as your life is lived in the now. The quality of your life is ultimately determined by your relationship with the present moment. I have noticed that most of my thinking is actually just pre-occupying myself by thinking about the past or the future while missing out on what life is really all about, what Enzo is here to teach me.

While life can be filled with clarity, focus, discipline, and execution, you can still live an empty, unfulfilled life if you aren't fully present in the now. Being preoccupied with your plans and habits, you can miss out on the magnificence of it all if you believe that the next moment is more important than this one. While planning is important, if you believe that your life will start when your plans and goals are accomplished, then you miss the whole point of life, because the only place that life exists is now, in this moment. There is no joy or meaning or satisfaction tomorrow or yesterday. You won't be happy tomorrow. You can only be happy now, in this moment. Now is where life is lived. If you don't experience the wonderment of life now, don't expect it later. Clarity, and the accompanying structure and discipline, makes room for what is important, for what matters most, and enables you to not only realize this but experience it.

Character

"Think only on those things that are in line with your principles and can bear the light of day. The content of your character is your choice. Day by day, what you choose, what you think, and what you do is who you become. Your integrity is your destiny. It is the light that guides your way."

Heraclitus

The training program for U.S. Olympic coaches at the Josephson Institute Center for Sports Ethics contains this illustration of virtue:

"In the 1936 Berlin Summer Olympics," Hitler said, "Americans ought to be ashamed of themselves for letting their medals be worn by Negroes. I myself would never shake hands with one of them."

Jesse Owens, the great American track and field star, had already embarrassed the German dictator by winning gold medals in the sprint and relay. But in his first two attempts at the long jump Owens stepped over the foul line. He recalls being scared stiff that he would foul on his third attempt and not make it to the finals. His fiercest rival in the event was Luz Long, the German athlete. Despite the risk of infuriating Hitler and the chance that Owens would beat him, Long took a towel and laid it a foot before the foul line and advised Owens to use the towel to assure that he would qualify. Owens did, and he ultimately defeated Long to win the gold medal.

Long's extraordinary display of sportsmanship, courage, and character went well beyond duty, but demonstrated the highest standards of ethical virtue in sports. As an aftermath, Luz Long was sent to the Russian front where he was killed. And when his daughter was married years later, Jesse Owens walked her down the aisle.

In a recent leadership development program, where I was addressing the topic of character in leadership, a participant came up to me at the break and introduced himself as one of the legal team. It so happens that when he started his first job as an eager young lawyer, with significant student debt, he had dutifully arranged for the student loan repayments to be debited from his bank account. When he observed, however, that the first three payments had not been withdrawn, he called the loan office. After a few moments, the clerk came back on the line and informed him that his file had been sent to storage and his loan was shown as having been paid in full. She seemed annoyed that he would have put her to the trouble of having to verify something that he must already have known.

The lawyer described his reaction at that moment as envisioning himself as the classic cartoon character with an angel on the one shoulder and a devil on the other, each advocating opposite responses. He listened to the angel and told the clerk that there must have been a mistake, that his loan was indeed not paid. She only grudgingly agreed to pull the file from storage. The bank eventually fixed the mistake, and he spent the next four years paying off the loan.

I've told this story in a variety of settings since I first heard it. There is always at least one person in every group who tells me that the man should have thanked the clerk, quickly got off the phone, and been grateful for his good fortune. The lawyer said that he was indeed grateful for his good fortune—because of the incident, not because of its outcome. Paying that debt may well have been the best investment he claims to have ever made because it was an investment not in his checking account, but in what he described as his "character account." The character account is not seen by the world, but it forms the roots for inner well-being and self-respect.

In the field of engineering, engineers are accountable for designing structures capable of handling conditions up to a certain limit. In the engineering world, the margin between safety and disaster is known as "structural integrity." Structural integrity is the ability of a structure to support a designed load without breaking or collapsing. It assures that the structure will perform its designed function.

Similarly, as the engineers of our own existence, our choices impact our ability to support the load of life. Through character, we begin designing a life of personal, structural integrity, a reliable existence that is capable of withstanding the inevitable demands of existence. After all, it's not the fierceness of the storm, which determines whether we break, but rather the strength of the roots that lie below the surface.

At the end of the day, we all must look at ourselves in the mirror. What we see is the result of the decisions we have made. Character is the undervalued virtue of human goodness. Character is about choosing what's right over choosing what's popular or easy or comfortable. If you don't stand for something, you will have nothing to stand on.

Recognizing the Character Traits We Value

In my leadership development workshops, I often use this exercise:

Think of three people you admire. They could be people who have made a positive difference in the world such as Nelson Mandela or Mahatma Gandhi, or people who have made a personal contribution to your own life, say your grandmother or a schoolteacher. For me, three people I deeply admire are my wife Val, my parents Joyce and Harlie Irvine, and Viktor Frankl, the Austrian neurologist and psychiatrist.

There's a second part to this exercise: think of the character traits that make each of your chosen people admirable to you. In my case, I admire Val for her unconditional capacity to love. I would not be the person I am today without Val's loving presence, acceptance, and support. I admire my mother for her wisdom, my father for his compassion, and I admire Viktor Frankl for his courage, resilience, and perseverance. From his harrowing survival of the Holocaust, he emerged with a philosophy of living that is centered on the pursuit of purpose and finding meaning amidst deep anguish.

Finally, I ask workshop participants to compare these fine, admirable traits with the typical success markers in our culture, the kind of character traits featured, say, in *People* magazine. After using this exercise with literally thousands of people, I have yet to observe anyone choose their admired people for the character qualities most frequently popularized in magazines and online, such as fame, beauty, power, youth, or wealth. It's fascinating that, culturally, we gravitate to those things that ultimately mean so little to us. We all have the power to pursue a pathway of greater depth that counteracts this pull, ultimately elevating us all to lives of greater meaning and fulfillment.

Improving Within Before Reaching Without

There's a story about a troubled mother in India, when Mahatma Gandhi was in office, who had a young daughter addicted to sugar. One day, the mother approached Gandhi and explained the problem to him and asked if he would talk to the young girl. Gandhi replied, "Bring your daughter to me in three weeks time, and I will speak to her." After three weeks, the mother brought her daughter to Gandhi. He took the young girl aside and spoke to her about the harmful effects of eating sweets excessively and urged her to abandon her bad habit. The mother thanked Gandhi for this advice and then asked him, "But why didn't you speak to her three weeks ago?"

Gandhi replied, "Because three weeks ago, I was still addicted to sweets."

Character means that the way you change the world is to change yourself. Before you reach out in an effort to change the environment around you, care enough to look inward to see what needs changing within you. Character is an attitude and an approach to life that is built on the foundation of personal responsibility. Whether that means doing your part to make a positive impact on climate change, making a difference in your workplace, or improving your marriage, the day you decide that blaming others is a waste of time will be the day you change your life forever.

If it is to be, let it begin with me.

I've noticed that the most successful leaders I've met in organizations aren't necessarily *pursuing* success, yet success comes to them. It flows naturally to them when they seek to bring value to others rather than chase success for themselves. They aren't just after the next promotion or trying to get ahead in the organization. Instead, they are busy growing and serving the people around them. While they undoubtedly have goals and intentions for their future, their focus is developing and using their strengths and unique talents to bring value to others.

A job title, the letters behind our name, the size of our office, or the worth of our portfolio, while perhaps worthy goals to pursue, are not true measures of human life. A more accurate appraisal of the worth of a person are the virtues of strong character: courage, humility, reliability, honesty, integrity, perseverance, prudence, unselfishness, and compassion. Developing unshakeable character calls you to shift from being the best *in* the world to being the best *for* the world, to strive not for what you can *get*, but what you can *be*, to endeavor to be a better person before you attempt to be a better leader. Respectful and civil societies, organizations, and families depend on their members to have strong character.

When your wealth is lost, something is lost; when your health is lost, a great deal is lost; when your character is lost, everything is lost.

Cultivating the Four Components of Character

"One of life's greatest paradoxes is that nearly everyone wants to improve their circumstances, but hardly anyone wants to improve themselves."

Milton Sills

In the context of authentic leadership, character means becoming a good leader by being a good person. It's about earning trust by being trustworthy. It's that simple, and it is that complicated. Here are four components to character that each of us has the power to improve through intentional, disciplined focus.

1. Personal Responsibility: Inspiring Through Ownership

Ron Bynum was the leader of a training organization that used a former summer camp as one of its facilities. One night he was reading at home when his phone rang with bad news: one of the buildings at his training facility had caught fire and burned down. Someone had left a towel near a heater in a dorm where some of the staff lived. The old wooden building had gone up in flames like a bundle of kindling.

When the staff gathered after the tragedy to debrief, everyone was pointing fingers in blame when Ron took the stage.

"I want to raise the question of who is responsible for this situation." He paused as the group continued to blame one another.

"The answer is very clear to me," he said. "I'm responsible."

Dead silence filled the room.

"Wait a minute," someone said. "How could you be responsible? You weren't even there."

"I'm responsible because I'm claiming responsibility. That's all that really matters. I've been in that dormitory a dozen times this summer, and I could have noticed that the towel rack was too close to the heater. But I didn't. So that's one reason I'm responsible. But the details are irrelevant. How about if we all take responsibility rather than blaming ourselves or someone else? Then let's find out what needs to be done."

The atmosphere in the room shifted in a second. Blame and recrimination stopped cold; the conversation turned into solutions. By stepping into responsibility, he steered everyone in a productive, solution-oriented direction. What more can be asked of a leader?

Personal responsibility is about owning our part of every problem that we are faced with. It means choosing citizenship over consumerism. Deciding to act as citizens means we are the cause of our environment, not the effect of it. We are not consumers of the cultures we live and work in, waiting to see what management has in store for us. Personal responsibility is deciding what this place will become. As citizens, we have the capacity to act on our intentions, even if the institutions we live and work in don't reward it. Personal responsibility is ultimately about growing up.

Quantum physics has discovered something that many mystics have long since known: that our perception of the universe actually invokes the very universe that we observe. If you change the way you view the environment around you, the environment around you changes. The world isn't as it is. The world is the way we see it.

Don't get me wrong. Bosses make a difference to the experience of an employee. Customer service people make a difference. Waitresses make a difference. And it is important to get feedback on how we are doing. But what I am saying is that we are all co-creating the world that we live in. We institutionally deny the fact that each of us—through our perceptions and our choices—is actually creating the culture that we so enjoy complaining about.

Deciding that I am creating the world around me—and therefore I am the one to step into healing it—is the ultimate act of personal responsibility.

2. Integrity: Being Accountable as Well as Ethical

Integrity comes from the word "integer," which means wholeness, integration, and completeness. Being integrated is a necessary condition for self-respect, and self-respect is the basis for creating a respectful environment as a leader. Integrity means you are integrated around principles that ultimately govern the consequences of your behavior. Integrity is keeping promises you make—both to yourself and to others. It's about being honest with yourself and others.

There are two fundamental kinds of integrity: *relational* integrity and *moral* integrity.

Relational Integrity

Relational integrity is accountability—the ability to be counted on. It implies that you can keep a promise, first to yourself, and then to others. A bond of integrity is created when you make a promise and keep it. You earn the trust of others when you do what you say you will do. You earn the trust of yourself when you can make a promise to yourself and follow through. Being a reliable person earns you respect. Relational integrity means you never make a promise you don't intend to keep. Build a bridge of promise, make sure you build it right, be sure you cross it all the way, and respect, trust, and well-being will be your reward.

Here are six ways to strengthen your relational integrity—your level of personal accountability.

- **Govern Your Life with Agreements.** I have a good friend who is in the middle of a divorce. After ten years of marriage, his wife walked out on him. Devasted and dishearted, he keeps his energy strong because of the agreements he made to his five-year-old son, to his family and friends, to the customers in his business, and most importantly, to himself. While he is facing his own demons, anger, and hurt, he maintains integrity by resisting the natural urge to assassinate his wife's character by keeping his comments about her away from his son, by showing up for his son, and sustaining the important relationships in his life. Agreements have the power to serve as a source of energy.
- **Think Carefully Before You Make an Agreement.** Remember, it's much easier to not make an agreement than it is to get out of an agreement you no longer want to keep. Just ask a divorce lawyer if you have any doubts about this point. Whether it's an agreement to get up in the morning and exercise, an agreement to take on a client project with a deadline, or an agreement to be a parent, think it through carefully and thoroughly before you make a promise.
- **Only Make Agreements that You Know You Will Honor.** Don't ever make a promise you don't intend to keep. Before making a promise, ask yourself: Do I have the *capability*? The *resources*? The *willingness*? Before you make an agreement be sure that your heart is in it.

- **Scrupulously Keep the Agreements You Make—Both to Yourself and to Others.** Corporations and lives across the country are littered with habitual excuse-makers and blamers. Do you honor your promises? Once you have made a promise, it no longer matters if it is easy or comfortable or whether or not you "feel like" keeping the agreement you have made. You honor it because it is the right thing to do. And by doing so, you will earn self-respect, well-being, increased energy, and trustworthiness among the people in your life. Two things I've learned in my lifetime about keeping promises. First, it takes less time to keep an agreement than it does to explain why you didn't keep it. Second, when you let someone down, you are the only person who cares about the reason why.

- **Have a Recovery Process.** You don't have to be perfect to maintain your integrity. Life happens, and there are times when we are simply unable to do what we promised. People get sick. People you depend on don't come through. Situations beyond our control happen. When circumstances or poor choices prevent you from keeping your agreement:

  - ✓ Let your creditor know *as soon as you know* if your commitment is *jeopardized.*
  - ✓ Take one hundred percent responsibility for your inability to keep your agreement.
  - ✓ Negotiate with your creditor at this point to minimize damages and re-commit to a new promise.
  - ✓ Learn from your experience, so it doesn't happen again.

- **Write Agreements Down.** Whether it's an electronic calendar, a smartphone, or an old-fashioned little black book, carry an "agreement book" with you wherever you go to clarify understanding. Taking agreements out of your head and putting them on paper frees up more of your creative energy. A frequent component of business disputes is the statement, "I wasn't sure we agreed to that … " These lapses in memory and responsibility can be avoided entirely by writing agreements down.

Moral Integrity

Not long ago, I was asked by a client to submit a proposal on culture change. While I felt confident to do most of the work, there was one aspect of the project that I decided to subcontract to another consultant. I mistakenly turned the entire proposal over to him, instead of just the portion that would be relevant to his area of the project. As a result, the consultant was able to learn that the client had a healthy budget and deep pockets. He proposed a project that would have made us both a significant amount of money.

I knew it was unethical to send this kind of proposal to the client. It simply wasn't the right thing to do. We would have been selling them a program they could—and likely would—have paid for but didn't need. My reputation was at stake, but more importantly, my character was on the line. I had long ago committed to only ask clients to pay for services that would bring them value.

So, I canceled the proposal and found another consultant with an ethical foundation and more integrity. The original consultant may have been accountable, but he wasn't ethical. That's the difference between relational integrity and moral integrity. Doing what is right means learning to accurately gauge the world around us. It means looking inward and being honest with ourselves and others.

While relational integrity is your accountability to others, moral integrity deals with the ethical side of the integrity equation. Deep inside each person lies a conscience—a "still small voice," "inner guide," or "moral compass"—that guides our concept of what is right and wrong, as well as our desire toward meaning and contribution. It is the guiding force of vision and discipline. One of the ways you can distinguish between actions guided by the conscience and actions driven by the ego is that conscience guided actions leave you satisfied, fulfilled, and at peace with yourself, while ego driven actions leave you discontented, dissatisfied, and wanting more. Character is about living an honest and honorable life in accordance with your conscience.

I have learned over the years of working with people that every time you "swallow" something that you don't believe in, you learn to swallow more, and your integrity is slowly eroded. Moral integrity means knowing we have a line that we will not cross under any circumstance. If you compromise your integrity, before you know it, you will learn to accept not having integrity. One of the most important accomplishments of my career is being known as somebody who is not only reliable but also honest and forthright in all my dealings. There is a difference between people who feel that the end justifies the means and the people who believe that the means are just as important as the end. I aspire to be one of the latter.

Think about the ethical boundaries you will not cross. As you do so, you may find the following three steps to moral integrity helpful.

- *First:* **You *discern* right from wrong, based on a strong conscience.** A key question gets to the heart of moral integrity: Does the intent behind your decision lead to the betterment of all constituents? Is it the right thing to do? Moral integrity is about intent, about an honest effort to do what is right instead of what is easy, comfortable, or popular. Moral integrity means at times you may risk personal or financial loss as you stand on principles that serve the greater whole.

- *Second:* **You *act* on your decision.** "That you may retain your self-respect, it is better to displease the people by doing what you know is right, than to temporarily please them by doing what you know is wrong," wrote William J. H. Boetcker, earlier in the 20th century. Mr. Boetcker knew something about character. While the foundation of moral integrity is intention, action is what makes it real. You must be willing to *do* what is right, even at the risk of discomfort, rejection, or financial or personal loss. Moral integrity means taking the long view. If it is morally right, it will lead to a better life, even if you don't get immediate returns.

- *Third:* **You make your decisions and actions *public* to all stakeholders affected by your decisions.** *Sunlight is the best disinfectant.* If there is any doubt that an action is ethical, bring it out in the open with those who will be affected by the action. Criminal, unethical behavior does not happen in the open. It's hidden in the dark.

Ultimately, you need to adhere to high levels of both types of integrity—relational and moral—to reach your full potential as an authentic leader.

Character reminds us that if you can't lead yourself, how can you lead others? How can you possibly have a positive impact on others if your own personal life is a train-wreck? Leadership development starts with character development: being honest with yourself, facing whatever personal issues you've been avoiding head-on, and cleaning up your personal messes, including the wreckage of your past.

As you take a careful "integrity inventory" in your life, as you assess the integrity gaps in your life, you may find that to sustain your integrity and self-respect you may have to leave a place of employment. On the other hand, I have met people who decide that to sustain their integrity, they choose to *stay* in a job but change the environment through having the courage of their convictions. Each person must find their own way to live with integrity and subsequent strength of character.

3. Composure: Practicing Poise Under Pressure

It is easy enough to be pleasant,
When life flows by like a song,
But the man worthwhile is one who will smile,
When everything goes dead wrong.
For the test of the heart is trouble,
And it always comes with the years,
And the smile that is worth the praises of earth
Is the smile that shines through tears.

It is easy enough to be prudent,
When nothing tempts you to stray,
When without or within no voice of sin
Is luring your soul away;
But it's only a negative virtue
Until it is tried by fire,
And the life that is worth the honor of earth
Is the one that resists desire.

By the cynic, the sad, the fallen,
Who had no strength for the strife,
The world's highway is cumbered to-day;
They make up the sum of life.
But the virtue that conquers passion,
And the sorrow that hides in a smile,
It is these that are worth the homage on earth
For we find them but once in a while.

Ella Wheeler Wilcox, 1906

Years ago I had a boss who was always in a panic. Though he was well educated, talented, and bright, he was unable to remain calm in the day-to-day challenges of his job. He was often needlessly dramatic about the smallest of problems. He was quick to anger and irritation and got annoyed easily. When he was in a good mood, you couldn't meet a nicer person. But you never knew, from one day to the next, which temperament he would bring to work.

For a while, most of us on the team were able to set aside our judgments about his erratic personality, and in those days I was too immature and scared to talk with him directly about the impact he was having on me. Where it came to a head was in a financial crisis. We were working in a non-profit agency that was publically funded, and when the funding was in jeopardy, he showed how stressed and worried he was about the future of the organization and our jobs. It was at this point that we lost all confidence in him and most of us ended up quitting.

A true test of character is poise under pressure. It's a self-confident manner that offers steadiness and stability to those around you. While it is both unrealistic and inhuman to expect our leaders to forever hold up a mantel of consistency and predictability that would save us from uncertainty, we also need to realize that emotional volatility erodes trust. If someone can't handle their emotions, what else are they incapable of handling?

Here's a list of ways to practice composure in your leadership and in your life.

- **Be Respectful.** I once met a respected HR executive who told me of a time she had two senior leaders sending disrespectful, degrading, derogatory emails back and forth to each other while copying the executive, each expecting to build a case for their own individual self-righteousness. This executive stormed into each of their respective offices and demanded an immediate meeting with them both. She was mad at them both, and she let them know it. She reminded them of the inappropriate conduct of using emails to fuel discourteous resentment toward a colleague. "I want you both to sit here and work it out like the two civil adults I know you are before you leave this office!" she exclaimed.

- **Contain Your Feelings.** Composure means "containing" your emotions in a way that is appropriate for the situation and respectful of the people involved, rather than repressing, denying, or spewing emotions indiscriminately. If this executive, for example, was stressed and angry about circumstances from her personal life and she misdirected this anger at these two managers, then it would have contaminated the whole scenario—and the office environment along with it. Immature children are incapable of containing their emotions. A four-year-old with an impulse to have a temper tantrum cannot be expected to be composed enough to wait for an appropriate time and method to express their frustrations honestly and respectfully. But we expect a greater level of maturity from a forty-year-old. Containment means when you are in a bad mood, don't make everyone around you in a bad mood.

- **Practice Self-Awareness.** Composure means being aware of your surroundings and being flexible, adaptable, and appropriate in your response. The ability to do this depends on self-awareness and the courage and willingness to take responsibility for your emotions. For example, I have learned in the hard school of personal experience, that when I get afraid, I get anxious. And when I get anxious, I get impatient and, at times, angry. When I am composed, I can stop and acknowledge that I am inappropriately angry and impatient. Hopefully, I can do this before I hurt anyone. Then I can acknowledge the anxiety and fear and take constructive action to either let it go or problem solve with my team on how to deal constructively with my anxiety in a way that moves toward productive outcomes. They have to see that I am taking responsibility for my anxiety, without blame, so as to remain confident and connected.

- **Do What's Right and Trust the Process.** Composure is doing what's right, not necessarily what's easy or comfortable. Between an impulse to respond and the actual response is a gap. When others panic, a leader with composure takes a step back during this gap and seizes the opportunity to choose an appropriate response. Your poise creates a sense of safety with others, secure and comfortable in your presence. Composure is the realization that, to be responsible and credible as a leader and as a person, there needs to be a pause and an accompanying realization that there is a choice. Before getting defensive or lashing out when I disagree with someone or when things don't go my way, composure means stopping, assessing the situation calmly and instead, taking the time to listen carefully to what needs to be said. Just because I have an impulse to gossip about a colleague doesn't give me the right to assassinate someone's character. Just because I want something doesn't mean I deserve it. In the midst of an impulse, if you can stop, get your bearings, and do the right thing instead of what is comfortable or natural or easy, then you are practicing composure.

- **Remember—You are Human.** I received the news that a tumor was discovered on the parietal lobe in my sister's brain shortly before a meeting where I was to map out a long-term leadership development project with an executive team. Minutes before going into the meeting I realized that, still reeling from the news of Kate's tumor, I felt a rush of emotions that put my composure with the client at risk. I sat in the car, called a close friend, had a good cry, picked up my briefcase, and went into the meeting. I could have been honest with my client about what was going on, but I made a judgment call that it wouldn't have been respectful. After all, it is a new relationship, and I didn't want to erode their confidence in me. There may very well be a time, in the development of our relationship, when I will share this with them, but I will make that choice when it is appropriate. While it would have been disrespectful to bring my emotional upheaval to this project, it also would have been dishonest to deny my feelings of grief and shock. Composure means having the maturity to know who to share your feelings with, where and when to share them, and how to share them. We all have a right to our feelings, and with that right comes a responsibility to deal with them suitably.

- **Be Courageous.** Composure requires a strong mind, some discipline, and perhaps a little wisdom. It also takes some courage to be both honest and respectful while keeping your emotions in check. For those who have a tendency toward being rational, composure might mean being a little more vulnerable. For those who show their feelings easily, perhaps a little more rationality is needed. When a tragedy in the world occurs, and the media is drawing us into spending hours in front of our screens, it takes discipline and courage to step away from the drama and take positive action rather than be seduced into pacifying our need for entertainment.

- **Don't Fight Back.** Composure is about taking the higher ground. Fr. Max Oliva, in his book, *Becoming A Person of Mercy*, tells a story of Jackie Robinson, the African American baseball player who changed American society by ending racial segregation in the major leagues. Born in Georgia in 1919, Jackie was the grandson of a slave and the son of a sharecropper.

> Branch Rickey, the Brooklyn Dodgers' innovative and courageous GM had decided to break baseball's color barrier and decided that Robinson was the right player to help him accomplish his dream. Rickey explained to Robinson that what they were about to do was greater than baseball. And the resistance would be fierce. Rickey

knew Robinson would be a good enough ballplayer, but he didn't know whether he had the "guts" to endure the hatred he would face, "no matter what happens."

Robinson was twenty-six years old at the time. He said much later that since he had been eight years old and experienced his first encounter with racism, his attitude had been retaliation and payback as a way to protect his personal dignity. When Rickey proposed his plan to him, Robinson asked if he was looking for a ballplayer who was afraid to fight back.

"Robinson," Rickey replied forcefully, "I am looking for a ballplayer with guts enough not to fight back."

Prejudice and bigotry were their constant companions. In the beginning, Jackie endured intense abuse even from players on other teams. After one particularly difficult game, Jackie said that torment from trying to ignore the insults nearly sent him over the edge. But then he remembered Rickey's admonition and endured the abuse.

Robinson would later write:

"I started the season as a lonely man, often feeling like a black Don Quixote tilting at a lot of white windmills. I ended up feeling like a member of a solid team... I had learned how to exercise self-control—to answer insults, violence, and injustice with silence—and I had learned how to earn the respect of my teammates. They had learned that it's not the skin color but talent and ability that counts."

Teammate Duke Snider said of Robinson, "Jackie made us better because of his ability, and he made us closer as a team because of his suffering."

- **Stay Humble and Grateful.** While composure is poise under pressure—the ability to stay calm and maintain the dignity of yourself and others in the midst of catastrophe—it also has to do with poise in the midst of any strong emotion. Remaining humble in the midst of triumph, grateful in the midst of excitement, and self-effacing in the midst of success are all ways that composure is expressed. It's inspiring to be around a leader who gives credit to her team for their success, a successful quarterback who gives credit to his linesmen, or a manager who receives an award and deflects the credit to those who have been influential in getting them there.

4. Grit: The Power to Persevere in the Pain

When the morning's freshness has been replaced by the weariness of midday, when the leg muscles quiver under the strain, the climb seems endless, and suddenly, nothing will go quite as you wish—it is then that you must not hesitate.

Dag Hammarskjold

In the classic 1969 Henry Hathaway movie, *True Grit*, John Wayne plays a drunken, hard-nosed U.S. Marshal who helps a stubborn teenager track down her father's murderer. In true John Wayne fashion, we see demonstrated a most valued virtue in the development of strong character, the virtue known as grit: tenacity, perseverance, and seeing things through to the end. Grit. It's a short word with great power. Grit is having stamina, sticking with the task at hand, day in and day out, not just for the day or the month or the years, but for as long as it takes. Grit is about passion and purpose and persistence. Grit is about living life as a marathon, not a sprint or a walk in the park. According to the Merriam-Webster dictionary, grit is defined as "firmness of character ... an indomitable spirit." Those with grit know that everything will be alright in the end, and if it's not alright, it's not yet the end.

It's easy to start, but it takes grit to finish. The role grit plays in success has become a recent focus for research. Grit's rise in popularity began with Angela Duckworth's TED talk in 2013. "It's not intelligence or talent or good looks," Duckworth tells us, "that determine whether or not you will be successful in life. It's grit."

While Duckworth may have popularized the notion of the value of grit, recognition of the importance of fortitude has been around for years. William James, Erik Erikson, and Aristotle, among other great teachers and philosophers, all believed tenacity was one of the most valued virtues.

While a good component of authenticity in leadership is learning to connect, to be vulnerable and humble, it doesn't mean that you don't have a spine. Leadership without a backbone, without grit, isn't leadership at all. At times leadership requires the toughness to stand for something, the toughness to finish, the toughness to refine our soul with the sandpaper of hardship. Grit grasps the acceptance of difficulty since it is through adversity that our humanity is elevated, the spirit is cultivated, and we are able to contribute to the world with a more developed soul.

Below are three characteristics of grit with accompanying strategies for fostering fortitude in your life. Take an inventory of just how gritty you are in your life and in your leadership. Get feedback from some trusted friends and advisors. Have the grit to look closely at your own grittiness.

- **A Compelling Vision.** While you will undoubtedly meet gritty people who cannot see the big picture, grit is fueled by the power of vision. A higher purpose, a reason beyond the emotions of pleasure, enjoyment, comfort, and failure will tap you into the inspiring virtue of grit. Every person has within them the ability to achieve great things. The incentive is vision. Dr. Martin Luther King, Jr.'s unwavering persistence in fighting for civil rights, justice, anti-discrimination, and peace, inspired a broken nation. An athlete training for the Olympics will persevere through the pain of getting up early, endure the brutal workouts, and see it all the way to the end. Why? Because of the power of the dream. Thomas Edison allegedly tried 10,000 times before succeeding in creating a light bulb. A gritty undergraduate college student will persist long into the night with the vision of becoming a doctor. A young entrepreneur endures the challenges and setbacks of failures to find a way to bring her vision to the marketplace. A recovering alcoholic keeps on their program with a vision of self-respect and the well-being of the family they love. A gritty patient with a spinal cord injury finds a reason to persevere through the emotional and physical suffering to emerge with experience that will serve the world.

If you can't get your head around this whole grit thing, or if you don't see yourself as a gritty person, perhaps the problem isn't grit. Perhaps you haven't dreamed big enough. Perhaps your dream is not compelling enough or coming from the deepest part of your being. A captivating vision beyond self-interest inspires and awakens the virtue of grit.

• **Courage.** Grit means a growth mindset, which means a willingness to fail. Managing the fear of failure is imperative and a good predictor of grit and success. The supremely gritty may be afraid to crash, but they embrace it as part of a process. They understand that there are valuable lessons in defeat and that the vulnerability of perseverance is requisite for high achievement. Theodore Roosevelt, a true exemplar of grit, spoke of overcoming fear by embracing it with vulnerability and courage in an address at the Sorbonne in 1910.

> *"It is not the critic who counts; not the man who points out how the strong man stumbles, or where the doer of deeds could have done them better. The credit belongs to the man who is actually in the arena, whose face is marred by dust and sweat and blood; who strives valiantly; who errs, who comes short again and again, because there is no effort without error and shortcoming; but who does actually strive to do the deeds; who knows great enthusiasms, the great devotions; who spends himself in a worthy cause; who at the best knows in the end the triumph of high achievement, and who at the worst, if he fails, at least fails while daring greatly ... "*

It takes courage to dream, and even greater courage to persist in the realization of that dream. It takes courage to take a dream beyond a wish to a firm and sustaining resolve. As one of my teachers, Jim Rohn, used to say, "There are two pains in life: the pain of discipline or the pain of regret. Discipline weighs ounces; regret weighs tons." It takes courage to identify the habits that will create and realize your vision, and even greater courage to get up in the morning and implement those habits—in the midst of a thousand excuses to stay in bed. It takes courage to stay focused on the day, and to execute your plans one day—and often one moment—at a time. It takes courage to keep making progress, to keep setting new standards, in the midst of the world telling you to settle for conformity and mediocrity.

Courage, however, isn't always apparent. Like deep roots that sustain the sturdy oak, courage lies below the surface. People are rewarded in public for what they practiced for years in private. You can't always see courage, nor can courage be accurately assessed by anyone else. It takes courage to finish a marathon, and sometimes it takes courage to quit. It takes courage to stand by a dying loved one at home through the last months and even years of their cancer, and sometimes it takes courage to ask for help and find a good hospice to help with the care. It takes courage to build a business, and it takes courage to find other priorities in your life that matter. It takes courage to do a job right, and it takes courage to let go of perfection and allow excellence to be good enough. It takes courage to get back on the proverbial horse, and sometimes it takes courage to walk away from the horse. It takes courage to stay in a relationship, and sometimes it takes courage to leave a relationship. It takes courage to love, and it takes courage to let go. Courage, a quality vital to grit, is developed with practice and identified by looking within.

- **Caring**. As I wrote in my book, *Caring is Everything*, caring enriches every facet of our lives. Caring helps heal those in need of healing. It inspires us to tend to our planet. It makes us better people. Caring guides us toward our authentic selves, to the lives we are meant to live. At a crucial time in human history—when countless individuals are met with violence, terrorism, and a disregard for human life, when politicians and public figures use fear to appeal to the darkest side of humanity, when so many of us are afraid, cynical, or stressed—the need for caring has perhaps never been greater. Caring, the most noble of human journeys, has a pervasive, enduring influence on the wellbeing of those around us. It impacts who we are as people, and the places where we work and live. Caring is everything.

Perhaps caring is just another version of vision, for without caring about something beyond ourselves there is no vision. Caring also stands alone. If you care enough, you will persist. If you care enough, you will find the grit. If you can't find it in you to dream, maybe all you need to inspire grit is to care. However, like courage, caring isn't always obvious. Sometimes you care enough to persevere. And sometimes you care enough to let go. Grit, like other qualities of character, cannot be "taught" to others like you teach algebra or organic chemistry. However, it can be "caught." It can be discovered. It can be fostered if we take the advice of Albert Schweitzer, theologian, philosopher, and physician: *"Example is not the main thing in influencing others, it is the only thing."*

To cultivate grit in others, and particularly children in their formative years, you have to care enough to love them through the hard times and support them through the pain. Sometimes you have to let go of the need to shelter them from failure and loss, pop the bubble wrap of coddling and overprotection, and simply care by loving them through the inevitable difficulties and disappointments of life. Grit requires an internal fortitude built through discovering the immense resources that live within us by walking through adversity. Grit is born in the realization that life is difficult. Once we accept this, then life isn't so difficult. In our efforts to protect those we care about from disappointment, it is good to ask ourselves if we are actually inadvertently harming them. Coddling and cultivating grit may indeed turn out to be incompatible bedfellows. The time has come to care in a new, grit enhancing way, not just about our children, but also about ourselves and everyone we care about.

Greg McMeekin, a 43-year-old lawyer with cerebral palsy, who in 2016 made history by being admitted to the Alberta bar, has grit. His persistence and tenacity allowed him to overcome his physical challenges in the thirteen years he spent getting his law degree, but he doesn't want only that to define him.

"I don't want to be known as a role model just because of my disability. I work hard, believe in being accountable, truthful, and in helping others."

McMeekin has spent most of his life defying boundaries others placed on him. He was the first person with a physical disability to enroll in a city public school, rather than one for special-needs students; he fought to change how others were treated as a member of the Calgary HandiBus Foundation and the Premier's Council on the Status of Persons with Disabilities. Caring, courage, and a compelling vision prove that McMeekin truly has grit. And it is people like McMeekin who inspire us all.

Centering

"Dwell as near as possible to the channel in which your life flows."
Henry David Thoreau

In a leadership retreat with an association of entrepreneurs and business leaders whose membership requirement was a seven-figure annual income, I asked, *"How much is enough?"* While they were intrigued by my query, no one was able to answer the question. After much discussion, the best I could get from them was, *"I don't know how much is enough. I only know that enough is more than I have now."*

In a world where our worth is defined by what we do, what we have, and what we achieve, our approach to living disproportionately emphasizes the value of the external—the belief that the happiness we desire will be realized if we get *more*—more money, more status, more recognition, more achievement, more possessions, more speed, more technology, more information, more intense experiences, more titles and degrees, more of virtually *anything*.

This prominence toward the external leads to continuous striving and accumulating along with a rise in personal and public debt and an accompanying increase in anxiety, depression, addiction, and obesity.

Lives driven by the externals result in confusion between *wants* and *needs*, *means* and *ends*, *obsessions* and *self-expression*, and *standard of living* and *quality of life*. The end result can be a corporate executive burning out, attempting to meet all the expectations of shareholders and customers, an anxious parent always trying to do what is right for their children, an entrepreneur never knowing what is enough, an employee experiencing a hollow feeling from having sold out to the demands of others, or an exhausted helping professional whose helping gets heavy.

Caught in the world of constant demands, we find ourselves in the proverbial rat race, so busy putting out the fires around us that we lack the clarity to kindle our own inner flame. Reacting to the demands and pressures of daily life is like being in a boat with oarsmen pulling frantically in different directions as we find ourselves amidst the frenzy, unfocused, continually available and interrupted, rushed, stressed, splintered, disjointed, disconnected, exhausted, and empty. The comedian Lily Tomlin said it best when she said, "Even if you win the rat race, at the end, you are still a rat."

In our unbridled pursuit of more, in a world that promises unlimited potential, success, and happiness, we, paradoxically, have forgotten what *enough* actually feels like. The mistaken notion that external acquisition is equated in some way to inner well-being is like churning sand all day thinking it will give us butter just because we worked hard. If we don't feel a sense of worth from within, no amount of accumulation of anything is going to satisfy us. As simply and eloquently expressed by the songwriter Bono, we "still haven't found what [we are] looking for."

A New Approach to an Old Idea

Centering offers an alternative approach whose emphasis is on the *internal* rather than the external. Rather than relying on the relentless and unending pursuit of more to define you and give you worth, you experience what enough actually feels like—from within. Until you know you are enough, until you are content with what is here, now, you will never be at peace.

Centering guides you to this sustaining life-giving inner wellbeing and way of living so that your pursuits, your achievements, and whatever you decide to acquire, is enough because you are enough. You have enough. You are enough. You do enough. When you grow and achieve and contribute from this centered place, everything changes. When centered, your roles, achievements, and acquisitions become an *expression* of who you are, enjoyed and appreciated, rather than a definition of who you are. Rather than being driven and obsessed to achieve in order to affirm your security and worth, the centering approach aligns with the ancient Chinese philosopher and writer Lao Tzu, who said, "*Be content with what you have. Rejoice in the way things are. When you realize there is nothing lacking, the whole world belongs to you.*"

Leaders who are content with who they are and thus what they have, are better leaders. Their egos don't get in the way of their primary ambition for the larger cause. They are humble because they know that their worth comes from within, not from their achievements or their possessions or office size or the titles behind their names. They are more composed under pressure so that others are apt to trust them. They manage stress better because they are clear about their values. They understand that they aren't going to please everyone, so they know how to say no to the wrong opportunities and to the nonessentials. Security and worth come from within them, so they have less need to over-control and micro-manage. They bring generosity rather than scarcity to the world around them. Within their ambition and goals is the realization that external success is different from human fulfillment, which comes from the inside. In the centering approach, contentment precedes success, so achievements become about self-expression rather than identity. Centered leaders, therefore, cease to be driven and emerge into a place of self-realization and service rather than obsession and self-interest.

If You Don't Go Within, You'll Go Without

Inside each of us, there is a sustaining center, a place where all that is most precious to us is embedded. Whether you call this center your soul, your true nature, your spark of divinity, your spiritual core, your unconscious, your higher self, your essence, your intuition, or your inner light, it cannot be easily seen or named. This inner guide, this still small voice, this absolutely trustworthy essential self that we come to know with undeniable certainty, is wholly sufficient, simply and completely enough.

Centering separates us from our roles, achievements and failures, possessions, and even relationships. Centering requires a conscious, consistent practice to discover inner peace, serenity, and clarity amidst what others would call chaos, demands, and stress. Helping, healing, and leading from your center generates effortless flow and maximum impact. Centering, in other words, provides a life of sufficiency.

It is this center that sustains us, that gives us connection in loss, humility in success, perspective in chaos, strength in weakness, and wholeness in fragmentation. It gives us sustained security when nothing in the world is secure, guidance and wisdom in the quiet moments, stability in an unstable world, and a true source of power and identity that comes from inner assuredness.

While the external is about *quantity*, centering is internal and about *quality*. Centering is the source of art, culture, imagination, and qualities of the soul. Centering is about finding contentment, independent of our successes and failures, poverty or prosperity, or the fleeting emotions of happiness or sadness. The work of centering takes us into a sustaining core of pure potential and presence where all that is most precious to us is embedded. This center is your truest self, the essence of your spiritual nature. Centering requires a conscious, consistent practice to find serenity and clarity amidst expectations and demands. Leading, achieving, and even helping and healing from your center generates effortless flow and influence. Centering is what allows leaders to amplify their impact with presence rather than the power assumed by a title. Being centered transforms achievement from a way of *defining* ourselves to a way of *expressing* ourselves. When integrated with active living and focused achievement, centering is the inner examination that makes life worth living. Activity without contemplation will catapult you into relentless frenzy. Contemplation without action can become escapism. Both contemplation and focused activity are required to live a full life.

It is here we must guard what is sacred to us for it is here that we feel most vulnerable and it is here we access our greatest strength. Centering reminds us we are a human *being* rather than a human *doing*.

The centering approach to life is built on a simple philosophy given to me by Norris Lowry, the wise philosopher in his own right, who helped on the farm and taught me many life lessons. "Happiness," Norris used to say, "is not a destination. Happiness is a method of travel."

William Stafford's journey with words began most mornings before sunrise. This simple poem, "The Way It Is," written 26 days before he passed, expresses brilliantly what it means to find an inner place of calm and steadiness—your center—in the midst of the vicissitudes of life.

> *There's a thread you follow. It goes among*
> *things that change. But it doesn't change.*
> *People wonder about what you are pursuing.*
> *You have to explain about the thread.*
> *But it is hard for others to see.*
> *While you hold it you can't get lost.*
> *Tragedies happen; people get hurt*
> *or die; and you suffer and get old.*
> *Nothing you do can stop time's unfolding.*
> *You don't ever let go of the thread.*

Coming Home

There was a time when farmers of the Great Plains would run a rope from their back door to the barn at the first sign of a blizzard. They all knew stories of people who had wandered off and froze to death, having lost sight of their home in a whiteout while still in their own backyards. "The blizzard of the world has crossed the threshold, and it has overturned the order of the soul," wrote Leonard Cohen. Today we live in a blizzard of another sort. It swirls around us in the form of ever-increasing demands and promises. Centering is finding the rope that will take you home to your true self.

I remember when my daughters were very young and I was building my speaking business. I would offer what I thought were profound messages to audiences who would give me accolades and praise. When I returned home, it didn't take long to discover that my family did not care about my brilliant stories or about how wise I was, only that I was home with them. I thought they didn't really care about me until the time that I failed to meet the expectations of a client and an audience rejected my message. I came home completely disheartened, full of self-doubt, and insecurity. The response from my family was the same unconditional love as when I came home with the perception of being a success. They didn't care that on that day I felt like a failure in the eyes of the world. All they cared about was being with me. Centering is finding that inner place of peace and contentment that knows your worth away from the world. Centering is about getting beyond the ego and connecting to a sustainable sense of sufficiency. Centering is coming home to yourself.

While there is no clear formula for being centered, I have found some strategies, what could be called guideposts, to help:

1. S-l-o-w d-o-w-n—and be Present to the Present Moment

"What day is it?"

"It's today," squeaked Piglet.

"My favorite day," said Pooh.

In its simplest form, start creating some space in your day to notice what's going on in your physical surroundings, as well as what is going on within yourself—your inner state, your thoughts, your feelings, your body. Stop, even once an hour, and ask yourself, "What am I thinking? What am I feeling? How's my body doing? How is my inner state? How about my energy level?" You can ask yourself, at that moment, whether what you are doing is giving you energy or depleting your energy. You may, at this point, decide to make some adjustments, but if you take the first step—getting centered by slowing down and tuning in—you are well on your way.

It has been said that the best present we can give to someone is the present of being fully present in the present. Of course, this gift of being present in the present begins with a gift to ourselves. As you become aware of the present, as you experience it, you change your relationship to yourself, to others, and to time itself. The rush of the past and the worry of the future are cast aside. There is no stress in the present. In the present we find center. A person who is busy reacting to the circumstances in their life, whose mind is racing without knowing that it is racing, who is fidgety and distracted and not aware of being distracted, cannot be attentive to another, so is limited in their impact on another. Presence—through centering—has a powerful impact. If you have ever had the experience of being with a person who is completely present to you, who gives you the feeling that you are the only person in the world right now—you'll know something of what I mean.

Any martial arts, yoga, meditation, or mindfulness practice will teach you simply to be attentive. Nonjudgmental attentiveness is the first step to centering. Being centered means s-l-o-w-i-n-g d-o-w-n enough to be here now. As you practice simple "present moment attentiveness," you will realize that there is actually no stress in the world and there is no stress in the present moment. Stress is in our minds, and it is only in our minds when our minds wander to either the future or the past. You cannot find peace of mind, well-being, or joy yesterday. You'll never find meaning, fulfillment, or satisfaction tomorrow. You can certainly learn from the past and prepare for the future, but the only time you will ever experience the true richness of life is now, this very moment. It is not the events in your life that makes you happy or unhappy. Life is lived in the *experience* of events. That's all we have in life: moments in which to be present. Being centered is ultimately about realizing that the only place life is lived, is now.

> Look to this day, for it is life,
> The very life of life.
> In its brief course lie all
> The realities and verities of existence,

The bliss of growth,
The splendor of action,
The glory of power—
For yesterday is but a dream,
And tomorrow is only a vision,
But today, well lived,
Makes every yesterday a dream of happiness
And every tomorrow a vision of hope.
Live well, therefore, this day.

                                        Sanskrit Proverb

2. Make Room for Stillness

Centering has very practical application. Whenever an answer, a solution, or a creative idea is needed, stop thinking for a moment by focusing attention on what is going on inside of you, what some may refer to as your "inner energy field." Become aware of the stillness. Get away, at least momentarily, from the burden of "thinking," and just experience some stillness. This may only take a minute or two, or it may require a walk in a nearby park. When you resume thinking, it will be fresh and creative. In any thought activity, make it a habit to go back and forth every few minutes or so between thinking and an inner kind of listening, an inner stillness.

"Beware the barrenness of a busy life," wrote Socrates over twenty-four hundred years ago. I have often reflected upon this statement. While an overbooked schedule is exhausting, I wonder if he was also referring to the nature of the active mind, the human tendency toward busyness inside our heads. Whether it's an over-extended timetable or a harried mind or a combination of both, when you practice centering it won't take you long to discover that life has no substance, meaning, or value when we are lost in thoughts. For example, if you are attentive you realize that when you are late and thinking of getting to your destination faster, you lose touch with the beauty that is all around you: with the sun that is going down behind the hill or with the flowers in the park beside the road, or the young child in the car seat beside you while you are sitting in traffic.

Without beauty, what is there in life? Without connection to what and who is around us, what purpose could we possibly find in this brief existence? At the end of our days, do we really want the inscription on our tombstone to read, "He did a great job of answering emails and emptying his inbox?"

The mind of the calm person is like the surface of a still pond. It reflects the beauty that surrounds it. Whereas the distressed mind, like the distressed surface of a pond, gives back a distorted reflection of its surroundings. Adhering to a practice that centers us will help smooth the surface of the mind.

3. Create and Use Sanctuaries

Blaise Pascal, the French scientist and philosopher, once remarked, "All man's miseries derive from not being able to sit quietly in a room alone." A sanctuary is defined formally as a sacred place, the holiest part of a temple; an area where wild birds and animals are protected; a refuge. In practice, sanctuaries are very personal. A sanctuary is a haven, a restorative place where you can find refuge from the demands of the world, a designated place to find solitude, silence, and space to stop and feel your emotions, turn off the noise of the world, and attend to the voice within. Regardless of what you call it, claiming sanctuary is part of our nature—it is both innate and necessary for us to want to retreat regularly. It is vital to give yourself permission to seek refuge amidst the requirements of life.

For some people, sanctuary is a religious place, a formal institution. For others, it could be a kitchen table, a meditation cushion, a special room in your home, a yoga mat, time with a pet, a special bench by a quiet river, or under beautiful trees. For others, sanctuary is a jogging trail. Mentors, allies, and trusted friends who create a safe and sacred place for us to open up without being judged or needing to be "fixed," can be a sanctuary. Sanctuaries can also be a place inside of us, a room in the inner sanctions of our mind, where you go when you meditate or pray or simply be still. All of these sanctuaries enable you to touch and listen to your inner wisdom.

After one of my presentations on sanctuaries, a woman came up and beamed: "I had an insight during your presentation as to why I have been angry at my husband for the past three years!" she exclaimed. "He has been renovating our bathroom!" You can imagine where this woman's sanctuary was. It turns out she hadn't had a hot bath since the renovations began three years before. She responded excitedly, "I'm going home to complete the construction myself!" A man standing beside us and listening in on the conversation laughed. "Guess where her husband's sanctuary has been for the past three years? I understand why he was not in a hurry!"

4. Remove the Distractions

Our five senses are potential barriers to going within and can potentially suffocate the inner voice. My friend, Ross Watson, blind from the age of eleven and now a successful community activist, politician, adventurer, and speaker, once gave me a lesson on how to listen. "Sight," he contends, "is such a powerful sense that it blinds us to so much of what is happening in the world."

Another barrier in our culture that "blinds" us to connecting with our inner life is the constant bombardment of noise. Silence has become elusive.

I remember having a friend from Los Angeles stay with us. One morning I took her for a walk along the river trail behind our home. As we walked, I was teaching her about some of our local wildlife and how you could tell the finches, blackbirds, and waxwings by the sounds they make. I kept asking, "Do you hear that?" and "Listen to that," but she didn't hear anything. It took days before she started to tune in to sounds that she didn't hear earlier.

5. Disconnect to Connect—Take Sabbaths

Millennia ago, the tradition of Sabbath created an oasis of sacred time within a life of unceasing labor. In today's world, with its relentless emphasis on success and productivity, we have lost the necessary rhythm of life, the balance between work and rest. Constantly striving, we feel exhausted and deprived in the midst of great abundance. We long for time with friends and family. We long for a moment to ourselves.

Technology, with all its capacity, has killed the 9-5 working day and left us, unless we choose otherwise, mentally tethered to our desks 24/7. There used to be a day when going or coming home from work meant that you left your work at work, weekends and holidays meant that you actually got a break from it all. A healthy life is about rhythms—"a time to be born and a time to die, a time to plant and a time to uproot … a time to tear down and a time to build, a time to weep and a time to laugh, a time to mourn and a time to dance … a time to search and a time to give up, a time to keep and a time to throw away, a time to tear and a time to mend, a time to be silent and a time to speak … a time to work and a time to be renewed."

Then there are the greater rhythms, seasons and hormonal cycles and sunsets and moonrises and great movements of seas and stars. There is a rhythm in the way day dissolves into night, and night into day. There is a rhythm as the active growth of spring and summer is quieted by the necessary dormancy of fall and winter. There is a tidal rhythm, a deep, eternal conversation between the land and the great sea.

In his book, *Sabbath: Finding Rest, Renewal, and Delight in Our Busy Lives,* Wayne Muller points out that Sabbath requires surrender. If we only stop when we are finished with all our work or when our inbox is empty, we will never stop, because our work is never completely done.

When you disconnect you learn, first and foremost, how addictive technology has become. It's difficult not to be obsessively checking emails, newsreels, sports scores, and the latest updates on social media. And what you also learn, if you allow yourself to go through the withdrawal and come out the other side, is that there is more to life than flickering pixels, online images, status updates, and Google alerts.

There is a dog to play with, a cat to sit with on your lap, a book to read. There are friends and family to spend time with, nature to be enjoyed. There is laughter and love and an abundant life that surrounds us. There are walks in parks. There are sunsets to see and ocean air to smell and perspectives to gain. There is a world that surrounds us that is actually a beautiful place. There is time to pray and dream and ponder and create and reflect and think and *be*. Let us be good to ourselves so that we might then be good to others.

6. Create Transition Rituals

A CEO I worked with once told me how he gets centered. "As soon as I get home I get changed and have a shower and wash off the problems and unfinished projects from the day. It signals to my brain that I'm done for the day. When I come out, I'm ready to get on with greeting my family and getting into household chores."

Over the years, I have gathered a variety of strategies that leaders use at the end or the beginning of the day to get centered. Some are intentional, and others are just a natural part of their routine. One leader expressed that she takes her husband dancing every Friday night as a way of bringing the week to a close. Dancing, for her, allows her to shake off any problems she brings home from work. One leader, if he had a particularly bad day in the office, went home, laid in the middle of the living room floor, put on his Bose headphones, and cranked up Beethoven's Ninth Symphony. After fifteen minutes he was ready to join his family. Other leaders go home and garden or take a walk in the park. Others go for a run or spend a little time reading. Still others find it important to debrief the day with a colleague or trusted friend or partner. I met a man once who puts his hands on a tree in his back-yard before coming into the house with his family. He calls it his "trouble tree." He gives all his troubles from the day to this big old oak tree, so he can be free of stress and strain when he greets his family. This is a similar ritual that many therapists and healthcare workers employ. When they shut the door to their office at the end of the day, they make it a point to consciously leave all the problems brought to them in the office.

"Ritual" comes from the Sanskrit word *rita*, meaning *that which illumines your transitions.* Transitional rituals are practices that illuminate your nature, bring you back to yourself, to your center, especially when you are making a transition from one role into another part of your life.

Most centered leaders I have met have a routine of starting the day with a ritual that connects them to themselves. It could be a spiritual practice, a time of prayer, spiritual readings, or meditation. For others, they like to start the day with some exercise, connect to nature, or simply quiet time reading the morning paper over a latte.

Of course, there are rituals when you first enter the office. Some leaders tell me this is their time to wander around, connect with staff, or find out what's going on in the plant. Some take half an hour to check emails and get the technology behind them for the morning, so they can move to the creative, connecting part of their work. Others take a few moments of stillness in their office before they turn on their computer.

With the increased attention to the importance of sleep, I hear more and more about transitional rituals before bedtime, habits that quiet the mind and relax the body. Evening rituals have to do with turning the TV off early, shutting off technology, taking some quiet time, reading, or listening to relaxing music before turning in.

Centering asks us to be intentional about the kind of rituals that bring us back to our deeper, sustaining self, especially when in the midst of so many demands in all of our various roles.

7. Find Inner Guides

Many believe that the soul is given a unique companion before we are born. This soul-companion guides you here. This "inner confidant," while forgotten, never leaves you and carries your destiny. Regardless of what you call your inner companion (the Romans called it your *genius*; the Greeks your *daimon* or *entelechy*; the Christians your *guardian angel*; the Romantics, like many poets, call it your *heart*; some refer to it as the *imaginal body* that carries you like a vehicle), it is your personal bearer, your support, your inner guide. Remember that he/she wants a relationship with you as much, if not more, than you want with him/her.

While you may connect with, and find strength from this inner companion, you may also find strength, guidance, security, and support from other "interior guides," such as relatives, teachers, or friends who have passed on. Napoleon Hill, in his renowned book, *Think and Grow Rich*, outlined his thoughts about imagery and visualization. He writes:

> The thirteenth principle is known as the sixth sense, through which Infinite Intelligence may and will communicate voluntarily, without any effort from, or demands by, the individual...

Just before going to sleep at night. I would shut my eyes, and see, in my imagination, this group of men seated with me around my council table... After some months of this nightly procedure, I was astounded by the discovery that these imaginary figures became apparently real.

Each of these nine men developed individual characteristics, which surprised me... These meetings became so realistic that I became fearful of their consequences and discontinued them for several months.

The experiences were so uncanny, I was afraid if I continued them I would lose sight of the fact that the meetings were purely experiences of my imagination... Whatever you believe that the adviser is a spirit, a guardian angel, a messenger from God, a hallucination, a communication from your right brain to your left, or a symbolic representation of inner wisdom is all right. The fact is, no one knows what it is with any certainty. We can each decide for ourselves...

Regardless of what you believe, I personally have found great strength in sitting quietly with the image of late ancestors, teachers that have gone before me that I admire, and particularly my parents who have passed on. When I am in need of specific kinds of guidance and direction, I often find myself sitting in silence and listening to their gentle wisdom.

> "The best and most beautiful things in the world cannot be seen or even touched. They must be felt with the heart."
>
> Helen Keller

8. Listen to Your Body

The body knows. It is an amazing, interconnected organism that will teach you a great deal about how you are living your life. Centering requires a connection to and an understanding of the language your body uses to communicate with you. Awaken to the wisdom of your body. Our quest for a centered, authentic life includes a new relationship to our physical body. For many people, the initiation into authenticity begins with a new awareness of their body, often in the form of an illness or a simple change in the way they see themselves. We may experience a lump in our breast or a questionable outcome on a prostate exam. That ulcer is there to teach you. That sore back, tight neck, the migraine headache, the intermittent sinus infection, are all giving you a signal. Of course, always get medical attention to assess and alleviate the symptoms and diagnose serious illnesses. Centering invites you to also inquire as to *why* those symptoms exist.

9. Stay Connected to Your Own Sources of Inspiration

To be inspiring, we must be inspired. Being centered recognizes that you can't inspire others until you, yourself are inspired. As leaders, we inspire others by being inspiring.

Albert Schweitzer, the philosopher and physician, wrote, "In everybody's life, at some time, our inner fire goes out. It is then burst into flame by an encounter with another human being. We should all be thankful for those people who rekindle the inner spirit." Great leaders inspire us by their presence and by their authentic lives. Mahatma Gandhi's life was authentic; when asked to describe his mission, he said, simply and honestly, "My life is my message."

There is a Greek word, politeia, which when translated means "your highest sense of purpose for others." I interpret politeia as the realization that while we may not be capable of curing the world of its suffering and sorrow, what we can do is find a way to bring our own wellbeing to the world. Francis Bernadone, referred to often as St. Francis of Assisi, had to face his own demons. From his pain emerged a prayer that expressed what he would wish to become, his own form of politeia:

> Lord, make me an instrument of thy peace. Where there is hatred, let me sow love. Where there is injury, pardon. Where there is doubt, faith. Where there is despair, hope. Where there is darkness, light. Where there is sadness, joy. Lord, grant that I may not so much seek to be consoled as to console, to be

understood as to understand, to be loved as to love. For it is in giving that we receive. It is in pardoning that we are pardoned. It is in dying to self that we are born to eternal life.

The remedy for absence is presence. Evil is an absence and, as such, it cannot be healed with an absence. By hating evil, or by hating someone who is engaged in evil, we contribute to the absence of light and not its presence. Hatred begets hatred. What we do to others, others will do to us. That's called karma.

The answer to an inhumane world begins with inner peace and the courage to open our hearts. In spite of the setbacks of war, hated, and greed, the world is sure to get better when we open our hearts. There is a First Nations saying that goes, "What we do not listen to, we do not understand. What we do not understand, we fear. What we fear, we seek to destroy."

What or what inspires you? What enables you to keep the fire of your own spirit burning brightly—so you can continue to bring light into the darkness? Being centered means staying plugged into the source that supports and sustains you.

In a world where pessimism, exhaustion, and an unwillingness to let go of past hurts damages souls and pulls people away from the virtue of human goodness, there is an array of ways to stay inspired. Read novels that will awaken and inspire your spirit. Listen to music that inspires you through its lyrics and melody. Watch films that touch you. A few inspiring films that illustrate authentic and courageous leadership include *Invictus*, *The Roosevelts: An Intimate History* (TV mini-series), and *Gandhi*. Expose yourself to guides, teachers, poets, artists, musicians, athletes, visual artists, songwriters, storytellers, authors, actors, friends, and colleagues who rouse within you a desire to be more of who you are meant to be.

10. Put the Serenity Prayer to Use

The Serenity Prayer is one of the most widely known prayers in existence. It was written and published by Reinhold Niebuhr in 1951, although he had used it much earlier in a sermon in 1943. This prayer is full of wisdom and guidance to help us stay centered.

God grant me the serenity
to accept the things I cannot change;
courage to change the things I can;
and wisdom to know the difference.

The serenity prayer gives a way to center, by offering three primary injunctions:

- **Change the changeable.** Life can get overwhelming. Staying centered means changing the world not by changing the world, but by changing the only thing you can: yourself.
- **Accept the unchangeable.** Bringing peace to the world means letting go of that which you are unable to change.
- **Remove yourself from the unacceptable.** There's an old aboriginal saying that goes, "When you are riding a dead horse, it's time to get off."

11. Manage Your Human Hungers

"Everybody has a hungry heart."

Bruce Springsteen

Nature gave us certain basic instincts for a reason. Without them, we would not survive as human beings. The desire for security, recognition, ambition, and comfort, or wanting to be needed or close to another human being, are hungers necessary for our existence. But when these natural desires are not managed, they can exceed their appropriate purpose and turn into an insatiable desire that creates unmanageability in your life and insulates you from your authentic self.

The key is to be aware of what you are truly hungry for and get to the source that will fill it. The heart's longing can be expressed through unquenchable hungers of the body. The insatiable desire for food, possessions, alcohol, sex, power, control, prestige, or relationships is often an indicator of a deeper yearning of the soul. If any of these hungers and subsequent cravings are creating unmanageability in your life, it is important to get some outside support and accountability. Therapists, coaches, mentors, twelve-step groups, or healthcare professionals can be helpful. Until the true source of the yearning is acknowledged, the thirsts will remain forever unquenched. If we fall prey to the illusion that satisfying the impulsive thirst will satisfy a deeper longing, what we pursue will leave us unsatisfied.

Human hungers can subtly take over and destroy your life. Unbridled ambition, for example, can tear apart health and relationships. The unbridled need for power can create an abusive, controlling egomaniac with an inferiority complex. Most of the harm done in this world is due to insecure people with an insatiable need to feel important.

The keys to prevent destruction and to use hunger as a positive force in your life is balance and moderation. These come from self-awareness, a willingness to face some of the darker aspects of yourself and having the courage to live a life dictated by your conscience, not your ego. Managing human hungers is the foundation of a sustaining center and subsequent authenticity.

12. Practice Gratitude and Generosity

"Find the joy in the moment and, if it can't be found, be in the moment and the joy will find you."

Bill Morris

"Life is difficult," M. Scott Peck maintains in *The Road Less Traveled*. "It is a great truth because once we truly see this truth, we transcend it. Once we truly know that life is difficult ... then life is no longer difficult. Because once it is accepted, the fact that life is difficult no longer matters."

I'd arrived late for the first speech at the conference and was headed for a seat along the side of the crowded ballroom. I was the wrap-up speaker, so I knew I had plenty of time to sit through presentations during the day to get a good sense of the audience. Sitting off to the side of the assembled seats was a man with crutches at his side. I pulled up my chair next to him without speaking to him, not wanting to disturb any of the nearby audience members. I'd been hoping to make a connection with someone in the audience, but it wasn't until now that I realized that I was sitting beside a guy without legs. As I glanced over, he gave me a welcoming nod and a smile. I reached out and shook his hand. He had a warm, inviting presence. He was calm and relaxed. Inner peace seemed to surround him. I was certainly more drawn to this man's contented manner than to the CEO's opening remarks. We didn't look at each other after our initial greeting, but I enjoyed sitting next to him for the remainder of the opening address.

After the speech was over, there was a break, and I turned and introduced myself.

"I'm Paul Franklin," he replied, smiling.

"What happened to your legs?" I asked.

"Afghanistan."

"How can you be so happy?"

"Gratitude. Every day is a new day because, in reality, I should be dead."

As with most of us, there are a handful of important years that have defined Paul Franklin's life. He explained that 1999 was the year he found his life's work with the Canadian Forces. A year later, he welcomed his son Simon into the world. He completed his first marathon in 2005.

According to Paul, the best year of his life, however, was 2006—the year a suicide bomb ripped through his vehicle in Afghanistan, killing Canadian diplomat Glyn Berry, and seriously injuring two fellow soldiers. Paul nearly died that year. He lost both of his legs, and he fought anger, hatred, unbearable pain, and fear, but he now maintains that this horrific tragedy eventually led him to his life's purpose: to improve the lives of Canadian military and civilian amputees. Now, so many years later, Paul makes a point of spending time with his son and with friends, while ensuring his family is well cared for.

Paul Franklin reminds me of the saying, "I used to complain about having no shoes until I met a man who had no feet." He also reminds me that to care enough about one's life and the people who care about us, to care enough to work through the anger and the injustice and the hurt, is to care enough to choose service and contribution over narcissistic self-pity. This honorable veteran is an inspiration and a great illustration of what it means to be grateful, and how gratitude is a powerful force for centering. You can read Paul's story in its entirety in the book, *The Long Walk Home*.

What I've learned in life is that what you focus on is what grows. When I focus on gratitude, my life gets better. When I focus on all my problems, the problems increase. When I focus on people's weaknesses, the weaknesses grow. When I focus on people's strengths, their strengths multiply.

I have also learned that what I bring to the world will come back to me. If I am generous, the universe will return it to me. If I am caring to others, caring will eventually, in its own time and its own way, come back to me. If I love, I will be loved. It may not meet my immediate expectations, but it will come to me.

If I am unable to feel centered, the best remedy is to get busy and be generous, and the joy, inner contentment, and serenity will find me. What you appreciate, appreciates.

Calling

What in your life is calling you?
When all the noise is silenced, the meetings adjourned,
The lists laid aside, and the wild iris blooms by itself
In the dark forest, what still pulls on your soul?
In the silence between your heartbeats hides a summons. Do you
    hear it?
Name it, if you must, or leave it forever nameless, but why pretend
    it is not there.

Terma Collective

While driving through the Rocky Mountains on a gorgeous fall afternoon only weeks after the death of my mother, I pulled the car over and stared breathlessly at the vast array of autumn colors scattered across the valley in front of me. I had driven through this pass hundreds of times, but that day bereavement was heightening my awareness like a new pair of glasses. I noticed colors and sunlight and ridges and the sparkling river as I never had before. I was feeling peaceful and serene when a thought abruptly interrupted me, "You need to go visit your uncle. You haven't seen him for a long time."

At eighty-four, Jack and his wife Evelyn were living a full life. Jack was so busy; you had to make an appointment to see him. When I returned to the city, I called and asked if he was up for a visit.

"Sure, I can squeeze you in," he replied. "I've got a lunch meeting on Saturday and then church at five o'clock, but why don't you drop by about two o'clock?"

Uncle Jack loves genealogy. So, my daughter Mellissa and I brought a box of old family photos and family history documents. We arrived shortly before 2 p.m. Spry as ever; he greeted us at the door with his usual warmth and spirit. We then spent a stimulating hour or so talking about family history.

Suddenly Jack turned pale and said he was feeling faint. His wife was out shopping, but after some coaxing, he consented to let us take him to the hospital. Within seconds of wheeling him into the emergency room, Jack suffered a major heart attack. Because he was there with all of the medical staff and equipment at his service, he survived. After an extended recovery, Jack lived another dozen good years.

As Mellissa and I sat quietly in the waiting room after Evelyn arrived and Jack was admitted, we felt the impact of being wandering messengers who had helped save a life. That we would choose that particular day to visit and be there to bring Jack to the hospital before his heart attack seemed more than coincidence. The sense that a deeper force was guiding us that day was undeniable.

The Danish philosopher Kierkegaard said, "We all come to life with sealed orders." There lies within us, if we slow down enough to listen, an inner urge, a leading, a feeling that a thing is right, an unspoken inner leading. It's a deep understanding that you are meant to be a certain kind of person, follow a specific line of work, or pursue a particular action.

I have known people who have just "known" they are meant to be a builder or an artist or a healer or a helper or a caregiver and have pursued work in the field of the arts, the trades, or the sciences. They have become architects or physicians, nurses or artists, caregivers or actors, engineers or dancers, mathematicians or teachers. "When the deepest part of you becomes engaged in what you are doing," writes Gary Zukav, "when what you do serves both yourself and others, when you do not tire on the inside, but seek the sweet satisfaction of your life and your work. What then? Then you know you are doing what you are meant to be doing."

There lies within each of us a kind of invisible intelligence that is calling us, guiding, supporting, and directing us toward the talents and capacities we have to offer the world and the life we are meant to live. I can't conceptualize or come close to articulating the source of this calling, this burning desire that is so often hidden by the noise of the culture, the demands of those around us, and our need to conform. I only know from my own experience of its existence. Authentic living is connecting to and living in alignment with that voice, with who we are meant to be and what we are meant to do. Calling is where the world's need meets the soul's desire. Authentic leading is guiding others to *their* voice. If we could live the lives we are each uniquely called to live, I truly believe there would be no more need to talk about words like "employee engagement," "motivation," or "empowerment." All these would naturally emerge—originating from within us.

The power to discover your calling lies in the potential that was bestowed upon you at birth. Latent and undeveloped, the seeds of both possibility and destiny were planted. Calling is about the clarity and courage to open these gifts. Learn what taps your talents, fills you up, fuels your passion, and rises out of a need in the world that you feel drawn to meet. Herein lies your calling, your voice, your soul's code.

The work of excavating our calling, of connecting with, and then courageously expressing who we are meant to be and what we are meant to do in the world can happen all at once, but more often it is an evolving process. The discovery of your calling comes from a combination of life experiences, careful observation, and maturity. For some people, it comes like a flash of light. For others, from evolving personal insights. For many, it is discovered when someone who really deeply believes in them sees their strengths and affirms them when they don't see their potential themselves. There is no right way to do this except to diligently stay open to new awareness and listen carefully for conscious driven action.

The Inner Vs. The Outer Calling

When it comes to living a purpose-driven life, it can be helpful to distinguish between one's *inner* purpose and one's *outer* purpose. Inner purpose is about *being*, while outer purpose concerns itself with *doing*. Inner purpose is about awakening to the person you are meant to be, and then bringing those virtues to the world in a way that serves others through a stronger presence. Outer purpose is about what you are meant to *do* in the world. Many people get hung up trying to figure out what they are supposed to *do* with their life. If this is your concern, be assured that while you spend some concerted time clarifying your reason for being, just bringing inner peace, compassion, joy, and gratitude—the qualities of a good person—to whatever you do will help guide you to your purpose.

I met a custodian in a high school who made every bit as much impact on the lives of students than any teacher in the school. On any given day, you would find students confiding in him, joking with him, and hanging out around him. Through his unconditional acceptance of everyone he met, "Mr. Joe," as the students called him, seemed to be trusted by everyone. He demonstrated, modeled, and set an example of personal pride and craftsmanship in everything he did. During the year I spent working with the staff at the school, there was a tragic traffic accident that took the lives of three students. It was "Mr. Joe" that many students turned to in their grief. "Mr. Joe" had no more than a grade nine education and no leadership title in the school. He was simply a caring custodian. Whether he realized it or not, he was living his calling. He was a good person. He modeled solid, lasting virtues. He loved, and he was loved. What else really matters?

Dr. Martin Luther King, Jr. brought some clarity about living your inner purpose when he said, "If a person is called to be a street sweeper, they should sweep streets as Michelangelo painted or Beethoven composed music or Shakespeare poetry. They should sweep streets so well that all the hosts of heaven and earth will pause to say, 'Here lived a great street sweeper who did their job well.'"

My life's work of speaking, coaching, writing, and facilitating workshops is aligned with my inner purpose. All are extremely fulfilling and greatly gratifying. However, my deepest sense of fulfillment comes from my inner work, the work that the world will never see, much less reward me for: my recovery from depression and addiction, learning to forgive and let go of resentments and pain, overcoming self-centeredness, and learning to love. This work ultimately has been the purpose of my life, the development of strong character and a caring presence. This has been my ultimate, authentic journey. This inner work has done more to impact my outer work than any effort I have put into my professional development.

Ikigai is a Japanese concept meaning "a reason for being." Connecting with one's *Ikigai* brings us closer to one's *outer* purpose. Everyone, according to the Japanese, has an *Ikigai*. In Japan, the word is widely used to describe a healthy passion for something that makes life worth living to the fullest. *Ikigai* seeks the answer to three essential questions: What do you love? What are you good at? What does the world need?

Finding your *Ikigai* requires a deep and often lengthy search of self. It takes time to unearth the gifts we possess, to match them with our life's endeavors, and discover a reason for being. "Human resources are like natural resources. They are often buried beneath the surface. You have to make an effort to find them," writes Sir Ken Robinson in his book, *Finding Your Element: How to Discover Your Talents and Passions and Transform Your Life*. When we discover and open our *Ikigai*, we should step back and examine them, perhaps with doubt, perhaps with delight, but certainly with awe and gratitude.

An important question that I am often asked is, *"Do I have to be able to make a living with my 'reason for being' in order for it to be a calling?"* For some, their reason for being lies in their careers. Their reason for being, for example, may be to heal others and their profession is nursing. For others, their calling is to build, and they become a general contractor or a carpenter. Others are called to teach, and this becomes their career. We would call that a *vocation*. A vocation is not a job; it's a calling. No job will be 100% aligned with your calling, but if the majority of your time in your paid work is spent in your *Ikigai*, this is your vocation. And you know that your paid work is your life's work.

On the other hand, you may be a lawyer or a bank teller or a plumber and your *Ikigai* is to make music, or to impact youth as a hockey coach and

mentor, or to lead an international environmental project. Your bass guitar
playing in the weekend band and your volunteer work would be called, in
this case, an *avocation*. An avocation is where your job—your paid work—
supports your *Ikigai*. Alternatively, you could find a deep sense of personal
satisfaction—your reason for being—as a cement truck driver and helping
build structures that make this a better world. All can be valid expressions
of your *Ikigai* if done with some awareness and clear intentions. Keep an
open, curious mind. You never know what the universe might provide for
you. You may currently be in a job that you dislike, but if you need this job
to meet financial obligations, perhaps you can find some aspect of your job
that responds to the soul's desire, or, when you are away from your job, you
can do something that fulfills you and connects you to your true passions.
While not everyone can become financially rich being authentic, everyone
has an opportunity to find enrichment by discovering their *Ikigai*.

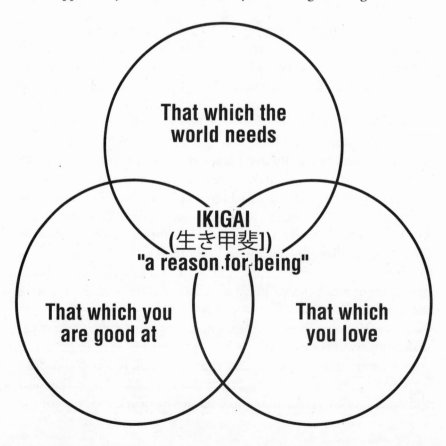

That Which You Love—Discovering Your Passion

"Let yourself be silently drawn by the stronger pull of what you truly love."

Rumi

"Don't ask yourself what the world needs," wrote Howard Thurman, theologian, Baptist minister, and civil rights leader. "Ask yourself what makes you come alive and then go do that. Because what the world needs is people who have come alive." Thurman was the author of twenty books on ethics and cultural criticism, a proponent of nonviolence and peaceful advocacy, and his work had a profound influence on Dr. Martin Luther King, Jr. Whether or not you see yourself as an artist or a builder or a healer or a teacher, there lies within every person a place where, when connected to it, we feel deeply and intensely awakened. The courage to listen to and attend to the strong pull to what you truly love is the courage to live life fully.

Finding What You Love—Some Clues

The conventional story in our society is that if you study particular disciplines and complete a prescribed post-secondary education program, your life will fall neatly into place. In reality, life is anything but linear and certain. Ken Robinson, in his book, *Finding Your Element*, cites studies that show no direct relationship between what you study in school and the work you do when you leave. You assume, for example, that engineers dominate companies in Silicon Valley and that there is a strong connection between innovation in these companies and leaders who specialize in mathematics and science. Vivek Wadhwa, a professor at the Pratt School of Engineering at Duke University, surveyed more than six hundred and fifty U.S. born CEOs and heads of product engineering at more than five hundred technology companies. Just over 90% of them had college degrees. Of those, only 40% had degrees in engineering or math. The other 60% had degrees in business, the arts, or the humanities. Professor Wadhwa found that there is no link between what you study in college and how successful or otherwise you are later in your life. He has been

involved in hiring more than a thousand people and found no relation between their fields of study and success in the workplace. "What
makes people successful," he said, "are their motivation, drive, and
ability to learn from mistakes and how hard they work." It is important to emphasize this principle because young people are often steered
away from courses they would like to take in school by well-meaning
parents, friends, and teachers who tell them they will never get a job
with those programs. Real life often tells a different story.

Katherine Brooks is director of Liberal Arts Career Services at the
University of Texas in Austin. She sees many of her students move in
completely different directions once they cast off from college and set
sail in the world. What determines happiness is if they are fulfilling
their passions. "The saddest thing to me," says Dr. Brooks, "is seeing
someone take the job because it pays well, then spend all their money
on toys to cheer themselves up for being so miserable in their jobs.
The people who are doing what they love hardly feel like they are
working at all, just living."

What do You Love?

We all have greater capabilities than we realize, and passion is a key
that unlocks the door to new possibilities. To know our passions, to
be able to listen to the calling of our hearts, we must learn how to
pay attention to energy. Finding your reason for being necessitates
a concentrated and often extensive search of just who you are. It is
not an overnight endeavor. Buy a journal that you are drawn to. Set
aside time each week—perhaps on Sunday mornings or an evening—
to intentionally go within and get some clarity as to what you love to
do, what it is that when you do it, you lose all track of time.

For a more detailed process for connecting with what you love,
view the companion workbook for tools such as a series of questions
intended to guide you toward discovering what you are good at.

What if I Have a Hard Time Finding What I Love?

Two barriers will block you from uncovering your passion. The first
one is time. If you haven't taken the time to slow your life down, to

pause, and to even ask yourself these questions, much less write down your reflections, it is going to be challenging to know what brings you real joy. Be wary of an over-scheduled life. It is easy to get so busy *doing* that we don't make the time to stop and listen to the voice inside that is calling us. Some people naturally and instinctively gravitate to what they love. Many of us, however, have been so busy meeting the needs of others that we don't stop and pay attention to what our souls desire.

The second obstacle to accessing your passion is unresolved pain. Many of us have been through trauma and pain in our past and as a way of coping have built a wall to protect ourselves. While this wall may have been an important survival mechanism at the time, protecting yourself from suffering may also keep the positive aspects of yourself hidden. If you are having real difficulty feeling any passion along with the accompanying emotions of joy, gratitude, pleasure, etc. you may want to consider getting some help from a guide to explore potential areas of past trauma and suffering that need some attention. Unacknowledged resentments, pain, suffering, grief, and trauma can be barriers to discovering what you love.

That Which You Are Good At—Discovering Your Genius

"There is a vitality, a life force, a quickening, that is translated through you to action, and because there is only one of you in all time, this expression is unique. And if you block it, it will never exist through any other medium, and will be lost. It is not your business to determine how good it is, nor how valuable it is, nor how it compares with any other expressions. It is simply your business to keep it yours, clearly and directly, to keep the channel open."

Martha Graham, World Renowned Dancer and Choreographer

There's a good joke about an insurance salesman who is driving along the highway in a rural community and sees a sign in front of a house, "Talking Dog for Sale."

He can't resist. He turns into the yard, gets out of his car, walks up the steps, and rings the front doorbell. The owner greets him nonchalantly and tells him the dog is in the backyard. The salesman walks around the side of the house, opens the gate, and sees a mutt sitting there.

"You talk?" he asks.

"Yep," the dog replies.

"So, what's your story?"

The old pooch looks up and says, "Well, I discovered this gift when I was pretty young and wanted to help the government, so I told the CIA about my unique talent, and in no time they had me jetting from country to country, sitting in rooms with spies and world leaders, because no one figured a dog would be eavesdropping. I was one of their most valuable spies eight years running. But I have to tell you that the jetting around really tired me out, and I knew I wasn't getting any younger, and I wanted to settle down. So, I signed up for a job at the airport to do some undercover security work, mostly wandering near suspicious characters and listening in. I uncovered some incredible dealings there and was awarded a batch of medals. Had a wife, a mess of puppies, and now I'm retired."

The guy is amazed. He goes back in and asks the farmer what he wants for the dog. The farmer says, "Ten dollars."

The salesman says he'll buy him, but asks the owner, "This dog is amazing. He's worth a fortune. Why on earth are you selling him for only $10?"

The farmer replies, "Because he's a liar!"

Everyone is talented, original, and has something to offer the world. The problem is that most people treat themselves and others like this old farmer treats his talking dog. We are so focused on the weakness and fixated on fixing that weakness that we completely miss our talents, strengths, and unique gifts: our genius. The history of humanity appears to be the story of people selling themselves short. Buckminster Fuller, the great American architect, designer, and inventor, once said that "All children are born geniuses; 9,999 out of 10,000 are swiftly, inadvertently 'de-geniusized' by grow-ups."

Uncovering Your Genius: Three Directions to Look

First, work with what comes *easy*. That which comes easily to us is a clue to finding our gifts. What do you do well that you *don't remember learning?* Building something? Working with numbers? Fostering relationships? Teaching? Creating? Selling? Healing? Writing? Mentoring?

Try to identify what aspects of these activities come easily to you. Managing the people in a building project? Creating a design, or doing finishing carpentry? Preparing and delivering a well-thought instructional design? Cleaning a wound or taking a few moments to put a patient at ease?

Second, work with your pain.

> *I walked a mile with pleasure, She chatted all the way,*
> *But left me none the wiser for all she had to say.*
> *I walked a mile with sorrow, And ne'er a word said she;*
> *But, oh, the things I learned from her when sorrow walked with me.*
>
> Robert Browning Hamilton

Within our wounds lie our gifts. Learning to walk through suffering with integrity and honesty connects us to our humanness and our ability to be there for others. In our suffering, we can make the world better. The singer and poet Leonard Cohen said it best, "Forget your perfect offering. There is a crack in everything. That's how the light gets in."

Your pain and suffering may help reach people that you otherwise couldn't, providing you with a unique gift that may be worth developing and offering.

And *third*, work with a guide. "The eye can't see itself," is an old Sufi saying. Just as a mirror reflects our face back to us, guides such as mentors, coaches, trusted advisors, therapists, and confidants reflect that which is so close we are unable to see. If you are serious about uncovering your genius, find a guide to help you.

You can't change what you aren't aware of. Once the clarity starts to come, you can begin to make new choices. One choice is to find a way to bring more of your gifts into your current paid work. It's unrealistic to expect that a hundred percent of your job be in your area of unique talents and abilities. Consider negotiating with your boss ways that you can bring greater value to your organization by aligning your job more fully with your unique gifts. You may want to consider saying no to some projects that are not within your strengths and take on projects that have greater alignment with your gifts. Delegate your weakness, at least whenever possible. Chances are, there is somebody in your organization that is good at what you aren't.

And ... if there is no room in your workplace to do more of what you are good at, then consider where you can honor your gifts away from your paid work. Ask yourself what you may need to say "no" to, to make room for your gifts.

View the companion workbook for tools to help, such as a series of questions intended to guide you toward discovering what you are good at.

That Which the World Needs—Discovering Your Contribution

"We have no more right to consume happiness without producing it, than to consume wealth without producing it."

George Bernard Shaw

I have a friend with a passion for climbing mountains. He has often spoken to me of how he has felt "called" to climb, that adventuring into the world's highest peaks was his reason for being. But it wasn't until his final trip up Everest when his mountaineering was used to inspire, teach, and touch the lives of an elementary school class in his community through the use of technology that he began to understand the full impact, meaning, and fulfillment in his work. Contribution took climbing to a whole new level. When his passion and gifts were transformed into service, something beyond his own self-interest, he was rewarded with a deep sense of satisfaction and fulfillment that he never thought possible.

For my mountaineering friend, shifting his focus to a classroom of young children entirely changed the climbing experience. There was something higher at stake. He felt connected to these young children in a profound way. And as much as he wanted these children to "experience" how it felt to climb Mount Everest, to understand the months of preparation, the long weeks of acclimatization on the mountain, the many laborious steps to reach the summit and get down again, and the important work of the mountain Sherpas who helped set up camps and climbing ropes, he was also able to experience his journey through their young eyes. A truly authentic exchange. Your reason for being is, by definition, an authentic calling, only when it, in some way, benefits and serves the world.

When we are looking at leaders, we often wonder if they are serving the institutions or themselves. Are they about service or self-interest? What is the motive behind their actions? Are they a taker or a giver?

To commit to something beyond ourselves and find a cause beyond our own pleasure and comfort is the antidote to self-interest and so many ills that ails the world today. To be part of creating something we care about will enable us to endure the sacrifice, risk, and adventure that the commitment entails. This is the deeper meaning of leadership and of service and can start where we work and live. Our leadership task today is to make the places where we work become places we believe in. Not because it is a requirement, but because it is a contribution. No one will do it for us. Others have brought us this far, and the next step is ours. The choice of service is the true essence of leadership.

After acquiring some clarity as to your passions and your unique gifts—what you love to do and what you are good at, take some time to consider how these will bring value to the world.

- What is the world asking of you? Where in the world do you feel needed?
- How can you be helpful? How will you serve?
- How can your unique talents and passion contribute to others and to the world?
- What gives your life meaning and purpose?
- What is your conscience directing you to do?

A Sense of Purpose—Answering the Call

"The two most important days in your life are the day you are born, and the day you find out why."

Mark Twain

In our vision, passion, and dedication, leadership can be consuming. If we have earned their trust, people come to us for answers and direction and solutions and inspiration. Those we inspire, guide, and serve will bring us their problems, their predicaments, and their pain. It's hard work taking people where they haven't been before. It's tiring to continue to challenge others to go beyond their comfort zone and into new possibilities, which only later will be recognized as growth.

"The sole purpose of human existence," wrote Carl Jung, "is to kindle a light in the darkness of mere being." Leadership needs something it can draw upon to inspire you to bring light to the darkness, courage in the discouragement, a reason to keep going when everything seems to be falling apart, and values that make risk-taking meaningful. That something can be a sense of purpose. Friedrich Nietzsche, the German philosopher, once said, "*He who has a why to live for can bear almost any how.*" Conversely, it has been said that when you lose your *why*, you lose your *way*. Clarifying and preserving a sense of purpose, first within yourself and then in the organization and the community that you serve, gives you that why, that reason for being.

In recent years, there's been an outbreak of attention in purpose-driven leadership and living. It's been said that an executive's most important role is to be a steward of the organization's purpose. Business experts make the case that purpose is a key to extraordinary performance, while psychologists describe it as the pathway to greater well-being. According to a 2014 Harvard Business Review study, doctors have even found that people with purpose in their lives are healthier and live longer. Purpose is increasingly being touted as the key to navigating the complex, volatile, ambiguous world we face today, where strategy is ever-changing, and fewer and fewer decisions are obviously black and white.

A sense of purpose, whether it's a clearly defined mission in life or an indefinable sense that you are on the right path, gives you a cause that inspires you. It inspires you to become the kind of person you need to be to get there, enabling you to take setbacks and failures in stride. "People say that what we're all seeking is a meaning for life," says Joseph Campbell in *The Power of Myth*. "I don't think meaning is what we are seeking. I think that what we're seeking is an experience of being alive so that our life experiences on the purely physical plane will have resonances with our own innermost being and reality so that we actually feel the rapture of being alive." Discovering a sense of purpose is a way to awaken this aliveness, first within yourself, then in the world around you.

When I was in high school, it was my dream to make the 1980 Canadian Olympic team as a track athlete. It was that dream that inspired me to get up early and train, to take better care of my health, to eat well, and to keep me away from alcohol and late nights. When I would lie in bed at 5:00 a.m. debating about whether I would get up and go for my morning run, it was the power of that purpose—the why, the vision—that would enable me to get my feet on the floor and my rear end out the door in -25°F weather. My father would often say, "The purpose of having a dream is not to achieve your dream. The purpose of having a dream is to inspire yourself to become the kind of person it takes to achieve your dream. Very few people will ever make the Olympics, and even fewer will stand on the podium, but anyone can become the kind of person it takes to get there." While I didn't qualify for the Olympics, having the dream, my *why* at the time, inspired me to live a healthier, more disciplined life. To this day, I have maintained many of those healthy habits ingrained in me over forty years ago. While my purpose has changed and broadened, the inspiration remains.

Having a sense of purpose is inspiring. It actually produces energy. Having a reason for being inspires you to develop yourself into the kind of person it will take to realize your purpose. Having a reason to get out of bed, to come to work, to accomplish any task, makes everything worth doing—with sincere and honest enthusiasm. In times of darkness or discouragement, or when you are facing what appears to be failure, you have a source of untapped strength in remembering and tapping into your purpose. When climbing a high mountain, you realize that you need the stony crags and rough terrain to aid you on the climb and that they are mere setbacks—and perhaps even aids—to help you get closer to the peak. The real challenge in life is learning to say "no" to what might look like a *good* opportunity but in the long run is the *wrong* opportunity. Having a sense of purpose keeps you focused. It gives you clarity about what is important.

The Yoga Sutras of Patanjali state, "When you are inspired by some great purpose, some extraordinary project, all your thoughts break their bounds. Your mind transcends limitations, your consciousness expands in every direction, and you find yourself in a new, great, and wonderful world."

There's nothing more attractive and inviting than someone who is confident in who they are and what they believe in. There's a grace and ease about them. Better yet, when you can live that way, you can share that grace with others. Life is more fulfilling. Contrary to that is someone who doesn't know themselves well, who depends on other people's opinions for validity, or on their titles and roles for identity. These types of people are unsure of their values and purpose. When that person is you, it can be confusing and painful.

Shine a light on what you desire. Take time to excavate your why. Whenever you set a goal, there is an unseen force or energy that moves you toward that goal. Visit the companion workbook for clues to help you along the path of discovery and contribution.

Creativity

We admire stories of creative leaders. We like to hear tales of CEOs, political leaders, and even front-line groundbreakers who bring about transformation with fresh ideas and innovative thinking. And there is good reason for it. Studies reveal that creative people are better able to lead positive change in organizations and are better equipped to inspire followers. Creativity, it turns out, is critical to a successful organization as well as a life well lived.

The desire to create, to bring something new to life, to express an idea or feeling, or even a way to resolve a problem, is one of the deepest longings of the human soul. It lifts us into a larger, more creative, powerful, and mysterious dimension than the everyday plainness of human existence. High on the list of the benefits of creative expression are stress relief and general wellbeing. It seems that when we become absorbed in our "art," in an expression of the vast array of human possibilities, that daily problems of the mundane begin to dissolve. We transcend our minute troubles, and the problems start to dissolve. The methods of self-expression are endless—music, writing, painting, needlework, drawing, coloring, leading, creating pottery, journaling, influencing, dancing, caring, gardening, selling, cooking, theatre, and many others. Everyone is born creative, and as unique human beings, we can choose a myriad of ways to express creatively that humanness. Awakening the artist within is about giving yourself permission to experience and express the privilege of this lifetime: to be who you are.

Here are a few thoughts about living and leading creatively:

- Creativity isn't something you pursue. It's not something you "do." It is something that emerges from within. It is not something you will find "out there." Creativity is in you. It's in our DNA. Pablo Picasso is said to have spoken these wise words: *"Every child is an artist. The problem is how to remain an artist once we grow up ... you don't have to be taught to be an artist; you have to be taught not to be one ..."*

- Artists don't necessarily produce "art." Being an artist is, instead, the way you see the world. Being an artist is about having the eyes to see things more clearly. Artistic living means seeing life more slowly. It means seeing beyond the obvious.

- You don't say that someone is "very" physical. We simply are physical. It is not a matter of degree. It's part of the human experience. So why should we say that a person is "very" artistic? Being creative is part of our nature, part of the essence of being human. Being artistic is not an optional add-on. It is not that some people are creative and others aren't, any more than some people are physical and others aren't. Some people may be in better physical health than others, but they are not more physical. Some people are aware of their artistic nature while others may be less aware, but they are no less artistic. If we are creative beings, we function best when we are cognizant of that.

- Everybody is artistic because everybody has something to express. Try not expressing anything for twenty-four hours and see what happens. You may find yourself losing energy, becoming despondent, or you may even feel like you will burst. Every time you write a letter, express yourself to someone, draw a picture, garden, embark on a project, decorate a room, buy clothing, get dressed, you have expressed yourself creatively.

- Art is a language, a language that we can learn. It is a mistake to think we can communicate everything verbally. In the language of art, words don't exist. This is why art can be used to express a range of emotions—grief, joy, inner peace—that words cannot reach. As we learn this language of art we connect with our authentic self and the world around us in new, expanded ways, thus deepening our capacity to influence others with greater presence, and most importantly, enjoy this experience we call human more fully.

- One of the indicators of a hurried, troubled, stressed world is that we disconnect from art and stop noticing the beauty, wonder, and awe of life. This limits our full capacity as human beings. Being disconnected from our humanness separates us from each other and from the environment. What we separate from we neglect or destroy. What are you doing to learn, deepen, and express the language of art in your life? What are you doing to stop and notice the beauty around you? When was the last time you were in awe?

- Toni Cade Bambara, the African-American author, documentary film-maker, and social activist, said the role of an artist is to make revolutions irresistible. This is where creativity assimilates into leadership. This is why I believe that leadership is an art form. In order to become a leader, you need to develop similar qualities to that of an artist—to tap into your creative intelligence in order to keep ahead of the crowd, stay nimble, and inspire those around you to want to push themselves toward a cause beyond self-interest.

- The purpose of art is to enhance the human experience. Again, this speaks to leadership as an expression of art. True leadership is more than "getting the job done." Leadership is ultimately about enriching the experience of being human.
- In an orderly, rational, linear world, that tells children to "grow up and act their age," results in far too many of us not supported nor encouraged to play or express our true nature. Without pure, non-judgmental self-expression we learn that conformity is not a path to creativity.

Creativity Takes Practice: Five Traits Creative Leaders Possess

Being a leader is difficult. That's why most of us end up taking direction from others in our professional lives. There's no inborn quality that leaders possess. They're ordinary people who decide at one point or another to do some things beyond the ordinary.

Erik Wahl, author of *Unthink: Rediscover Your Creative Genius,* provides us with five traits that creative—and the best—leaders possess:

1. **They rattle cages.** Change is a constant. In the natural world, in politics, in business, the only thing that stays the same is the fact that nothing stays the same. Some people wait until they're propelled into leadership positions by forces around them. But the best leaders—from Joan of Arc to Dr. Martin Luther King, Jr. to Nelson Mandela—provoke themselves into action first, then the people around them. They're constantly imagining new possibilities. They instigate change that they envision even when others don't.

   Yet perhaps the only major difference between these great leaders and the average person is that they're willing to do something rather than let circumstances dictate life for them. That typically means rattling cages and shaking up long-standing beliefs and institutions—which is never easy or universally well received. But that's precisely what makes them great. To rise to your true leadership potential, chances are you'll need to rattle a few cages as well, starting with your own.

2. **They listen to intuition.** There are things we know to be true
and things we feel to be true. Thanks to our education, most
of us tend to lean on our existing knowledge base to solve
problems and make decisions. But the best leaders are those
who realize that the things they sense—those possibilities that
lie just beyond the realm of the known—hold a special value,
too. Listening to them is how real breakthroughs happen.

Most of us have problems balancing logic with intuition.
But the truth is that those faculties aren't opposed to one
another. In fact, you need to figure out how to get them
working together if you're to become a truly creative leader.
Intellect without intuition makes for a smart person without impact. Intuition without intellect makes a spontaneous
person without direction.

3. **They don't get held back by perfectionism.** One of the big-
gest stumbling blocks for anyone trying to accomplish something is perfectionism—the illusionary need to get it exactly
right before taking the next step. The best leaders realize that
perfection is impossible, and pursuing perfection often stands
in the way of what's most important: progress. Creativity grows
in the fertile soil of uncertainty and ambiguity. Leadership
requires making consistent strides, no matter how big.

Don't buy into the notion that you can take a giant leap
if you spend enough time carefully mapping it out. By the
time you get done planning, others will have lapped you twice
and already taken that leap you spent months mulling over.
Instead, opt to "just go" and let the sparks fly. You *will* make
mistakes. But in the process, you'll learn quickly and keep
moving—refining your skills and igniting new levels of creativity you didn't know you had.

4. **They have convictions and stick to them.** There's something
compelling about a person with conviction, whether or not
you agree with everything he or she represents. Conviction is
rare because, in our longing for stability, security, and certainty,
we often make the mistake of looking outside ourselves for

direction when we should be looking inside. Over time, we can lose sight of who we truly are and what's really important to us.

Conviction can be cultivated, though, and it starts with you. While those who live with great conviction can always inspire you, they don't know your passions and beliefs. Only you can ask, "What makes me come alive?" From there, the gaps between who you are and who you can be will become clear. You might find you need something dramatic like a career change, or just answering that question might help propel you further down the path you're already on. The key is to find something that you feel you're meant to do and give yourself to it.

5. **They don't do (only) what's expected of them.** The ability to come up with new ideas is a defining characteristic of great leaders. They're able to step out of the common view and imagine new possibilities that set the course for others to follow. Each of us has a tremendous capacity for originality—we're each unique, after all—but activating it can be difficult. Why? Because our lives are full of other demands such as our jobs and our families, and we spend most of our precious time and energy just trying to keep up.

In order to free your own originality, you need to be willing to stop doing only what's required and expected of you and start doing the things that only you can do—those ideas and projects you keep shelving until you've got time for them. But the truth is there's never a convenient moment to tackle them. There's never going to come a time when you'll be 100% certain you'll succeed if you do them. Get started on those things today and work on them every day thereafter.

Ultimately, the real difference between you and the creative leaders who inspire you is action. You have the innate capacity to develop all the qualities they possess. The key is to start. Start today. Start now. Don't wait around until life demands something of you—it always will. That's not what leaders do.

I recently watched a superb documentary called *The Pixar Story*. This remarkable movie chronicles the tumultuous journey of Pixar when it first started in 1979 through its current day monumental success. The story centers around John Lasseter, one of the founders and creative directors of this innovative organization. This documentary is filled with tremendous lessons:

- The importance of embracing change.
- Cultivating a passionate and committed team.
- The power of optimism and infectious enthusiasm.
- Story drives everything.
- Beauty is built on sacrifice.
- One doesn't manage creativity. One manages *for* creativity.
- Overnight success takes a long time.

In short, one doesn't manage creativity; one manages *for* creativity. Below are twelve strategies for releasing creativity within yourself and your team. You'll discover that anything that is good for creativity is equally good for your life.

1. **Start within.** Creating a culture that unbridles creativity begins with unleashing creativity within yourself. It starts with you. Go through this chapter thoroughly and reflect carefully on how much you are unleashing your own creative potential. You can't, as a leader, take people where you haven't been. Here are a few ways to deliberately and consistently feed the creative aspects of your being:

   - Create solitude. Create boundaries in your life daily—or at minimum weekly—where you turn off technology and are unavailable. It was Pablo Picasso who said, "Without great solitude no serious work is possible." Create a sanctuary where you can get away from the expectations of the world to create and reflect.
   - Take time daily to move toward a particular art form that you may be drawn to—literally. It may be an area that you were one day told you weren't good at and that you gave up

years ago. Experiment with painting, drawing, sculpting, meditating, gardening, woodworking, dancing, playing a musical instrument, singing, or writing prose or poetry. No evaluation. No judgment. No grade. No goal—except to turn it into a habit. You don't have to perform or show any of this to anyone if you prefer not to. It's all about your own personal expression. Even Einstein played the violin to balance his astounding scientific mind. My good friend and Canadian renounced artist, Murray Phillips, had me buy a good sketch pad, an artist's pen, and had me sit and draw something every day for several weeks. The discipline slowed me down, helped me pay attention to what was around me and what was within me. Sometimes I drew my desk. Sometimes a lamp. Sometimes a tree outside my office window. Nobody saw what I drew. Like pouring my heart out in a journal, it was only for me. After doing this for a few months, I noticed the spontaneity in new ideas that started coming to me. This book was written during the same period that I was methodical about my drawing. The discipline of creativity has untold benefits.

- To encourage, support, and guide you, sign up for an art, music, writing, or meditation, class. Hire a teacher. Join a choir. Get involved in a local amateur theatre group. Consider learning a musical instrument. Take a course in improvisation. Become part of an artistic community, other artists who share your passion.

- Buy—and use—Julia Cameron's book, *The Artist's Way*. Buy a journal and write in it daily.

- Get a good night's sleep. Being well rested, on a consistent basis, will have a positive impact on your creativity. Make sleep and rest a priority in your life.

2. **Adopt an artist's mindset.** Photographers and painters understand the vital importance of s-l-o-w-i-n-g down and being still. Create pauses in your day to see the beauty around you. See the light, texture, and colors in your everyday world.

Observe closely without judgment, evaluation, or criticism. Buy a sketch pad and a good quality pencil and practice drawing something every day. If you prefer painting, buy a brush and easel. Nobody's going to see what you create. Creativity has nothing to do with performance. Creativity, artists will tell you, is about seeing the world deliberately and gradually. Artists know the wisdom of the ancient Chinese philosopher, Lao Tzu, when he said, *"Nature does not hurry, yet everything is accomplished."* Drawing or painting something in front of you—a tree, a plant, a desk, a shelf, a rug, anything—will help you observe more closely, feel more deeply, and adopt an artist's mindset. Enliven your sketches with colored pencils. Hang around people who know they are artists. Observe how artists think and how they observe the world. And keep in mind the creative expression that comes with activities like cooking, gardening, or simply visiting museums, marveling at cloud formations, or be enchanted by a starlit sky. Consider a commitment to explore some type of creative expression and practice it faithfully.

3. **Grow your visionary capacity.** Within you lies the ability to construct the future, long before it is realized physically. Challenge yourself to see beyond your current sight. Creative leadership needs vision to help direct ideas to their best use. This does not necessarily mean looking for something on the horizon that you have never seen before. You can also take the time to look at something old in a new way. You can do a superb job of constructing your vision of the future based only on resources and talents present in your current reality. Resist the natural human tendency as a leader to get bogged down in the operational weeds. Visionary leaders tend to think more about where they want to end up rather than the path to get there.

4. **Look beyond your own circle of peers.** It's natural to surround yourself with people who are like you. Consider expanding your network of reference. This will broaden your horizons and challenge your thought processes. Individuals

not in your field of expertise may be just the ones to propel you toward your future. Branching your creative leadership out to new people gets perspective from multiple views. However, you aren't really looking for confirmation of your ideas in a new circle. Instead, you are looking for people who will push the boundaries of your own current reality with different experiences—people who approach tasks with varied mindsets. Finding people outside your regular circle enables a larger scope for creative thinking.

5. **Be a force of nature.** George Bernard Shaw, the renowned Irish playwright, at the age of ninety-three, said:

> This is the true joy in life, the being used for a purpose recognized by yourself as a mighty one; the being a force of nature instead of a feverish, selfish little clod of ailments and grievances complaining that the world will not devote itself to making you happy. I am of the opinion that my life belongs to the whole community, and as long as I live it is my privilege to do for it whatever I can. I want to be thoroughly used up when I die, for the harder I work the more I live. I rejoice in life for its own sake. Life is no 'brief candle' for me. It is a sort of splendid torch which I have got hold of for the moment, and I want to make it burn as brightly as possible before handing it on to future generations.

No matter where you find yourself in the hierarchy of the organization, the opportunity is yours to be creative. Don't paint by numbers. Go over the lines. Paint a masterpiece. It is, after all, an expression of your life. Once you have a vision of your desired future, step out of your everyday routine and begin planning how to bring it about. Your creative leadership will garner attention and inspire others to set their sights on the future.

6. **Get on the bench.** While I've never been able to verify it, I heard once that when Wayne Gretzky sat on the bench between shifts on the ice, he could lower his heart rate from

180 beats per minute to below 50 in less than a minute. Even professional athletes have to unplug from the intensity of the game and get on the bench. For many of us, it's a luxury to get some uninterrupted private moments during the day when we can lean back, rest, and reflect. We are always "on the ice," in the midst of nonstop emails and demands from others. Without time to rest, our brain is thrown into a state that opposes the open focus where innovation flourishes. In the tumult of daily demands and to-do lists, there is no room for creativity that comes from focused attention. The stories of significant discoveries are rife with tales of brilliant insight during a walk, in the shower, or on vacation. Downtime lets the creative juices flow. Tight schedules kill innovation and connection. Take some unproductive time daily to simply tune in and attend to the natural world around you. Or just stop for a few moments at your desk. Sit back. Close your eyes. And take a little non-thinking time for yourself. Create a "creative cocoon" for yourself. Get off the ice of demands every so often and get onto the bench.

7. **Play.** At the end of the classic musical *Mary Poppins,* the gruff and joyless Mr. Banks arrives home, having been "sacked, discharged, flung into the street." Yet he seems undeniably and unexpectedly overjoyed—so delighted that one of the servants concludes he's "gone off his crumpet." Even his son observes, "It doesn't sound like Father." Indeed, his father is almost a new person as he presents his children with their mended kite and launches into the song, "Let's Go Fly A Kite." Liberated from the miserable monotony of his job at the bank, Banks's inner child suddenly comes alive. The effect of his cheerfulness is marvelous as he bolsters the spirits of the whole house, infusing the previously melancholic Banks family with joy, camaraderie, and delight. Play, the manifestation of humanness that has no ulterior motive except pure self-expression, can restore sanity and creativity to our daily lives. Roald Dahl, the brilliant British novelist and screenwriter, said it best when he said, "A little nonsense now and then, is cherished by the wisest man."

The word *school* is derived from the Greek word *schole*, meaning "leisure." Yet our modern school system, born in the Industrial Revolution and pushed by a current obsession by the pressure for achievement, has removed the leisure—and much of the pleasure—out of learning. Sir Ken Robinson, who has made the study of creativity in schools his life's work, has observed that instead of fueling creativity through play, schools can actually kill it. In his 2010 TED talk, he observed: "We have sold ourselves into a fast-food model of education, and it's impoverishing our spirit and our energies as much as fast food is depleting our physical bodies… Imagination is the source of every form of human achievement. And it's the one thing that I believe we are systematically jeopardizing in the way we educate our children and ourselves."

Brendan Boyle is a toy inventor, consulting associate professor at Stanford University's Institute of Design, and Partner at IDEO, a global design company that builds learning platforms and tools to unlock creativity. Play, Boyle reminds us, has a PR problem. Some think of play, he says, as frivolous—a distraction, or worse, a waste of time. In the office, play is often regarded as a break from "real work." But what if the opposite of play isn't work, but boredom? What if work could actually benefit from play?

As a partner at IDEO, Boyle instills a playful culture, not only in mindset but also in daily behaviors. Play, he says, allows people to experiment, empathize, and take creative risks. Having play ingrained in their culture makes it an incredibly satisfying place to work. It keeps everyone engaged in their projects and makes IDEO employee's better innovators.

8. **Support people to pursue their passions and their gifts.** The keys to creative output are intellectual challenge and independence. Creativity flourishes in the soil of passion. Encourage people to be more revolutionary in their thinking. When people are well aligned to a project, granting them independence holds less risk. Ideally, creative workers should be able to set their own agendas as much as possible. The more people

choose the projects they are engaged in, the greater the level of creativity. Scientists at Novartis, a Swiss multinational pharmaceutical company, spend a portion of their time working on drugs for "niche" diseases, where the intellectual rewards are often high. Screening for such projects consists of two questions: is it scientifically tractable, and does it meet an unmet medical need? Not "What is the market?" but "Is there a patient suffering who could be cured with today's knowledge?"

9. **Embrace constructive conflict.** There might be those who don't agree with your vision of the future. Dealing with conflict is difficult for most of us. However, if you implement creative leadership skills, you can bring about a positive outcome. One of the most important things to remember is to focus on similarities first. Look at what it is that both parties desire and focus on the good points of each side. From this vantage point, it will be easier to understand the other person's point of view. Most leaders have to deal with conflict all the time, internally with employees and externally with clients. Tapping into your creative leadership helps you bring the other side's perspective of the conflict into consideration. Practice coercing others not by force, but by thinking outside of your box, putting yourself in their shoes and finding common ground.

10. **Be an appreciative audience.** Just because creative workers are intrinsically motivated doesn't abdicate the leader's responsibility to ensure a creative culture. A good leader can do much to challenge and inspire creative work. Mark Addicks, Chief Marketing Officer at General Mills, believes that people are highly attuned to a leader's engagement with an attitude toward a project. "The way in which a leader asks a question and shows genuine interest in both the project and the people can move a team very positively," he noted.

11. **Embrace the certainty of failure.** Managerial reactions that impact the level of creativity on a team the most are reactions to failure. To foster creativity, positional leaders have a responsibility to reduce the fear of failure. The goal should be to experiment constantly, fail early and often, and learn as much

as possible in the process. Research with firms in Silicon Valley shows that organizations that have the hardest time managing creativity are, ironically, the ones that have been most successful. Why? Because they tend to develop an aversion to failure. Not only do firms become more conservative as they grow, but fear also makes managers more likely to deny that failure has happened and more eager to erase all memory of it. Amy Edmondson, a professor at Harvard Business School, underscored what a lost opportunity that constitutes. Any business that experiments vigorously will experience failure—which, when it happens, should be mined to improve creative problem solving, team learning, and organizational performance. How can an organization capitalize on failure? Above all, Edmondson said, "… its management must create an environment of psychological safety, demonstrating to people that they will not be humiliated, much less punished, if they speak up with new ideas, questions, or concerns, or make mistakes."

12. **Provide the setting for "good work."** "The potential for passionate engagement in one's work is highest when the work itself is seen as noble," said Howard Gardner, a professor at the Harvard Graduate School of Education who has conducted research on "good work." Good work is excellent technically, meaningful and engaging to the worker, and carried out in an ethical way. Creativity, it turns out, is impacted by how we actually feel about our work.

Community

"That which is most precious to us is often so close to us that we don't know that it is there."

Georgia O'Keeffe, an American painter

In 1835, the Frenchman Alexis de Tocqueville traveled through the young United States and published *Democracy in America*, where he described "habits of the heart" that gave citizens of the United States a distinctive culture. The one personality characteristic that impressed him most about the U.S. was individualism. Tocqueville admired this character trait immensely but strongly warned that unless this individualism was continually balanced by other habits, it would inevitably lead to the fragmentation of American society and the social isolation of its citizens.

For all but the last small percentage of recorded history, we have lived tribally in communities, with everyone dependent on each other. Around the time of the Renaissance, tribal existence began to diminish, and individual rights and freedoms took priority over obligations to the community. While this, in part, resulted in the release of great creative energy and brought about extensive artistic, scientific, and financial advances, it came at a price—the possibility of ultimate loneliness. Integrating individuation with connection, the internal community and external community is the great story of life itself.

Leading, they say, is "lonely at the top." While it is undoubtedly lonely, leading is not designed to be done alone. The lone-warrior model of leadership, born in a culture of over-individualism is, in the words of Ron Heifetz, "heroic suicide." We all have blind spots that require the perspective of others. At times in our lives, we need support in letting go of the weight of the world we carry on our shoulders. At times we have dreams that need to be shared. At times we require guidance to find our own voice amidst the clamor of the culture. At times we need assistance to step away from the fray and get a different viewpoint, particularly when the pressures mount. At times accountability partners are required to help us stay on track.

Confidants

In 1984, when I was in the early stages of opening my practice as a family therapist, I took a course from the world-renowned psychotherapy pioneer, Dr. Carl Whitaker. He was adamant about the advice he shared, counsel that has stayed with me ever since. "Never see a family alone," he said. "They are way too complicated. Even if you can't always get a co-therapist to be there when you meet with the family, at least have a confidant to talk to between sessions."

Since working with leaders, I have given them the same advice: Never lead alone. Just as authentic living requires support and perspective beyond your own view, so too does leadership require a confidant. Just as you can't write a book alone, you can't lead alone. From time to time, we need to turn the manuscript over to a new set of eyes.

Confidants are people in your life who create a safe space to be who you are, who will listen to your truth and will, in turn, tell you the truth and help hold you accountable. From time to time we need a shoulder to lean on and new eyes to see the view. A confidant is a person to reach out to when you need to cry and complain. A confidant can hold you up when you are trying to hold everybody else up. We all need confidants who can help put us back together at the end of the day and help us let go of what is hurting us and see the world through a new set of lenses. We also need confidants with whom we can share our dreams, our fears, our values, our deepest aspirations, and who will help us see our gifts when we don't see them in ourselves. A confidant is someone who can remind us why what we do is worth doing—someone who cares more about our soul than our ego.

Confidants, often spouses, lovers, trusted colleagues or friends, provide support and perspective. They help ask questions like, "What just happened? What's going on? What can be learned from the mistakes and failures? What can you do now? Can you learn something for the future? What do you really need? What are your options?"

Where do you go when you need to talk? Who do you turn to when you are worried or afraid or want to share a dream? Where do you go when you are exhausted or discouraged or full of self-doubt? Who inspires you? Who helps you discover your gifts when you can't find them within yourself? Who do you turn to when you have lost perspective and need support? While there is a time for quiet reflection, thinking, and individualism, there is also time for community. There is a time to be alone, and there is a time to be together.

Allies

As you have already learned in this book, if you aren't taking people into unfamiliar territory you aren't leading, you are only managing.

And we need allies who share our vision, support our values, and stand beside us on the journey. While you never want to initiate change merely for the sake of change, leadership comes with being a change agent. Leadership, at times, requires the introduction of initiatives that go counter to the familiar, that shake up the status quo, that take people into a state of disruption. Allies can ease the personal turmoil that comes with it.

Allies, whether supporters outside your organization or colleagues within your culture, provide perspective, wisdom, encouragement, and honesty. It is vital, in the work of leadership, to know we aren't alone. It is imperative to know that someone shares our passion and understands and supports our dream.

Allies, however, go beyond being confidants and encouragers. We also need the trust of key stakeholders in the realization of our vision. We cannot achieve a vision alone. Eleanor Roosevelt's life was marked by many deep and persuasive friendships. She, like all great leaders, knew how to build alliances with influential people in the press and in the political arena that supported her cause. She learned to use her position of First Lady and Presidential confidant to promote issues of concern to her. Not all of these allies were explicit, but she knew how to get the right people at the right time on her side.

All successful leaders know how to earn trust and create value for others to realize their vision. Learning to build alliances is the realization of the power of synergy.

Communities

One of the most beautiful qualities of true friendship and community is to understand and to be understood. Communities and the relationships they bring are very precious. To think you can take the authentic journey without a community is like thinking you can survive a Canadian winter without a coat.

Community comes with many faces, all carrying unique expressions of human connection, support, guidance, and accountability. There are work-based communities, religious communities, recovery communities, informal communities, monastic communities, learning communities, political activist communities, and family and neighborhoods. Among this wide range of manifestations, a sustaining community breaks through the superficial exchange to an authentic connection that can be distilled to a few key elements. Rarely does one community consist of all of these, and some element of each is contained in most lasting communities. Many people in your community will serve in more than one of these alliances.

- **Friendships.** Friendships are people you simply enjoy being with. Friendship is what makes life worth living. The challenge with friendships is that we tend to stay in friendships that are comfortable. The strength of this is that they are safe. You feel relaxed and at ease around true friends. The test of a true friend, however, is that they support you to grow. As I have repeatedly told my three daughters over the years, you want to choose very carefully who you allow to influence you. Sometimes you have to disassociate. Sometimes you have to have limited association. You always want to find good associates. Who you associate with is who you become.

- **Confidants.** Someone you can empty your heart to at the end of a day and who will stand beside you through the storms is a confidant. George Eliot, the English novelist, understood something about the true nature of confidants when she wrote, *"Oh the comfort, the inexpressible comfort of feeling safe with a person; having neither to weigh thoughts nor measure words, but to pour them all out, just as they are, chaff and grain together, knowing that a faithful hand will take and sift them, keep what is worth keeping, and then, with the breath of kindness, blow the rest away."*

- **Leg-Up Influencers.** Every so often a difference maker comes into your life, often unexpectedly, usually not designed or planned, and is there to give you a "leg-up" on a challenge you may have been facing. Before I was big enough and strong enough and had enough money to buy a saddle, people were around to lift me up on the old seventeen hands tall (over five and a half feet) gelding I rode as a kid. A leg-up person, I have been told by many, is a guardian of your soul, someone who gives you more support, encouragement, and affirmation than negative criticism, who comes along just at the time you need it most. None of us would be here today were it not for the influence, care, and sustenance of a leg-up person who came into our life at the time we needed it the most. Teachers, grandparents, leaders are all potential influencers in the leg-up area of our lives. Building community means intentionally recognizing and acknowledging the leg-up people in our lives, both past and present.

- **Coaches.** A coach is a guide who will take you into unfamiliar territory and lead you back to yourself. Coming at strategic points in your life when you are either lost or require support and guidance with current personal or leadership challenges, coaches are essential influencers in the growth of a leader and the development of authentic presence. The best coaches guide you to your own truth.

- **Therapists.** A therapist is a professionally trained expert who can help you unlock the often unconscious barriers, the blind spots in your life that are holding you back from realizing your fullest potential. Almost everyone who has the depth of authenticity required to lead in today's complex, demanding world has engaged either a therapist or a coach to guide them at defining passages on their journey. As a general distinction, therapists have a propensity toward the past, while coaches lean toward the present. Both approaches, especially when integrated together, can bring you value.

- **Mentors and Coaches.** Mentors are people who have walked before you and can pass on their experience, perspective, wisdom, and vision. Mentors are different from coaches in that, while perhaps not specifically trained in the guiding process, they have had *experience* in the terrain you are traveling and can at least share with you how they found their way. You can be a good hockey coach, for example, in your skillful ability to find and access the strengths of your players and build chemistry, strategy, and execution on your team, without necessarily having been a hockey player. To be a mentor, however, is different. Mentoring means passing along your experience and wisdom to your protégé.

- **Mastermind Groups.** A mastermind group is a permanent group of five or six people who meet regularly—at least once or twice a month—for the purpose of problem-solving, brainstorming, networking, encouraging, and motivating each other. The concept of a mastermind group came originally from Napoleon Hill, author of *Think and Grow Rich,* "When two or more people coordinate in a spirit of harmony and work toward a definite objective or purpose," Hill wrote, "they place themselves in a position, through the alliance, to absorb power directly from the great storehouse of Infinite Intelligence." Regardless of whether your mastermind group is designed to help you with your personal or professional life, the key is to choose people who are where you would like to be in your life—virtually a group of mentors for each other. With regards to creating a mastermind group, Jack Canfield, in his book, *The Success Principles*, says, "I don't know anybody who has become successful who has not employed the principle of masterminding."
- **Fellowship.** Whenever a group of people comes together in suffering, in love, and in faith, a fellowship is born. Whether a community is centered around religion, recovery, a common cause, or simply support, fellowships usually have three fundamental elements: 1) Citizenship—contributing together for the greater good, for an effort beyond self-interest; 2) Service—the opportunity to give back to others what you have been given, so that community remains rejuvenated; and 3) Accountability—a connection with those who hold your feet to the fire and support you to stay on track.

Guides

At times we need confidants that will help us go deeper, that will help us release a logjam that we can't seem to do ourselves, that can take us further along the authentic journey. At times our community comes in the form of a guide—a coach, a mentor, a therapist, or a recovery or support group. I've worked with, and continue to work with coaches, mentors, and teachers in virtually every aspect of my life: physical, mental, and spiritual health, as well as relationship and personal development. Therapists and guides have been there during times of pain and transition. I've had coaches that have worked with me to help me excavate and clarify my sense of purpose, my unique gifts, my calling in the world, and helped me grow my business.

When a guide is required, I have found four essential qualities or criteria to consider. As you go through this list, you will hopefully find it helpful in all of the confidants that you choose.

Characteristics of a Good Guide:

- **Guides you to your own voice, rather than imposing their agenda on you.** Regardless of what form they take, guides are there to help get you to our own authentic self and your own truth—not to dictate what you should do or be. They affirm you and care about you without necessarily agreeing with you. They are not afraid to be honest and are able to do so without diminishing you. They help expose you to the truth that lies behind your blind spots, and they offer hope, but they don't tell you how or whether to proceed. A good guide will help you discover what matters to you and lead you to the truth about yourself and help you stay on track. They have no interest in imposing their values or agenda on you. A true guide is not there to evaluate, judge, advise, or interpret your words, but simply to be present and help point you toward your own truth and meaning.

- **Oriented toward personal responsibility.** While supportive, I've never found it helpful to get support without looking at how I am contributing to every problem I face. I don't need people in my life who are there to please me or try to rescue me from my unhappiness by telling me what I want to hear. Support means listening and empathizing, as well as challenging you to get past the blame, to approach the presenting situation through the eyes of accountability. Fulfillment in life comes not from what you get but from who you become. Once you decide, once and for all, that all blame is a waste of time, you discover who you really are.

- **Encourages individuality.** Parker Palmer, a generous mentor, once reminded me that the quest for community can be one more form of manic activity if it is not rooted in a continual practice of silence and solitude. We need to balance time alone with the commitment to being in relationship with others. It is not healthy to be submerged in any relationship at the expense of your own identity. All identity is anchored in and sustained by relationships, and all healthy relationships are anchored in and sustained by a strong identity.

- **Builds on strengths.** Unfortunately, most of us have little awareness of our talents and strengths, much less the ability to build our lives around them. Instead, guided by well-meaning parents, teachers, and managers, and by psychology's captivation with pathology, we become experts in our weaknesses and spend our lives trying to mend these flaws while our strengths lie dormant and neglected.

While I've always been leery of labels and my own profession's obsession with pathology, Marcus Buckingham and his team at the Gallup International Research & Education Center shifted my perspective and approach with clients. Their approach is to identify your gifts, delegate your weaknesses, and align your work and contribution around your unique abilities. After all, we can't be strong in everything. Rather than trying to strengthen weaknesses, let's change the approach to strengthening strengths instead. A strength-based approach to personal and leadership development will bring fulfillment and meaning to your life and your leadership while moving you away from self-criticism. The best guides work from this approach.

Mentors

Defining moments in our life often occur at a point of suffering, crisis, or desperation. While these moments are often crossroads where we simply seek something new, they are usually experienced at times of being lost. Regardless of the form they take, these are vitally important junctures on the authentic journey. Mentors are guides we reach out to when we can't find the way ourselves.

There are many forms of mentoring. There are teachers, people who inspire and impact your life, knowingly or unknowingly, through their wisdom, their presence, their perspective, and the example they set. Some teachers may never meet you, but influence you through their writing or their work in the world. Teachers, of course, can have a direct impact on you when you are directly taught and guided by them.

You can be mentored either informally through a mentor's teachings and presence or formally through an agreed upon relationship. Informal mentors are guides who help you along the way without a formal agreement to do so. Their influence simply rubs off by association. Wayne Gretzky and Michael Jordan were informal mentors to generations of athletes in the hockey and basketball worlds and beyond. Then there are the Nelson Mandela's, the Eleanor Roosevelt's, the Mahatma Gandhi's, and the Dr. Martin Luther King, Jr.'s who have impacted, and continue to impact, thousands through their teaching and mentoring, and lives they lived. The world-renowned family therapist, Virginia Satir had a profound impact on my life and my work. Geoff Bellman, Peter Block, Robert Bly, Jack Canfield, Stephen Covey, Gabor Maté, Og Mandino, Earl Nightingale, Parker Palmer, Jim Rohn, Eckhart Tolle, and David Whyte are some of the people who, through their presence and teachings, have made a significant difference to me personally. Every field has influential pioneers, groundbreakers, and discoverers that could be called both teachers and mentors.

Finally, there are formal mentors, recognized by both parties as entering into a mentoring relationship. The best mentors, when formalizing the relationship, are specifically chosen by their protégés, sought after deliberately for a specific area of growth that is needed. Mentoring, at least when it is formalized, starts with a request, "You have what I want. Will you guide me and teach me, through your experience, how to get from where I am to where I want to be?" Formal mentoring begins with an agreement, a mutually beneficial covenant with each other.

The protégé benefits from the experience and wisdom of the mentor, while the mentor too, must find benefit in the form of feeling valued, appreciated, and privileged to be able to give back what has been learned. Mentoring is also for mentors. We all reach a stage in our life when we need protégés to acknowledge, appreciate, and seek our wisdom. This is a necessary stage in one's life and work cycle. Without giving back what we have learned in life, we stagnate. At times there may be a financially agreed upon arrangement between mentor and protégé, but regardless of the parameters of the covenant, it must be viewed as reciprocally valuable to both parties.

Your Wall of Influence

A life well lived, it has been said, is marked by the wisdom, friendship, and love gathered along the way. Since my brother's untimely death last year, after an arduous journey through brain cancer, I am developing, on a wall in my study, a "wall of influence," a collage, a collection of photographs of the twenty-five most influential people in my life. These are the people who have shaped me, impacted me deeply, and helped make me who I am today. They consist of teachers, parents, grandparents, coaches, mentors, trusted friends, and of course Val, my three daughters, my grandchildren, and my two siblings.

Take some time to stop and think about who would be on your "wall of influence." Who are the people who helped shape you and make you who you are? Where has the role of community fit into your development as a leader and as a person? If you are honest and courageous enough, there may be people on your wall that had, at the time, a *negative* impact on you, that taught you how you *don't* want to be—as a leader, a boss, or a person. Those who cause us pain can also, in the light of time's perspective, be a force for good in our life.

My early years were filled with my father's passion for sports and his love for the outdoors. Dad was a nationally ranked gymnast, and when I was in elementary school he would take me every Saturday morning to the old YMCA in our community, and we would work, just him and me alone, on the parallel bars, tumbling mats, and climbing ropes. In adolescence, he was my track coach and scoutmaster,

and we would canoe, camp, and hike together. He introduced me to Earl Nightingale, the "dean of personal development" on the radio in our red Valiant on the way to church. He was a man of deep faith and few words. He also had great courage, I discovered years later, as he battled mental illness in the form of manic depression and disabling anxiety. Following an extended time in a psychiatric hospital, he confided in me, "At the time it looked like a breakdown. I know now it was a break*through*."

I was born into a dynasty of both courage and humanness. There was no pretense of perfection, just a willingness to face the suffering in an authentic human way. As in most families, nobody in my family has had it easy, just as no one in life has a trouble-free existence. It was filled with both dysfunctional and functional elements.

Authenticity never guarantees it will be easier or more certain, just more meaningful and fulfilling. I have been taught and inspired to somehow embrace it all, appreciate it all, and use it all as fertilizer in my authentic garden. My mother inspired me with her wisdom, her pioneer spirit to be an entrepreneur in the 1960s. I now know it was a bold move for a woman in those days to work outside the home and be focused on her career. And she modeled a deep commitment to life-long self-development. I continue to be inspired by the books I inherited from her library.

Soon after her death in 1999, I found among her personal belongings a three-hundred-page handwritten history of her seventy-eight-year life, written over a forty-year span. The best way to honor my mother is to share some of the last three pages of this chronicle with you. These last pages were written just months before her death.

> … Regrets eat at the soul—especially regrets over material things. I watched my father's pain because he had no inheritance to leave his children. What wasted energy!
>
> I do know that I have a much greater legacy to leave my children than money or material things. That is the legacy of my writing about my own personal journey. In this sharing, I hope I can help them to be open to living life more fully. The freedom to be—fully to be—who we are is the greatest gift any of us can give ourselves. And we must give it to ourselves. No one can do this for us.
>
> My hope is that my journal writings will help my progenitors accomplish this task!
>
> As I reflect upon my seventy-seven years, I am enveloped in memories and love for this experience of "living life." What a gift it is. I am so grateful to the Creator of this miracle. My whole journey has been a mystery, a miracle, and a marvel. I feel strongly that an unseen hand had orchestrated it and has handed it to me as a gift! I know it has been a process, with peaks and valleys, with joy and deep pain, with laughter and tears, and with many wonderful experiences and the whole gamut of human

emotions. Most of all it has been a privilege, and I thank the Great Creator for such a wonderful gift.

... Every parent, no matter how hard they try, will be both a blessing and a curse to their children. My hope is that my children will appreciate the "blessing," if not immediately then later in life, and perhaps more importantly that they will take the "curse" and, like an oyster irritated by a grain of sand, over time use it as a catalyst to build layers of character and under-standing—thus producing a pearl.

Joyce E. Irvine

In my Authentic Leadership programs and retreats, I give the partic-ipants an assignment to start identifying the people on their wall of influence and then pick one that they have yet to acknowledge and write them a thank you letter. And then, if the person is still alive, mail the letter or, better still, deliver it to them directly. It's amazing what comes out of this assignment. This assignment alone is one of the most meaningful of any that I give to people. I recently heard back from one of the leaders who wrote a letter to his grade three teacher, acknowledging the impact she had on his life. He then spent a couple of months tracking her down and found her in a senior's center. She was in her eighties by then and had been retired for almost thirty years. He wrote me soon after and spoke of how they cried together, and how important it was for his own leadership develop-ment to acknowledge his teacher and ultimately affirm his own qual-ities he brought to *his* leadership. I am now calling these "thank you projects." They are quite life changing, to say the least.

A few years ago, in a similar situation, an executive wrote a letter to her father, expressing for the first time, a message of gratitude and acknowledgment of the influence he had in making her the leader and the person she is today. Later in the afternoon, she received a text to call her sister. It turns out that very day, her father had suffered a heart attack and was in the intensive care unit in a hospital a three-hour drive away. She was able to get there before her father passed. In the course of the last two hours of his life, she read him the letter she had written that morning and was able to express her sincere, honest, and heartfelt gratitude to her father.

As you reflect on the question of who would be on your wall, gratitude will be a powerful guiding force. The challenge will be to take that appreciation and transform it into contribution, impact, and deep fulfillment. You will then be able to answer the question, "Whose wall, will you, one day, earn the right to be on?"

Learning to Navigate

A dvancing along the journey to authenticity requires anchoring yourself with a strong orientation based upon all six compass points.

As you continue to enhance your understanding, self-knowledge, and self-improvement in each of these areas, you will develop an increasingly accurate travel arrow pointing toward your own True North.

Here are some tips as you learn to navigate:

Becoming Real

The process of becoming real, developing as an authentic leader and contributing to a great organizational culture is not accomplished in a linear, tidy fashion. Like building a cohesive marriage or family, it's a human, imperfect journey that involves attention, vigilance, disciplined action, and perseverance. The journey is not about perfection but rather about consistent reflection, action, learning, and adjustment, driven by a commitment to continual improvement.

Focusing on Presence

Leaders aren't defined by the size of their office or the titles behind their name. Leaders are defined by the difference they make. While you might get promoted to being a boss, you don't get promoted to being a leader. You have to earn the right to be called a leader by your ability to influence and your capacity to achieve results through others. Learning the fundamentals of authentic leadership will enable you to lead with presence, not position.

Developing Your Map

To survive—and thrive—you have to adapt and embrace change. When you have made the decision to dive in and explore your core authentic leadership capability, you become an agent of change. But where is your roadmap? Where are your tools? There are many approaches you will learn in the course of this book, but a critical place to start is to be open to possibility. Be honest with yourself, be receptive to learning and growing, and start moving forward one step after the other.

Patience and Dedication—Move at Your Own Pace

Exploring *The Other Everest* and embracing the wisdom within is a process, not a destination. You will find the path to improvement and achievement at the same time you are creating it. This is your journey. Your direction—your "True North"—based on exploring your authentic values and desires, is unique to you. Be patient with yourself and move at your own pace. Dedication is more important than speed.

Field Notes

Opportunities for reflection from Part II: Journey to Authenticity ...

1. *Clarity is about living in alignment with your values. How would you assess your own clarity and how can you improve?*
2. *Character is about having the courage to face the demands of reality. How would you assess your own character and how can you improve?*
3. *Centering is about knowing your worth away from work. What are some of your key strengths that define this worth?*
4. *Calling is the nexus point where the world's need meets the soul's desire. What would you describe as your calling right now—is it something the world needs that aligns with what you truly want to be doing?*
5. *Creativity is about awakening the artist within. Be truthful with yourself—how are you doing at providing yourself with opportunities for self-expression through creativity?*
6. *Community is about "connecting with your tribe." Think about what you may need now in the way of community in your life. Where do you need to start reaching out to strengthen and expand your community?*
7. *Who would be on your personal wall of influence? Think about how, precisely, these people influenced you and what qualities they have that you admire. How can you better acknowledge these people and the contributions they have made to your life? How can you further sharpen these qualities in yourself?*

8. *Whose wall will you be on? Let this question guide your continual commitment to influence others with greater presence and love.*

9. *What are the top three "notes to self" you can take away from this section of The Other Everest?*

Those using the companion Workbook: The Other Everest can find additional teachings and exercises in the workbook to help absorb and utilize the information from Part II.

PART III

Summits of Success

Milestones Toward the Peak of Achievement

As you make progress in developing the elements of leadership presence that are reflected in the six compass points, you simultaneously increase the opportunity to amplify your impact through leadership practices.

A core part of leadership is action. As you become more strongly oriented in understanding the nature of your authentic leadership, you can start to focus more on the work of applying your authentic leadership capacity to drive toward your own definitions of success and achievement.

There are five core pillars of authentic leadership action that flow from harnessing and directing the elements of leadership presence described in the previous section of this book. They serve as milestones in your authentic leadership journey, propelling you towards new summits of success as you make progress.

These milestones include: Build Trust, Create Clarity, Engage Talent, Embrace Change, and Ensure Results. Collectively they help you build a high-performance culture in your role as a business or organizational leader.

Build Trust

"Trust is the glue of life. It's the most essential ingredient in relationships, the fundamental principle that holds together all connections."

Stephen Covey

When we brought Enzo home from the Humane Society, we knew that he had been neglected during the first ten months of his life. Confined to a small kennel with little human contact, he was shy, withdrawn, and fearful. For the next several months, it became our family project to earn Enzo's trust. Like a wild animal, he taught us to sit quietly and wait for the treasurable trust we sought to emerge. In the process, Enzo became a teacher of trust as we have helped him find his legs, his gift, and passion to run and work and to allow us into his heart.

Trust is the most important issue facing the world today and lies at the foundation of every relationship. It's the keystone of success in work and in life. It's the new global currency. It crosses cultures and generations. Building, restoring, and sustaining trust in your family, your community, and your workplace is your number one leadership challenge, and your number one leadership priority. Without trust, there is no leadership, no relationship, no life as we know it in this interconnected universe. Trust lays at the center of everything we do—from driving through a green light to eating the food we purchase to allowing the words of this book influence you.

Trust in a culture is the key factor that enables people to unleash their unique capacities. Trust frees creativity, enabling you to focus your energy on creating and discovering, rather than on defending. Trust transcends fear. Trust transforms tension, caution, and over-control into confidence, imagination, and the flow of energy. Trust provides an environment that nourishes, rather than depletes. When trust is high, people and systems function well. When fear is high, energy is blocked. Trust turns bureaucracy into accountability, institutions into communities, fear into freedom, politics into forthrightness, and employment into authentic engagement. Trust converts "task doers" into true contributors, superficial exchanges into genuine conversations, and "command performance" into sincere commitment. Simply put, we're happier—and maybe even healthier—when we are trusted and when we can trust. Trust makes the world a better place to live and work.

Derived from the German word *trost*, trust means "comfort." It implies an instinctive, unquestioning belief in and reliance upon someone or something. It is the experience of being comfortable and unguarded around another person or situation.

There is an emotional component to trust, which speaks to the quality of the relationship between us. Is there alignment around our values? Does it intuitively "feel right" to trust this person? Character plays a big part here. We aren't going to trust people who lack integrity, honesty, or who aren't in some way aligned with our values. A "belief in" someone requires that I am able to, in some way, connect with you, that we can find common ground to work together, that there is some kind of explicit or implicit chemistry between us. Believing in another implies that you can answer the questions, "Do they believe my best interest and the best interest of our relationship is important? Do they care?"

Trust is also a "reliance upon" someone. This is the rational side of the trust equation. Can this person be counted on? Do they keep their promises? Do they do what they say they will do? Do they show up on time and get the job done? Just as we aren't likely to trust people who don't care, we aren't going to extend trust to incompetence. If you get the sense that someone doesn't care, if they don't put a measure of pride in their work, then they likely will show a degree of incompetence. Simultaneously, even if they care and try hard, to trust a person you still have to see competence. Trust is ultimately about results.

The Trust Playbook: Twelve Things I Know About Trust

Trust presents a paradox in that it needs to be earned, but to be earned it has to first be given. Yet trust without wisdom is naiveté. That is why trust is often given in small amounts over time. As we experience success trusting an individual, we are more and more willing to trust further. Overall, twelve precepts seem clear.

1. **Trust cannot be coerced or controlled.** It can only be invited. Building trust isn't like building an IKEA bookshelf. There's no step-by-step course of action that guarantees an outcome. Trust is more like gardening. It's organic and dynamic, creating the right conditions and providing the needed care. Trust is more about "fostering" than "building."

2. **Trust is to a relationship what oxygen is to life.** A relationship depends on trust for its existence, and it's easy to take it for granted until it's not there. Trust isn't only the absence of dishonesty, cruelty, or betrayal. It's also the presence of connection. Trust must be nurtured, built up, and protected. Trust is a rather delicate flower. What can take years to build can be destroyed in one decision.

3. **Trust is not built in a day.** It is built daily—with consistent, repeated action. While trust has an emotional component to it, trust is not an emotion. Trust is an action. Trust is an ever-moving, ever-changing way of being in the world. Trust is demonstrated by the way you behave in response to another person or circumstance. In your most trusted relationships, trust is generally not even talked about. Instead, it's demonstrated.

4. **Trust is both a prerequisite as well as an outcome.** While vulnerability requires trust, trust also requires vulnerability. While competence is necessary for trust, sometimes admitting that we don't know and that we need help is the best way to build trust. People need to feel safe in order to trust, and you feel safer after you have taken risks. You may be deceived if you trust too much, but you will live in anguish if you don't trust enough. These are some of the paradoxes of trust. Behavior begets behavior. Trusting others invites trust. The best way to find out if you can trust somebody is to trust them.

5. **Trust is a decision.** Trust is a choice, and it's a vulnerable choice. It takes courage to trust. While children trust instinctively, this is a naïve trust. It isn't until we have been betrayed and choose to trust again that we can realize what it means to have the courage to trust. While trusting people can be risky, not trusting people is a greater risk.

6. **Trust must be constantly earned.** If you want to be trusted, you must first give others evidence that you are trustworthy: Be sincere. Be honest. Be reliable. Don't make promises you don't intend to keep, and do what you say you will do. Make excellence and continual improvement a life-long habit. Be generous. Care.

7. **Mature trust is smart trust.** Years ago, an employee embezzled thousands of dollars from my bank account. Responsible for making deposits, she was pocketing essentially all the cash that went through the business for more than a year. What I learned from the experience was to put proper accountability processes in place. Blind trust is naïve. Extending trust is noble, but make sure you're intelligent and responsible about it and do your due diligence. It's the kind of trust that Stephen M. R. Covey calls "smart trust."

8. **Trust in others begins with *self*-trust.** The world does not look bright if you are wearing dark colored glasses. We don't see the world as it is; we see the world as we are. You won't trust others beyond your capacity to trust yourself. If you are having a hard time trusting a person, look first in the mirror.

When we believe in and can rely on our own resources, we are far more apt to trust others.

9. **Trust is a releasing process.** Max De Pree, founder and former CEO of Herman Miller, not only practiced intentional caring for his employees but demonstrated trust in their commitment and value to the company. He once received a note from an outstanding industrial designer who worked for him for many years. The note said, *"Your trust is the grace that enables me to be creative."* When leaders give and expect trust, the organization reaps undreamed-of benefits. Trust may well be the most inspiring force in organizations. It is the power that transforms *contractual* relationships into *covenantal* relationships, from relying on the contract to holding to the promises. By freeing creativity, trust enables you to focus your energy on creating and discovering rather than on defending. It releases your courage. It opens you to play, feel, enjoy, experience your pain, and be who you are. The full life is a spontaneous, unconstrained, flowing, trusting life. Trust gives you freedom while fear takes it away. Freedom is not out there. Freedom comes from within. Freedom comes from the decision to trust. Trust opens the doorway to the human spirit.

10. **Trust is not black or white.** It's a dynamic, ever-changing, moving target. Trust is a state of mind that is situational and determined through experience. There is no such thing as "absolute trust." Trust is a continuum, not a dichotomy. If you ask someone to help you with your groceries, you may trust their strength, but it doesn't mean that you would trust them with the keys to your house. You might trust a contractor to renovate your bathroom, but you wouldn't trust them to do your job for a day. Trust is where competence and character intersect. While you might trust someone because they are competent, you may not trust them if they don't show up to work on time. On the other hand, they may be reliable but incompetent.

11. **Healthy boundaries are required in all trusting relationships.** If you can't say "no," you will be unable to fully give yourself to "yes." Trust requires that you respect yourself enough to risk disappointing others. Full trust requires that you can't base your own worthiness on others' approval. In the words of Brené Brown, "Only when we believe, deep down, that we *are* enough can we say '*enough!*'"

12. **You don't have to be perfect to be trustworthy.** Trust is more about humanness than it is about appearances. If you genuinely care and are committed to a relationship, most people will extend their trust to you. And most broken trust can be repaired.

"Communication is more a function of trust than of technique."
Stephen R. Covey

Assessing Trust

There are a number of principles I have learned about trust that are critical to understanding and sharpening your capacity for trust building.

Trust is built with care and compassion. It's built with honesty and stability and strong character. Trust is built through paying unwavering attention to the small things and knowing what's important to people. Trust is built with integrity and a can-do attitude. Trust is being there for another person when it isn't easy or comfortable.

Here are some questions that assess whether a person is trustworthy:

- Do they deliver results?
- Do they stand by me under pressure?
- Do they tell me the truth?
- Do they fulfill their promises?
- Do they care?

When leading groups of senior executives through a discussion about trust over the years, "lack of trust" is a familiar presenting problem. When asked how you know if there is trust in a relationship, responses that come from the groups I've worked with include:

- "It's intuitive. It's a gut feeling. You just *know* instinctively whether you can trust someone."
- "I trust people who do what they say they will do, who I can count on. I need people to be accountable."
- "We build trust by doing things together over time and getting to know how each other handles situations, decision, and stress."
- "Competence. Pure and simple. I need to know that you can do your job. Without ability, there is no trust."
- "Integrity. That's what I need from a person in order to trust them. I need to see honesty and ethical actions."
- "For me, it's all about relationships. How the person is able to relate to me and to the people around them."

These answers remind me of the familiar story of the blind people asked to describe an elephant. The one who had a hold of the elephant's legs described the elephant as being like the trunk of a tree. Another, who was holding on to the elephant's tail, said the elephant was like a rope. Another one, while holding the trunk, described the elephant as a large hose. The one who was feeling the ear proclaimed that the elephant was like a blanket. The person feeling the belly expressed that the elephant was like a wall.

By stepping back far enough and getting the whole picture, we can see that each person was correct—albeit limited—by their own perception. The challenge with many groups is that much of the mistrust they hold toward each other is based on incomplete knowledge of each other's perceptions. For example:

- You may not see being late for meetings as any big deal. But for a person who values reliability, you may be unintentionally eroding trust.
- The perceived competence you have in yourself may not be good enough to instill confidence in those who rely on you.

- You may be working hard at listening, being open and transparent, and building relationships with people on your team while unintentionally eroding trust with your staff when they don't see you following through on the promises you make.

Trust, like the elephant, is a large animal. It's complex. There is a relational component as well as a rational component to trust. Trust is about intuition as much as it is about reliability. It deals as much with integrity as it does with capability; vulnerability as much as sincerity. Whether a person trusts us may well be based on past experiences and perceptions that we have no control over. Expounding upon and understanding trust always comes with its own set of biases. What is important is the need for continual investigation, vigilance, and dialogue.

Trust, in all its complexity, is the bedrock of success in work and in life. Think of all the various teams you have been on in your life—sports teams, school teams, family teams, or teams in your workplace. Teams with high levels of trust are better in every way—they are more productive; they are more creative; the energy is high; people are motivated to be on them; and they are more fun! Contrast this to the experience of being on a low or no trust team, and I'm sure you will agree that the difference is not incremental—it's huge.

Trust enrolls people in a worthwhile vision. It then enables full passion, commitment, freedom, energy, health, effectiveness, and engagement. Trust makes everything happen in organizations. If you can earn and build trust, you can lead. If you can't, you won't be a leader. It's that simple, and it's that complex.

It can be said that trust is the barometer of individual and group health. With it, we function naturally, spontaneously, and directly. Without it, we need constraints, rules, contracts, and policies. It's not the breadth of the change that will determine your success as a leader. It's the depth of the trust with your people. Building, restoring, and sustaining trust is your number one leadership challenge.

How do you know when people trust you?

1. **People who trust you seek your advice.** An indication of trust is that people feel safe enough around you to be vulnerable. They can risk admitting that they don't know, that they need help, and that they respect you as a trusted source. While you certainly don't have to have the answers, it is an indication that you have earned trust when people come to you for guidance. While it isn't the only way to measure trust, it's a good starting point.

2. **People are honest with you.** People will initiate tough conversations with people they trust. You know you have earned trust when others—particularly your direct reports—share good news or bad, negative and positive feedback, and when they are direct, candid, and straightforward with you—all of which are vulnerable choices. You can be polite with anyone, but the seed of trust lies within *genuineness*. Are people giving you open and honest feedback, bad news as well as good?

3. **People challenge you.** As a corollary to #2, you know you have established trust, especially when you are in a position of authority, when others respectfully challenge your point of view, your approach, and your decisions. Are you being challenged by the people who report to you?

4. **People are competent.** While you can foster competence for a time in a non-trusting relationship, it won't last. Trust breeds competence. Trust builds results. Trust fosters capability. Are you getting the results you need from your team?

5. **People are relaxed around you.** I recently coached a manager whose boss exploded every couple of weeks. He constantly lived in tension, never knowing what would set the boss off or the mood he would bring into the office. Being relaxed is not the same as being complacent. It means being calm in the midst of activity, poised under pressure. You are more effective when you aren't wound up and stressed. You are more productive and do better work when enjoying yourself. Tension, stress, anxiety—all indicators of a lack of trust—can destroy a

workplace. Are you aware of the level of tension in the people around you?

6. **People stick around.** It's been said that people don't leave organizations; they leave bosses. The number one reason people leave marriages is because they no longer feel good about themselves in the presence of their spouse. People leave bosses for the same reason: they no longer feel good about themselves in their presence. You don't feel good about yourself when you are around people you don't trust. How's the retention rate of your direct reports?

Herein lies the first clue to fostering trust around you. Start with a willingness to *give* what you desire from others. If you are committed to building trust in the relationships with people around you:

1. **Seek the input and advice of others.** Genuinely look for opportunities for others to help you, guide you, and support you. Extend trust. Ask questions. Be curious and coachable.

2. **Be open and honest with people.** Tell people what you know; tell them what you don't know. Show your humanness. You don't have to be perfect to build trust; what you do have to be is real and honest.

3. **Challenge yourself in the presence of people.** Let people know your weaknesses and what you are doing to work on them. Invite them to challenge you and thank them when they do.

4. **Be competent.** Be committed to mastery and excellence. Be a life-long learner. Stretch beyond mediocrity to mastery. Be dedicated to your on-going development. Be open to feedback. Nobody trusts an incompetent person.

5. **Be relaxed.** Tension is an indicator of mistrust. Composure earns people's trust. People lack trust in a stressed, unpredictable, unstable leader. You can be firm, clear, and tough, but be calm, composed, and caring in the process.

6. **Stick around.** People don't trust quitters. We are apt to trust people who have this quality of grit. We trust people are who dependable, reliable, and persistent.

7. **Above all, be trustworthy.** Being trustworthy means being accountable, which indicates you can be counted on. Being trustworthy is about being a person of character. Character isn't how you act when life is going the way you want it to. That's easy. Character is how you act when everything around you is falling apart. Character is how you act when you are scared and angry and tired and frustrated. That's when people watch you and decide whether they will trust you.

Fostering Trust

While there's no formula for fostering trust, there are ten strategies that may be helpful in your commitment to creating trust around you.

1. **Be honest.** Probably the greatest single trust-building behavior is honesty. It's obvious that we don't trust people who lie, cheat, or steal. But just because you don't lie, cheat, or steal doesn't guarantee that you are going to be trusted. That's because there's more to honesty than meets the eye. A senior VP once told me about her CEO who made a promise to his senior leadership team and then, when under the pressure of his board, took a complete 180 and threw his executives under the bus. He lost the trust of not only the team but also of pretty much his entire company. Honesty also means talking straight and being transparent. A big part of honesty and subsequent trust is how a leader stands by others under the test of pressure.

Honesty is also about having the courage to talk straight, to be direct in your communication. Most people don't tell outright lies. Instead, they engage in what Stephen M. R. Covey, in his book, *The Speed of Trust*, calls *counterfeit* straight talk. Counterfeit straight talk, according to Covey, includes behaviors such as beating around the bush, withholding information, double-talk, flattery, positioning, posturing, and the smooth manipulative behavior of "spinning" communication to get what you want. Another dangerous counterfeit is "technically" telling the truth but leaving a false impression. This is mincing words and legally splitting hairs. All these behaviors invariably weaken trust. We all have periods of insecurity. But when we don't have the courage to be honest about it, smooth, indirect, manipulative communication results and trust is diminished.

Being honest doesn't justify cruel, abusive communication. You can't go around beating people up under the guise of honesty. Trustworthy leaders are committed to balancing honesty with respect, and temper honest, straight communication with skill, tact, and good judgment. Wrestling with these two vital values is integral to learning to be trusted. Trust starts with the courage to be honest and the courage to face the brutal facts. You earn trust when you maintain unwavering faith that you can and will prevail in the end, regardless of the difficulties, while at the same time have the discipline to face the truth of your current reality, whatever it may be.

2. **Connect before you expect.** In my years as a family therapist, parents would often bring in their children with a list of things they wanted me to "fix." After listening to a variety of requests, such as motivating them to clean their room or get their homework done, I would ask a simple question: While I know it's important to teach kids to be responsible, how much time in the past week did you spend with your children when you weren't trying to get them to do something? When you were just hanging out and connecting with them? A sign of troubled families was when the answer was very little to none. The only way parents in these families knew to relate to their children was to try to get them to do something. My own teenage daughters have always been my best teachers. When I'd been traveling for an extended time and disconnected from them, my tendency was to come home and see all the things they weren't doing to help around the house. When I was tired and detached from them, I'd notice how they hadn't been keeping their rooms clean enough or their chores weren't

done adequately. Then I'd try to use my positional authority as a father to get them to conform to my will. This type of approach, or management by pressure, is what Ken Blanchard used to call "seagull management," which means you ignore people, and then you fly around and crap on them. The obvious result of this line of attack is resistance, disengagement, and power struggles. You have to connect before you expect. In more than thirty years of facilitating leadership development workshops, I have learned that relationship and connectedness are the pre-conditions for change. Every meeting, every process, every training program has to first get people connected. Otherwise, the content falls on deaf ears. Trust without connection is not trust at all. It's compliance. If you are committed to building trust, connect before you expect.

3. **Listen. Listen. Listen.** If you have any hope of connecting—and thus building trust and influencing—you always have to start with showing genuine interest. My mother used to tell me, "Don't seek to be interesting; seek instead to be interested." If you are going to connect you have to come into a relationship with a sincere intent to connect. If you aren't genuinely interested in the other person, people will sense it, and you won't have a hope of connecting. You show genuine interest when you listen and are fully present. When you come into a new team, listen. When you start a new relationship, listen. Before you take on a project, listen. Before you act, listen. Ask questions. Be curious. Be genuinely interested.

A good rule when you are inviting people to open up is: "No fixing, no advising, no setting people straight." Also, allowing brief, reflective silences in the conversation, rather than rushing right in with an agenda gives people a sense of being heard and listened to. Most people listen to respond rather than listen to understand. At the beginning of an interaction or a relationship, the goal is not agreement. You aren't listening to debate or argue or persuade or manipulate. People will see right through all these motives. You are listening, at least initially, with a genuine intent to simply *understand* and be curious. You convey understanding by clarifying before responding. If you genuinely seek to understand before being understood, the door to trust will open. Responding to the speaker, not with commentary or advice, but with honest, open questions that have no other intent than to help the speaker reflect more deeply on whatever he or she is saying makes an impact in the conversation and fosters trust.

4. **Take ownership.** Oprah Winfrey was raised in rural Mississippi by her grandparents and abused by a relative as a youth. But she chose to rise above her circumstances. As she puts it: *"I don't think of myself as a poor deprived ghetto girl who made good. I think of myself as somebody who from an early age knew I was responsible for myself, and I had to make good."* People who take ownership of their lives, who view all blame as a waste of time, who choose to be victors rather than victims, inspire others. People are more apt to trust those who take responsibility for their lives than people who blame and complain. People who resist the human tendency to blame and complain are more confident, self-assured, and more at peace with themselves. People who take ownership are more inclined to respect themselves and thus are more apt to earn the respect of others.

Rather than allowing people to wallow in victimhood, owners ask, *"What are you doing to contribute to the thing you're complaining about? What's the promise you're willing to make?"* We are more apt to extend trust to owners as they stand on solid stable ground.

Another aspect of ownership is the self-respect required to apologize. No one will ever think less of you by holding your hand up high and saying, "I'm responsible for that." To be human is to err. When you make a mistake, owners admit it, say you're sorry and tell the people who are impacted how you are going to remedy the situation. Having the self-regard and thus the humility to acknowledge when we are wrong and apologize for our errors is an indicator of strength, character, and integrity. Real leadership is impossible without a willingness to apologize and acknowledge when we make a mistake. It's a trust-building action to have the courage to take an honest look at ourselves, to take a truthful appraisal of the impact of our actions on others, and to have the willingness to make necessary changes.

Besides taking 100 percent responsibility and apologizing when we are wrong, owners are also what I call *anti-entitlement people*. Being anti-entitlement means that you believe you need to bring value to others before you deserve anything in return. You *earn* a raise before you presume one. You *earn* good service before you expect good service. Being anti-entitlement means you choose service over self-interest, gratitude over privilege, and obligations over rights. There appear to be two kinds of people in the world: those who help, and those who hinder; those who give, and those who take; those who lift, and those who lean; those who contribute, and those who consume. In the dictionary you'll learn that to consume is to "destroy, squander, use up ..." while to contribute is to "build, serve, make better ..." In a consumer society, you'll stand above the crowd of mediocrity and earn the trust of the people around you when you decide to be a contributor. Saying, "I'm responsible for that," will never diminish you. Take ownership for your side of the street. Become part of the solution to every problem that's in front of you and watch trust grow around you.

5. **Be accountable.** A close cousin to being an owner, being accountable is about earning trust by being a person who can be counted on. Keep your promises. Show up on time. Do what you say you are going to do. Never make an agreement you don't intend to keep. While not everyone may value this virtue and hold you in higher regard when you keep promises, why take the chance? Not only will you earn the trust of others by being accountable, most importantly, you will earn the trust and respect of yourself.

Being accountable also means starting the day with what Stephen Covey used to call a "personal victory." Personal victory precedes public victory. Get the hard tasks out of the way first thing in the morning. Feel good about yourself by conquering a difficult task early in the day. No one takes pride or develops self-respect by procrastinating or taking the easy way out. If exercise is hard for you and you decide it is important, start your day with a private victory of exercise. If you want a respectful workplace or relationship, start by earning *self*-respect. When you respect yourself, others will respect you. Grow where you are planted. Don't expect that a better job or a better relationship or a better place to live will make you happier. What will make you happier is to take pride in doing what's in front of you now. Serve where you are. The grass isn't greener on the other side of the fence. The grass is greener where you water it.

6. **Say thank you.** Just as ownership and accountability inspire trust around you, so too does the attitude of gratitude. The story goes that a couple of mischievous boys wanted to play a joke on their grandpa, so while he napped, they rubbed some Limburger cheese in his mustache. When grandpa awoke, he sniffed a little bit and said, "It stinks in here!" He arose from his favorite chair in the living room and walked into the kitchen. As he sniffed around, he declared: "It stinks in here too!" Leaving the kitchen, he walked into the hallway that led to his front door. Sure enough, as he sniffed, he muttered: "It even stinks in here!" Flinging the front door open, he took a breath of what he expected to be fresh air. But once again the Limburger cheese filled his nostrils, and grandpa shouted in disgust: "The whole world stinks!" Question: Did the whole world stink? Of course not! In fact, the real problem was right under grandpa's nose! People don't put their trust in people with a bad attitude. They know if they aren't willing to let go of what is under their nose, how will they take care of what we entrust to them.

Gratitude has transformative power. Gratitude is the antidote to hatred, fear, and entitlement. Next time you see a police officer take a moment and thank them for their work. Next time you see a tired cashier at the grocery store, take a moment and express your gratitude. Thank a colleague for their contribution to a recent project. It's easy to be grateful when you get what you want. The real challenge is being grateful when you don't get what you want. It's not a good life that makes us grateful; it's being grateful that makes a good life. When you surround yourself with thoughts of gratitude, you'll soon find yourself surrounded by high trust relationships.

7. **Give credit.** I once coached a line manager who told me how he had worked three months on a research project. He presented his hard work and subsequent data and findings to his boss right before leaving on holidays. Upon his return two weeks later, he found out that his boss had presented his research to her board and taken all the credit for it. "This has happened more than once," the manager told me. "I just can't trust her." It was Harry Truman who said, *"It is amazing what you can accomplish if you don't care who gets the credit."* While trustworthy leaders are secure enough within themselves not to care who gets the credit, they also value themselves and others enough to *give* credit rather than take it.

8. **Be loyal in people's absence.** A trusted partner promises, "What I share with you, you will hold in confidence. What you share with me, I will hold in confidence." Trust also means that one respects not only my story, but the story of others in my life. I will notice how you treat others who trust you, and that will shape the trust between us. I, like all of us, have gossiped about people. I have a good friend who was honest with me when she said her trust in me diminished when she heard me criticize a mutual acquaintance in their absence. As uncomfortable as it was to hear the truth, I am grateful for friends who are honest. I'm also grateful for people in my life who are loyal in people's absence. It is in these people I put my trust.

9. **Humanize your workplace.** A new vice president in Farm Credit Canada, the leader in loans, business, and financial services to Canadian agriculture, started his presentation to his new division with a story about the influence of his grandfather in shaping his values, character, and work ethic. Accompanied

by a short slide show of his grandfather on his homestead, farming in the 1950's, he talked to the group about what he learned about farming and leadership from working alongside his grandpa when he was a boy. Within ten minutes he had his entire team, most of whom he had never met, eating out of the palm of his hand. Authentic leaders understand that their first job is to create a foundation of trust with their team. The best way to do this is to own up to vulnerabilities. The worst thing you can do is defend against your fears, doubts, and insecurity by implying, "I've done this a million times before and I've got this under control." That alienates people. You have lots of time to show your competence. It's humanness that opens the first door to trust. While trust comes through vulnerability, being vulnerable doesn't mean that you show all your fears, doubts, and insecurities and expect the group to look after you. Being vulnerable and human means sharing your values, your hopes, your dreams, as well as your expectations and needs from the group. Authentic leaders know that you don't earn credibility and trust by pretending to be more than you are. You earn trust through honesty, humility, and humanness.

The word organization comes from the word "organ." Organizations aren't machines that can be managed like a piece of equipment or with a technical procedure. Organizations, at their core, are about heart, soul, and human beings. Work has to provide opportunities for personal growth, as well as financial growth. If it doesn't, we are spending far too much of our lives there. Humanizing the workplace means making the shift from "management by chopping people's heads off" to "leadership through respect." Humanizing the workplace means getting out of your office, wandering around, asking questions, observing the operation, and learning about what people do. Humanizing the workplace means opening up to your employees, encouraging them, letting them get to know you a bit, and sharing your expectations and approach to leadership.

A manager of a power plant who gave me this concept of "humanizing the workplace" told me about an employee he had taken aside, soon after he was brought in to look after the plant. After he had observed him for a few shifts, he acknowledged him for the quality of his work, his attention to detail, and the example he was setting for his team through a strong work ethic and positive attitude. After hearing this feedback, the employee fell silent. With tears in his eyes he responded, "In my twenty-five years working at this plant, you are the first person to tell me I'm doing something right."

Humanizing our workplace isn't about gimmicks or fads. It's about respecting ourselves enough to show genuine respect for others. It means creating a caring environment and embracing a commitment to help people grow, just as much as it means getting good results. Humanizing your workplace is about creating a space where people feel safe to take risks, to make mistakes, and to fail. It's a sustaining, simple, down-to-earth philosophy that liberates us from "chopping people's heads off" to focusing on what really matters. In short, it isn't about being right; it's about being *real*. It also means resisting the tendency to manage by email. Humans need face-to-face contact. Get out on the floor. Walk around. Ask questions. If you can't get with people face-to-face, at least pick up the phone and talk to them. As Maya Angelou, the American poet, singer, and activist reminds us, "People may not remember what you did, or what you said, but they will always remember how you made them feel."

Humanizing your workplace includes a willingness to leave your ego at the door and make others feel important, which means bringing a servant attitude to everything you do. It means deciding to be a "we" person rather than a "me" person. Albert Schweitzer, the French-German theologian humanitarian, once said, "I don't know what your destiny will be, but one thing I do know. The only ones among us who will be really happy are those who will have sought and found how to serve." Servant leadership is being committed to serving those in your care, ensuring that they have what they need to get their job done and grow in the process. Serving leads to freedom, self-respect, and well-being within and around you. You can't make everyone on your team happy. What you can do is support their success by helping them meet their needs.

Care enough to invest in the lives of the people around you. Organizations don't give a leader power. Power comes from the people you serve. You earn power by earning the trust of others. And if you don't use this power well, they will take it away from you. They take it away by making leading difficult for you by resisting and refusing to be influenced, even if they pretend to follow you because you have a legislated title. When you choose to extend yourself by serving, sacrificing, and caring for others, you increase your capacity to influence. When you care, you invite people along on a journey and inspire them to join you. You offer them a seat on the bus—not because they *have* to but because they *want* to. A leader who knows how to influence through genuine caring will be a leader who is in great demand and is trusted. The paradox, of course, is that caring leaders don't do it to be in demand. They do it because they care.

10. **Keep getting better.** People who set high standards of excellence for themselves inspire trust around them. Competence is valued, and those who strive for continuous improvement are more likely to be trusted. People are more apt to put their trust in those people who value excellence. Set high goals. Be a life-long learner. Read more books and fewer emails. Bring curiosity to everything you do. Have a disciplined approach to self-improvement. Trusted people learn from their mistakes. They are committed to self-awareness and personal development.

People who are trusted not only have high standards for themselves, they hold high standards for those they serve. And they make these standards clear. Caring means building a platform where people can grow. You don't build trust by having low standards or letting people off the hook. You have to care about people *and* the results they produce. Trust requires high support and accompanying high expectations. You foster trust by supporting people to go beyond what they thought they could do. Then hold them accountable for what they have agreed to. These expectations are part of a leader's value system that must be communicated to those being led. It is important to define your top priorities with your workers and clarify the results and the attitude that you need from them. Then model what you expect—so you will be credible to hold them accountable.

11. **Appreciate the big value of small.** According to the Greek storyteller Aesop, a little mouse ran up and down a sleeping lion who awoke, grabbed the poor helpless rodent, and opened his big jaws to swallow him. "Pardon, O King," cried the little mouse, "Please forgive me. I promise never to climb on you again. And if you let me go, who knows what I may be able to do for you someday." The lion was so intrigued by the idea of a mouse being able to help him that he lifted up his paw and let the critter go. Sometime later, the lion was caught in a trap, and the hunters tied him to a tree while they went in search of a wagon to transport him to the king. Just then the little mouse happened to pass by and seeing the lion's sad plight, quickly jumped at the opportunity to help him. He gnawed away the ropes, setting the lion free.

We live in a society that values *big*. Big profits. Big paychecks. Big companies. Big titles. Big fame. Big offices. In this world of big, it's easy to get the crazy idea that you aren't valuable if you are small or perceive yourself to be small. But Aesop's tale of the lion and the mouse teaches a wise lesson. The tiny mouse is every bit as valuable as the lion. According to Aesop, importance is not based on size, but rather on the value you bring to others. It's a simple matter of changing the context. The person who brings the most value is the most valuable. Value isn't measured by the size of your office, the size of your paycheck, or the size of your business. Value is measured by your contribution to others. If you want to earn people's trust, bring value to them.

Bob Galvin, speaking of his father, founder of Motorola, has said: *"Dad once looked down an assembly line of women employees and thought, '[They] are all like my own mom— they have kids, homes to take care of, people who need them.' It motivated him to work hard to give them a better life because he saw his mom in all of them. That's how it all begins—with fundamental respect."*

Paul Galvin knew something about appreciating the big value of the small. Appreciating the big value of small means fostering trust by paying attention to the little things. It means reaching others through the values of humility and curiosity. Tom Peters tells us that the four most important words in the English language are, *"What do you think?"* Employees can teach us a great deal when we slow down and listen to them, when we ask them what they think. Appreciating the big value of small means paying attention to what people need and to the impact our actions have on others. Paying attention is about self-awareness, humility, and gratitude. When we are sincere, four additional words that will never let us down are, "I'm sorry" and "thank you."

12. **Make your workplace your home base.** A few years back I spoke at a Detachment Commander's meeting of the Royal Canadian Mounted Police in Gimli, Manitoba in Central Canada. Several months after the session, one of the leaders from the group emailed to tell me that he appreciated and valued what I had to say. He then told me that whenever he was transferred the first thing he would do with the members of his new Detachment was to sit them down together and say, very simply:

> Your detachment (or post) is *Home Plate*... This means you are safe. The fight is out there on the streets, roads, and fields. But when you get to Home Plate, you should feel sheltered and protected. The fight should never be in our office, but out there. Too often the most stress we feel is inside. This is wrong, and it was something I, as a

noncommissioned officer, would always work on to make sure everyone could breathe a sigh of relief when they were in the office… We are a team, and no one rounds the bases without the help of all the team to get to Home Plate. Once there, we are all safe and if anyone wants to bring the fight to our Home Plate then let them come. We as a team will be ready and able to handle them.

Sgt P.L. (Larry) Sharbell, Operations N.C.O.

While offering some strategies for building trust, the reality is that there is no formula for fostering trust. What trust is, is a life-long human journey. At the end of the day, what matters is that you care enough to struggle enough to make trust a priority. Leading with an orientation toward trust, toward the undervalued virtue of human goodness, is what creates a workplace worth working in and a life worth living.

Create Clarity

"There is nothing so useless as doing something efficiently that should not be done at all."

Peter Drucker

While the uncertainty and ambiguity of life must surely be embraced, leaders must also lead with clarity. Leading without clarity is like putting together a jigsaw puzzle without having a picture of the end result. Even though there is no guarantee that you have all the right pieces or how you are going to build it, it's always better to have a clear picture of why you are coming together and what you intend to create together.

Without clarity of purpose, without knowing why we do what we do, life is a series of meaningless reactions to requests. Without clarity of vision, without understanding *where* we are going as an organization, people flounder. Without clarity of focus, without a clear sense of your priority, workplaces are merely "busy factories" consumed by the whirlwind of urgent demands. Without making your values explicit and clear, how will you know who to attract and hire, who to retain and promote, and how you are expected to act while doing your work? Without clearly understanding the key drivers of sustainable performance and success, your core leadership requirements, your organization's key strengths and gaps, and how to hold each other accountable, your organization will flail. Without clarity, organizations fall short of focus, inspiration, and results.

While volumes of leadership books have been written about visioning, planning, and execution, my intent is to distill what I have learned about strategy over the past three decades into five fundamental questions that every employee needs clear answers to. These five questions constitute what I call your organization's *One Page Strategic Plan.** Answering these five questions succinctly but meaningfully puts every employee literally on the same page, anchoring every aspect of an organization in a set of commonly-held beliefs and commitments. Clarity around these questions becomes the deeply ingrained principles and fabric that forms a framework for employee behavior and organizational decisions and actions.

Note that you can apply these in any leadership capacity, whether you are building a multinational company, a community association, a non-profit organization, or a family. For those committed to taking the time to clarify and use these questions with your team, visit the companion workbook where you will find guiding questions, suggested processes to follow, and plenty of examples.

Also, note that the One-Page Strategic Plan is an internal document. It is designed to get your team on board. Once you construct the plan, you can hire a marketing agency to help you create external messaging to communicate your mission, vision, and values to customers and a broader community.

---

*I credit seven thought leaders who have influenced my thinking about clarity, strategic thinking, and execution, namely Jim Collins, Stephen Covey, Chris McChesney, Sean Covey, and Jim Huling, Vern Harnish, and Tim O'Connor.

Clarity Playbook: The Five Clarity Questions

1. Why do We Exist?

In the earlier days of Hewlett Packard, a customer was taken on a tour of the manufacturing plant by one of the plant managers in their medical instruments division. While walking through the facility, they passed by a small group of employees in the middle of a short stand-up meeting. The plant manager stopped to say hello to the staff, introduced the customer, and they entered into short discussions. During one conversation, the customer asked one of the employees what her job was. Without hesitation, she replied, "My job is to save babies' lives…"

After further conversation, the customer learned that this woman worked on an assembly line and her task was to stuff printed circuit boards that were used in fetal heart monitors sold around the world. But it made quite an impression on the customer to hear the assembly line worker describe her job in this way!

Leadership can be a consuming endeavor. People need inspiration and renewed vitality to step away from the drudgery of the whirlwind of the urgent day-to-demands into a place of purpose. Leadership requires the capacity to step out of the fray and remember what sometimes makes menial work meaningful and inspiring.

"Why do we exist?" is the question that clarifies what your organization stands for and what you bring to the world while inspiring all with a reason to come to work. A clear mission statement will articulate the purpose of your organization: why it exists, what it does, and for whom. It should communicate the impact that your organization is committed to making in the world—the why behind everyone's efforts. What do its products and services contribute to the world? How will you measure success? How does each employee's contribution make a difference?

The core purpose is an organization's most fundamental reason for being. It should not be confused, according to Jim Collins, with the company's current product lines or customer segments. Rather, it reflects people's idealistic motivations for doing the company's work.

Disney's core purpose is to make people happy—not to build theme parks and make cartoons.

When you realize that assembling a computer is linked to a device that is saving lives, or that laying bricks builds a cathedral, or approving permits enables community development, a sense of purpose emerges and inspires dedication. Clarifying and preserving a sense of purpose enables you to take setbacks and failures as learning opportunities. It gives you perspective. A sense of purpose actually becomes a force, the necessary power to act in the face of discouragement and monotony. A sense of purpose gives meaning to life and transforms success into significance.

A sense of purpose, often captured in a mission statement, should resonate with all stakeholders of an organization and help them feel proud and excited to be a part of something bigger than themselves.

Your why is the purpose, cause, or belief that inspires you to take action. Your why is a true reflection of what your organization stands for and believes. It provides you with clarity, meaning, and direction. It is a filter through which you can make decisions, every day, to bring your cause to life. A why statement is a statement that captures your impact on the world as well as your unique contribution to the world. The impact is the condition you wish to leave the people and world around you. The contribution is the actionable part of your why. Together, these two elements provide fulfillment for you, your organization, and those you serve.

The author Laurie Beth Jones reminds us that bees hum while they work. They don't complain. Your why—in the form of a mission that clarifies your reason for being, is what inspires people to get on board, or alternatively, get off the bus.

2. What is Our Vision?

Antoine de Saint-Exupéry, the French aviator and author, said, *"If you want to build a ship, don't herd people together to collect wood, and don't assign them to tasks and work, but rather teach them to long for the endless immensity of the sea."* This statement differentiates *managers* from *leaders.* On May 25, 1961, when then-President John F. Kennedy announced before a special joint session of Congress the dramatic and ambitious goal of sending an American safely to the moon before the end of the decade, it inspired an entire nation.

Managers assign responsibilities and ensure the job gets done. Leaders, on the other hand, inspire people with a vision. A vision turns a mere job into an opportunity to make a difference in the world. A vision turns a task into inspired action. A vision turns a chore into a contribution, a job into a passion, a responsibility into a dream. A vision for the future, well-articulated, is a powerful force.

A vision provides focus and clarity about where we are headed and how we define success. A well-articulated envisioned future has two elements:

- A Big, Hairy, Audacious Goal (BHAG)—ambitious plans that inspire the entire organization. They typically require 10 to 25 years of work to complete.
- Vivid descriptions that paint a picture of what it will be like to achieve the BHAG. They make the goal vibrant, engaging, and tangible.

Your vision will outline your aspirations for the future. It should describe what success will look like—or—how the world will be improved after you implement your strategies and achieve your full potential. It should inspire you to push well beyond your existing comfort zone.

While a mission is centered around *why* you exist, a vision outlines the goals and aspirations for the future. A vision should describe what success will look like or how the world will be improved after the organization implements its strategies and achieves its full potential. While your mission is centered on the "here and now," your vision is about the future.

Organizations without a vision create anxiety, a lack of confidence, unease, tension, and apathy. An organization without a vision leads to a waste of time, resources, talent, and motivation, a sure way to run an organization into the ground. A vision is vital to giving people a sense of security and direction. It builds a framework for decision-making and providing clarity about the opportunities you want to say "no" to. A vision tells you what is most important.

Clarify what you want, shine a light on it, and an unseen force will move you toward that goal. A vision turns drudgery into destiny, transforming mere job descriptions into inspired action. A clear and compelling vision brings purpose into focus, imparting an exciting, realistic, and inspiring picture of what you and everyone else are committed to accomplishing together.

3. What Do We Stand For?

Tim O'Connor is CEO and partner at Results Canada Inc., currently one of Canada's fastest growing companies. In speaking of their mission, vision, values, and how they shape their amazing culture, Tim said, "Our passion and purpose is to help companies unleash their business potential through disciplined execution."

"We also believe in our own culture which is embodied in our simple core values." These values include:

Simplicity is Genius
Simple solutions, approaches, templates, and tools will always outperform more complex ones. We endeavor, in everything we do, to simplify.

Make a Difference
Every interaction with a Results team member should make a difference in the way someone thinks, feels, or acts. That can be as big as a strategic decision that results in a huge financial win, or a welcoming smile that changes someone's day.

Passion for Learning
We are constantly on the lookout for new data, ideas, and research that can help us and our clients be better.

Live What We Teach
We hold ourselves accountable to every best-practice we recommend to our clients.

Extra Mile
Often we go beyond the usual "call of duty" to help support our clients and our teammates.

Experiencing a growth phase amidst a challenging Alberta economy, Tim talked about his hiring practices. "Among other things," Tim explained, "we ask key questions that get to values alignment. For example, as you know, one of our core values is a 'passion for learning.' We always ask a potential hire what book they are currently reading. If they haven't read a book in the past few years, they aren't likely going to fit our culture."

This question gets to what values our employees embody. It defines how we need to act to realize our vision, how we will engage every employee, and how will we be sure we have the right people on the bus.

Clarifying what you stand for, whether expressed in your core values or guiding principles, or what Jim Collins calls your "core ideology," defines the "enduring character of an organization—a consistent identity that transcends product or market life cycles, technological breakthroughs, management fads, and individual leaders." HP's core ideology, which has guided the company since its inception more than 50 years ago, includes a deep respect for the individual, a dedication to affordable quality and reliability, a commitment to community responsibility, and a view that the company exists to make technical contributions for the advancement and welfare of humanity. Great culture builders understand that it is even more important to know who you are than where you are going, for where you are going will change as the world around you changes. Leaders die, products become obsolete, markets change, new technologies emerge, and management fads come and go, but what you stand for endures as a source of sustained guidance and inspiration.

Your core values—the enduring principles of an organization—require no external explanation; they have intrinsic value and importance to those inside the organization. This core ideology provides the cement that holds an organization together as it grows and changes and evolves.

The Walt Disney Company's core values of imagination and wholesomeness don't stem from market requirements but from the founder's inner belief that imagination and wholesomeness should be nurtured for their own sake. Service to the customer—even to the point of subservience—is a way of life at Nordstrom that traces its roots back to 1901, eight decades before customer service programs became stylish. For Bill Hewlett and David Packard, respect for the individual was first and foremost a deep personal value; they didn't get it from a book or hear it from a management guru. Ralph S. Larsen, CEO of Johnson & Johnson, put it this way: "The core values embodied in our credo might be a competitive advantage, but that is not why we have them. We have them because they define for us what we stand for, and we would hold them even if they became a competitive disadvantage in certain situations."

Values tell you how you are expected to work together and behave. Values establish a code of conduct, an organizational charter, a creed: what is acceptable and what is not acceptable behavior—both in an organization and in our lives. Values define your leadership as well as what you need from your hires. Having a set of core values gives people a sense of respect, a shared credo that reflects how they feel about themselves and the pride they have about the work they do. Values get to your highest priorities.

While Tim's firm is certainly about principles like integrity, respect, and excellence, he is wise enough to know that having these as his core values merely describes what his firm is already doing. What these values demonstrate is not just the maintenance of status quo but how to inspire the company to go beyond the ordinary. Tim understands the purpose of values. They aren't just nouns; they are verbs. They become aspirational. They call you to action. They push you to strive. They transform value "statements" into something we actually value. They become *eulogy* virtues rather than mere *resume* virtues, the stuff we want our organizations and our lives to be known for.

Dr. Martin Luther King, Jr. said, "If a man has not discovered something that he will die for, he isn't fit to live." While you may find this statement extreme, values can change your culture when they force you to reflect upon the question: "What would I actually die for?" Getting close to the answer to this question will take you to a whole new level of values.

Notice how old tired values like "integrity," "respect," "fairness," "honesty," "accountability," and "teamwork," can be renewed with words that provoke, create some fun, and inspire renewed action. For example, Zappos's 10 core values are:

- Deliver WOW Through Service.
- Embrace and Drive Change.
- Create Fun and a Little Weirdness.
- Be Adventurous, Creative, and Open-Minded.
- Pursue Growth and Learning.
- Build Open and Honest Relationships with Communication.
- Build a Positive Team and Family Spirit.
- Do More with Less.
- Be Passionate and Determined.
- Be Humble.

Several years ago, I spoke to a group of executives on the importance of developing clear values and developing an accountability process for getting the value statements into every employees' day-to-day actions. "Values only have value when you have pushed hard enough to have your values tested, when you have to make a choice," I told them. During the question and answer period, a question arose about a top employee, a salesman who brought in more income than his entire sales team combined. However, he was offensive and rude to his colleagues in his pursuit of delivering his all-star numbers.

"There's no way I'm going to fire a person who is achieving these kind of results…" the executive exclaimed.

"That's fine," was my reply. "Just be sure you cross off *respect* from your value statements. Be honest with yourself and others. You can't fake culture. It has to be real. If you value financial results more than you value the treatment of people, then let people know this explicitly, so they know where they stand."

Your values have to be more than a set of fancy statements. Instead, they must reflect the bone-deep ideology of what you actually stand for.

4. What Is Our #1 Priority?

Beware the tyranny of the urgent: many priorities means nothing is a priority.

Recently I was on a United Airlines flight from Calgary to Oklahoma City, via Houston. It was on the morning of Calgary's first snowstorm of the year, and we were sitting on the tarmac for several minutes before passengers started to get restless, anxious, and impatient about the delay. You could feel the tension in the cabin as rumors about the delay turned to murmurs. Then the captain came on the intercom and demonstrated some good leadership.

> "I want to apologize for the delay, folks," he said. "You can see the snow on the wings, and we are waiting in line for the de-icers to do their work. Unfortunately, they are a bit backlogged with the demands this morning. There are three or four planes ahead of us, so it appears it will take about half an hour before we will be ready.
>
> We also are having some difficulty with our computer system communicating with air-traffic control, so we have to reboot the system. That will take about an additional half hour.
>
> What I want you to know from the flight deck is that we have only one priority: *your safety.* And I promise you *that we will not take off until we know this aircraft is 100% safe to do so. You can count on us for this.*
>
> What I ask is that you have patience with us in this process that will enable us to make this a safe flight for all of us."

All the frustration that was surfacing amidst the passengers began to subside with this direct, simple, and honest message from the captain. In less than a minute, impatience was transformed into support. We shifted from being irritated with the airline to being sympathetic to the captain and committed to helping him make it safe for us. The tension in the cabin was dissolved in a few short moments of listening to a clear and calm message sent by the leader at the front of the aircraft.

This is what leaders do when they are clear about their priority and are honest with those they serve.

Your #1 priority gets clear when you can clearly define:

- Where the organization is headed in the next three to five years.
- What results need to be achieved in the next twelve months.
- Where I need to focus my attention this week. What's important now?

The word *priority* didn't always mean what it does today. In his book, *Essentialism*, Greg McKeown explains the surprising history of the word and how its meaning has shifted over time.

> "The word priority," writes McKeown, "came into the English language in the 1400s. It was singular. It meant the very first or prior thing. It stayed singular for the next five hundred years.
>
> Only in the 1900s did we pluralize the term and start talking about priorities. Illogically, we reasoned that by changing the word we could bend reality. Somehow, we would now be able to have multiple 'first' things.
>
> People and companies routinely try to do just that. One leader told me of this experience in a company that talked of 'Pri-1, Pri-2, Pri-3, Pri-4, and Pri-5.' This gave the impression of many things being the priority but actually meant nothing was."

The captain on United Airlines flight 1599 knew what his priority was in the context of his job. A clear focus leads to clear leadership. This priority was transferred to his entire team. While the flight attendants served us drinks and were expected to be pleasant and supportive to the passengers and helped us make connections to our next flight, their only real priority was passenger safety.

You know when you have achieved clarity with your team when you wander around and people know what their #1 priority is, what is most important, right now.

5. How Will We Execute?

You can have a great vision, but trust will deteriorate over time if the people around you realize you can't execute a plan to reach that vision. It won't take long to begin losing faith in the vision with poor execution. Leadership and management go hand-in-hand.

Whether you call it a strategy, a goal, or simply an improvement effort, any initiative you drive in order to move your team or organization forward will require behavioral change. To achieve a goal, you have never achieved before; you must start doing things you have never done before.

Chris McChesney, Sean Covey, and Jim Huling's book, *The 4 Disciplines of Execution*, provides a great roadmap for execution. These disciplines are not designed for managing the whirlwind of urgent demands but are strategies for executing your most critical strategy in the midst of your whirlwind.

- **Focus on what is vitally important.** Basically, the more you try to do, the less you actually accomplish. None of us want to do less. As high achievers, we want to do more, even when we know better. And yet, there will always be more good ideas than you and your teams have the capacity to execute. Focusing on what is vitally important requires that you, as a leader, focus on *less* so that your team can achieve *more*. When you narrow the focus of your team to one or two vitally important goals, you distinguish between what is truly the top priority and what is the whirlwind.
- **Act on lead measures.** Acting on lead measures, according to McChesney, Covey, and Huling, is the discipline of leverage. It's based on the simple principle that all actions are not created equal. Some actions have more impact than others when driving toward a goal. Effective execution is about identifying and acting on the high leverage measures.

   To understand lead measures, it's important to understand lag measures. *Lag measures* track dimensions that are in the past. A lag measure would be how many sales you had at the end of the month, what was your profit, how much weight you lost, how your customers rated you, or how engaged your employees were.

   Lead measures, on the other hand, measure the future. They can be influenced by team members, and they are predictive. Lead measures might be how many customers you are going to speak with each day in the coming week, how many test-drive appointments you are going to set up, how many leads you are going to extract from existing customers, how many follow-up contacts you are going to make. Knowing that 80% of sales close on the fifth to twelfth contact makes

lead measures predictive. You know how many contacts you
need to make this week to achieve your eventual lag measurement. Lag measures are ultimately what matter. But it's lead
measures that will get you there.

- **Keep a compelling scoreboard.** People play differently when
  they are keeping score. It's not about you keeping score for
  them. The next discipline, discipline 3, is the discipline of
  engagement. In principle, the highest level of performance
  comes from people who are emotionally engaged. And the
  highest level of engagement comes from knowing the score.
  The kind of scoreboard that will drive the highest levels of
  engagement with your team will be the one that is designed
  solely for (and often by) the players. Included in a compelling
  scoreboard must be a "line of sight" through which everyone
  is able to see how his or her daily actions link to the organization's goals. One of the keys to keeping people engaged is
  making the connection between their day-to-day efforts and
  the vision of the organization.

- **Create a cadence of accountability.** Once the vision has
  been set, the few priorities clearly identified, the lead measures distinguished, and the scoreboard established, a cadence
  of accountability is now set into motion. The cadence of
  accountability is a rhythm of regular and frequent meetings
  to assess progress and ongoing support requirements to help
  team members follow through on the lead measures. It's about
  team members holding each other accountable for producing
  results—in the midst of the whirlwind of demands.

Remember, the power of clarity comes from creating safe and respectful conversations for people to tell the truth, talk about what matters,
and take personal responsibility. According to Gallup's 2015 *State of
the American Manager Report*, "Clarity of expectations is perhaps the
most basic of employee needs and is vital to performance."

Helping employees understand their responsibilities may seem
like "Management 101," but employees need more than a written job
description to fully grasp their roles. They need to comprehend why

they are doing what they are doing, what they need to be focused on, and how their work fits in with everyone else's work—especially when circumstances change. The best leaders don't just tell employees what's expected of them and leave it at that; they don't save those critical conversations for once-a-year performance reviews. They make it a habit of regularly opening up conversations with employees about the mission, the vision, the values, the responsibilities and progress, what we expect from each other, and what it all means to their people.

A spacecraft from the earth to the moon requires a clear navigation system to keep it on course, even if the majority of the journey is spent with the shuttle actually being "off course." Wind at launch, variations in engine thrust, friction, and velocity are just a few of the factors that require continual adjustments in order for the rocket to remain on track. Creating clarity for the journey toward authentic organizational excellence requires the same degree of rigor, intentional focus, and follow-through. It's not about an illusion of being perfect and on course all the time. It's a human, imperfect journey of continual resetting of the compass and persevering. With a commitment to clarity comes inspired focus, collaboration, and sustained results.

Engage Talent

"To win in the marketplace you must first win in the workplace."

Doug Conant, Former President and
CEO of the Campbell Soup Company

I was recently wandering around the offices of a client, helping him assess employee engagement in his division, when I noticed the screen saver that one of his administrators had with a large number on it.

"What's with the number?" I asked the young woman sitting by the computer.

"… Oh, this tells me how many days I have left until I retire …" she responded with an embarrassed smile. "It motivates me to come to work, especially on Monday mornings when the number drops by two days over the weekend."

Perhaps this could be a fun strategy if retirement is just around the corner. The problem with this employee was that the number on the computer was 7,219!

Employee engagement is the desire and capacity of employees to go the extra mile to help their organization succeed—while finding meaning and significance in the work they do. Engaged employees look forward to coming to work in the morning and are equally happy to return home at the end of the day. Engagement is measured by the connection an employee has to their work and to their workplace. They say great things about the organization when they are away from the office. They aren't planning to leave to take another job, and even if they do leave, they will leave the organization better than they found it. Engagement goes beyond mere "satisfaction," to deep caring and commitment. It's about wanting to give more than is required or even expected. Employee engagement is about pride, passion, and being supported in your work. It's about knowing that your work matters and makes a difference. Engaged employees care. They care about their work. They care about the people they serve. They care about their colleagues.

Fortune Magazine cites the ability to attract and retain talented employees as the number one indicator of corporate excellence. This is especially true during times of growth, excessive change, and demanding environments. Most research indicates that up to 70% of North American workers are not fully engaged in their work. Up to 60% of employees said that they intend to pursue job opportunities somewhere else in the next year, and up to 20% are actually working toward leaving the organization that currently employs them. This means that roughly two-thirds of employees are less than highly motivated to be productive, ultimately affecting customer satisfaction, profitability, innovation, and rising costs. With the cost of losing and replacing an employee estimated to be 50-200% of an employee's salary, employee engagement not only has personal and performance implications, but it also greatly impacts the financial success of your organization.

Engagement Playbook: Assessing Employee Engagement

There are several ways to assess how engaged your employees are. One common approach is to send out employee engagement surveys. While surveys can be very useful tools, you will find they are limited. Surveys give you a "photograph," a current picture of people's existing level of engagement. They don't give you the "movie." They give you a picture of the climate but not necessarily how the weather patterns are contributing to the current temperature. They don't give you the context, the whole story, the reasons below the surface of engagement. Surveys are limited, especially if you rely solely on the data to assess how engaged people are. Reading employee engagement surveys is like reading a newspaper or watching the news. It's interesting, and while there's an element of truth in them, it's not the whole picture. It's a small spectrum of what's actually happening. Surveys turn your organization into a noun, while conversations make culture a verb, a living breathing entity.

To get a more accurate assessment of what's happening in your organization, you have to, on a regular and consistent basis, get into the cafeteria and the hallways and the offices and cubicles to get to what's really going on. You have to wander around, listen carefully to people, and pay close attention. As the great philosopher, Yogi Berra once said, "You can observe a lot by watching." You have to watch, observe, and tune in to what is happening. There is no substitute for conversation and connection. While there appears to be an inherent distrust in management, leaders need to put in the extra time to counter this, to make contact, to create openness, to make it safe for people to be honest. In reality, to effectively assess employee engagement, you have to get out of your office. You have to make contact with people. You have to listen carefully. You have to be in touch.

If you *are* going to survey your employees, here are a few tips:

- **Don't use surveys to abdicate leadership.** At first, people aren't likely to be completely honest with you when you walk around and ask them questions about themselves and their work. We seem hard-wired—mostly through our experiences—to be distrustful of those in authority in our lives. But don't use that as an excuse to abdicate leadership and rely on anonymous surveys. It is good for your culture when people see you, as a leader, out there attempting to break down old outdated barriers and doing your part to create openness.

- **Shorten your surveys.** People are getting surveyed out. I've seen employees answer low because they are angry about having to do so many surveys. Dr. Theresa M. Welbourne (www.eepulse.com) is designing employee engagement and 360-degree feedback surveys that take three minutes to complete. Dr. Welbourne believes that you can get pretty much all the information you need in about three minutes. She just might be on to something.

- **You don't have to survey everyone to get an accurate picture.** Television ratings are not determined by calling every single person watching TV. Pick a good cross-section of people to survey and give the rest a break. Switch it up so you aren't surveying the same people every time.

- **Don't mistake *climate* for *culture*.** Climate is how people feel about the organization and their work (what you get from an employee engagement survey). Culture is what *causes* them to feel that way. Employee engagement surveys may tell you what the climate is, but they don't necessarily get to the culture. Every culture has both the "visible" culture and the "real" culture. The real culture is what people talk about when the boss isn't there. Humorously, I tell leaders that if you want to find out about the real culture, don't send a survey to your employees. Send it to your employee's spouses or best friends. It is what people talk about when they go home at night that will give you the best picture of how engaged they are. Culture and leadership are measured by what people talk about when the boss isn't in the room. Get out of your office, away from your computer, and get connected.

Three Categories of Engagement

When it comes to engagement, employees tend to fit into three categories*:

- **Engaged.** Engaged employees express passion for their work and feel a profound connection to their organization and their work. They speak highly about the organization when they talk to their friends and family. They are involved in, enthusiastic about, and committed to their work. Engaged employees support the innovation, growth, and revenue that their companies need. Engaged employees are strongly connected to business outcomes essential to an organization's success, such as productivity, profitability, and customer engagement.

- **Non-Engaged.** Non-engaged employees are essentially "checked out," sleepwalking through their workday. They are putting in time, but don't have much energy or passion in their work. These employees are not hostile or disruptive. They show up and kill time, doing the minimum required with little extra effort to go out of their way for customers. They are less vigilant, and more likely to miss work and change jobs when new opportunities arise. They are thinking about lunch or their next break and will know how many days there are until the weekend and how many years they have left until they retire. They are either actively pursuing work somewhere else or, even worse, have decided to "quit and stay."

- **Actively Disengaged.** Actively disengaged employees aren't just unhappy at work; they're busy acting out their unhappiness. Every day, these workers undermine what their engaged co-workers accomplish.

---

*Most research on engagement (the Gallup organization has done the most investigation and documentation in this area) will confirm that, worldwide, most employees (between 50-60%) fit into the "non-engaged" category, less than 30% are engaged, and between 10-20% are actively disengaged. In other words, over 70% of the workforce is either under-performing or actively undermining their work.

After observing and researching leadership for more than thirty years, I've boiled down engagement to three fundamental conditions that form the foundation of an engaged organization:

- **Leadership.** Positional leaders set the tone for an engaged culture.
- **Ownership.** Every employee is ultimately accountable for their own engagement.
- **Energy.** Engagement is ultimately about energy.

Positional Leaders Set the Tone for an Engaged Culture

Leadership is vital to building an engaged culture. Positional leaders set the tone. Leadership means caring enough to clarify and create the conditions required to make a workplace worthwhile. To build an engaged culture, bosses have to care about more than just getting the job done. They have to care about *how* the job gets done and about the people doing the job. They have to care about what motivates people and attempt to respond to these needs. Leaders make a difference. Engagement is now a business issue, not just a topic for HR.

Every Employee Is Ultimately Accountable for Their Own Engagement

I rarely fill in surveys for hotels or airlines when I travel. But recently, I took five minutes to respond to an online survey from Air Canada. They wanted to know how my flight went. In the process of filling out the survey, I learned something about engagement.

I had a great experience on this flight, and I told them so. But taking the survey made me think about a much bigger issue. What actually makes a great experience possible—whether on an airline, in a hotel, restaurant, workplace, or even a marriage? I have had some bad experiences with all of the above in the past. What is the common denominator? When I am honest with myself, I can see that every time I've had a lousy experience, it usually has more to do with the lousy mood I'm in that day than the person offering the experience.

Don't get me wrong. Bosses make a difference in the experience of an employee. Customer service people make a difference. Servers make a difference. And it is important to get feedback on how we are doing. What I'm suggesting is that we are all co-creating the world we live in. We don't live and work alone. We institutionally deny the fact that each of us—through our perceptions and our choices—is actually creating the culture—in our airlines, hotels, restaurants, workplaces, and marriages—that we so enjoy complaining about.

Quantum physics has discovered something that many mystics have long since known: that our perception of the universe actually invokes the very universe that we observe. If you change the way you view the environment around you, the environment around you changes. The world isn't as it is. The world is the way we see it. When your own mind behaves as your good friend, you get all the benefits, and you see friends everywhere. But if your mind behaves as your enemy, you hardly find a friend anywhere. If you aren't at peace with yourself, you see everyone as your enemy. There's a saying, "If you're a thief, you don't trust anyone." It all depends on the "glasses" that you wear. You see everyone and everything through your own mind's eye. The world is nothing but your own projection of how you view yourself.

The only person you can change is yourself. We all need to examine our level of expectations of others carefully, especially when they become a defense against personal responsibility. While bosses undoubtedly make a difference, employees are ultimately accountable for their own level of engagement. There is nobody to blame. You are the one that is going to spend upwards of seventy thousand hours of your life at this thing called "work." You are the one that lives with you twenty-four hours a day. While customers and colleagues spend time with you at work, you are the one that goes home with you at the end of the day. You are the one who must live with your decisions and actions.

Culture isn't something that you do *for* or *to* people. Culture is something you co-create—by the perceptions you bring and the decisions you make and the actions you take. Employee engagement is a shared ownership. But it's not all up to the boss. Employees too must take ownership for their own personal level of engagement. As an employee, you bring your body to work every day. But do you also bring your passion, your dreams, your unique gifts, your values, your commitment to serve? It's not all up to the boss. Employee engagement is a shared responsibility that requires ownership. There's only so much a boss can do.

Engagement Is Ultimately About Energy

According to Tony Schwartz, in his book, *The Way We're Working Isn't Working: The Four Forgotten Needs That Energize Great Performance,* leaders are the stewards of organizational energy. Leaders either inspire or demoralize others, first by how effectively they manage their own energy, and next, by how well they mobilize, focus, invest, and renew the collective energy of those they lead. The more we take responsibility for the energy we bring to the world, the more empowered and productive and fulfilled we become.

But in order to be able to take responsibility for managing your energy, it's helpful to learn to recognize how different stimuli impacts your energy. How can you tell when you are being drained of energy? Do you feel it in your chest? Your stomach? Your shoulders? Your back? Leading means learning to tune in to your energy levels. What activities drain you? What activities are life-giving? What relationships drain you? What relationships enhance you? As a leader, make it a point to be a student of energy.

Building an engaged culture requires an awareness of at least four kinds of energy and how your perceptions, choices, and environment impact your vitality. Getting engaged, and getting others engaged starts with self-awareness.

Physical Energy

What you eat for breakfast affects your energy, as does your blood sugar levels throughout the day, the amount and kind of exercise you get, and the quantity and quality of your rest and sleep. If you drink soda pop all day, your energy will be different than if you drink water. Even though these substances may affect each person uniquely, they still impact us, and anything that impacts you physically will affect you mentally. It is not my intention to tell you how to eat or induce guilt. These are decisions you have to make for yourself. Working under artificial lights for eight hours, with no sunlight, will impact your energy, just as working in an environment that does not allow for clean, fresh air. Getting outdoors for a couple of breaks during the day may have as much impact on your level of energy and subsequent level of engagement, as an employee engagement program.

Physical energy is about becoming aware of how your environment and your choices impact you. Because energy capacity diminishes with both overuse and underuse, it is important to balance energy outflow with a consistent habit of energy renewal. While we are all impacted differently by such variables as nutrition, rest, sunlight, or exercise, understanding engagement means understanding how these factors affect you and those around you. Energy is not limitless. And physical energy fuels engagement.

Relational Energy

We all know that the quality of our connections impacts our energy. Be mindful of the people in your life that drain you and those that inspire and sustain you. The kinds of friends you have away from work will impact your level of energy, and thus your engagement when you come to work. Do you bring energy to your work? Or, because of a destructive relationship in your personal life, are you coming to work empty, void of energy? Who you choose to be around, just as *how* you choose to be around them, will affect your energy. Pleasing people and carrying their problems will drain energy. Ask yourself if the relationships in your life are life-giving or life-depleting. Remember to take responsibility for the choices you make rather than blaming your colleagues and the culture you work in for your unhappiness.

Mental Energy

A pessimistic outlook on life drains vital energy, while optimism is a life giver. Blaming your boss for your lack of energy can be just as much of an energy drainer as having the bad boss to begin with. It's a good habit to learn to be optimistic. If optimism doesn't come easily to you, it's good to practice being grateful and positive. Learning to be disciplined, to do the difficult tasks first, to tell the truth, to keep a promise, or to stick to a challenging undertaking when it is easier to give up, are all habits that renew essential energy. One simple habit is to take a daily (or at minimum weekly) inventory of what you are grateful for. Or, start to recognize the positive in others and practice being grateful for what is around you. It's amazing how a small habit can change your mental state and your level of engagement at work.

Authentic Energy

Discovering and living in accord with your deepest values, your authentic self, is energy enhancing. A purpose-guided life is an engaged life. Those who have found a *reason* for coming to work and a *reason* for being—beyond merely completing a task or carrying out a chore or getting a paycheck—are the ones who know the power of true engagement and enjoy their work. Knowing and doing more of what you love—at work and at home—fills you up and gives you energy, so you have an overflow to give to others. Life-giving hobbies that engage you in the evening and on weekends will impact your level of energy and engagement when you come to work.

Guiding People to Their Authentic Self—Getting to the Heart of Engagement

> *"Let yourself be silently drawn by the strange pull of what you really love. It will not lead you astray."*
>
> Rumi

Over a hundred years ago, the German poet, Rainer Maria Rilke, wrote a poem that sheds some clues about letting go of the inauthentic self and moving into our true nature.

> *This clumsy living that moves lumbering as if in ropes … reminds us of the awkward way the swan walks.*

*And to die, which is the letting go of the ground we stand
and cling to every day, is like the swan, when he nervously lets
himself down into the water, which receives him gaily and which
flows joyfully under and after him, wave after wave, while the
swan, unmoving and marvelously calm, is pleased to be carried,
each moment more fully grown, more like a king, further and
further on.*

The swan in this poem doesn't cure his awkwardness on the land by moving faster, working harder, criticizing himself, or by developing a better performance plan. He frees himself from the stress of his environment simply by moving toward the element where he belongs. Simple contact with the water breathes life into his tired body. Marsilio Ficino, the Renaissance philosopher, says it this way: "It is useful for us to search for that region which best suits us, a place where our spirit is advanced and refreshed, where our senses remain thriving, and where things nourish us."

There lies within every person a place where, when connected to it, we feel deeply and intensely alive. At such moments there is a quiet voice inside that says, "This is the real me." If you have ever worked in an organization where you had to play the role of what the culture expected of you and were unable to be yourself and where it wasn't safe to talk about incongruence, then you will know something about disengagement. Nothing will erode engagement more than a team of people who are just "playing a role," "acting nice," "looking good," and pretending to be engaged when the boss is around. Employees today are simply not going to stick around just because they have a paycheck—even if it's a good paycheck—if they can't be who they are. Your best employees today have a low tolerance for compliance and insist on engagement. They are aware of opportunities elsewhere and are perhaps more mobile than ever.

Leadership as a Catalyst for an Authentic Workplace

Leadership is about transforming your culture into a community. A community is a place where work is meaningful, not just menial, where you support people to be genuine contributors, not just "task doers," where people are honestly valued, rather than used up, where you invite intentional conversations, not just superficial exchanges.

Communities are places where "units" are transformed into "neighborhoods," where there is a sense of belonging, shared vision, pride, ownership, and a commitment to service; where "command performance" is replaced with a bone-deep commitment to courageously seek participation.

Community is where paint-by-number management programs are replaced with a profound, yet simple respect for realness, honesty, and the dignity of everyone, which in turn results in an authentic expression of the human spirit.

Fostering this kind of culture is akin to being a gardener. It can't be legislated, controlled, motivated, or coerced. No plants ever grow better because you demand that they do so or because you threaten them. Plants grow only when they have the right conditions and are given proper care. Creating the space and providing the proper nourishment for plants—and people—is a matter of continual investigation and vigilance.

Seven Strategies for Engagement Success

1. **Connect to personal values.** Human beings don't put their hearts into causes they don't value. We don't commit energy and intensity to something that is misaligned with what we deem important. Research done by James Kouzes and Barry Posner, found in their book, *Encouraging the Heart*, show how values make a difference in how people behave inside organizations and how they feel about themselves, their colleagues, and their leaders.

   They found that it wasn't the fancy, well-articulated value statements on the walls or the glitzy videotapes played at the leadership retreats that get people engaged. Clarity of organizational values is vital to building an aligned culture, and great videos can be inspiring, but these have low impact when it comes to engaging people in that culture. When it comes to engagement, such efforts to spell out organizational values are essentially a waste of time and resources unless there's also a concerted effort to help individuals understand their own values and examine the fit between their values and what's important to the organization.

In order to engage employees, leaders must include employees in open discussions about what matters to them, what matters to the organization, and the level of alignment between the two. The emphasis in traditional leadership approaches is to align people to the organization's values. But you also have to align the organization with people's values.

2. **Find and foster flow—through listening, attention, and challenge.** We all know the feeling of becoming so absorbed in our life that we lose track of time. The author Mihaly Csikszentmihalyi, in his books *Flow* and *Finding Flow*, demonstrates the results of hundreds of interviews with successful painters, dancers, poets, and others who had careers which allowed them this vital engagement on a regular basis. His research showed that while all the paths of these careers are unique, the outcome is the same: *there is a connection between the person and their work.* Csikszentmihalyi described the feeling of flow this way:

> Imagine that you are skiing down a slope and your full attention is focused on the movements of your body, the position of the skis, the air whistling past your face, and the snow-shrouded trees running by. There is no room in your awareness for conflicts or contradictions; you know that a distracting thought or emotion might get you buried face down in the snow. The run is so perfect that you want it to last forever.

Finding Flow contends that we often walk through our days unaware and out of touch with our emotional lives. Our inattention makes us constantly bounce between two extremes: during much of the day we live filled with the anxiety and pressures of our work and obligations, while during our leisure moments, we tend to live in what he calls "passive boredom." The key, according to Csikszentmihalyi, is to challenge yourself with tasks requiring a high degree of skill and commitment. Instead of watching television, play the piano. Instead of mindlessly surfing the internet, read a book that challenges your thinking and absorbs your attention. Get out of a dull routine at work and take a class that pushes you. Transform a routine task by taking a different approach. In short, learn the joy of complete engagement. Engagement, explains Csikszentmihalyi, comes when we are challenged, not to the point of being immobilized by the pressure of the challenge but by the push just beyond our comfort zone.

3. **Care enough to find out what people care about.** The best way to help people find their authentic self, their voice, their "flow," is simply to ask them.

- Talk to the people on your team about the idea of flow and what activities put them into a state of "flow."
- If their flow is related to their life away from their work, see if there are elements of flow they experience at home that they could envision bringing to work. If, for example, they find their flow in hobbies such as cooking or woodworking or gardening, find out what it is about these activities that get them into a state of "flow." Is it creativity? A sense of accomplishment or contribution? A sense of cultivating caring, or building community?
- Finally, if they are interested, help them explore ways they could bring more of these elements of flow into their work. What projects could they take on that would bring more creativity and flow into their work? Are they making a meaningful contribution to others in a way that is most fulfilling? Even if you can't build the bridge between flow at home and flow at work, you have at least shown that you care and foster gratitude for having a job that enables them to do what they love when they get home.

4. **Catch people being excited.** Observing where people's enthusiasm and energy lie shows the source of their potential. Sometimes it is very powerful just to sincerely say, "I believe you have great potential in this area. I see real strengths in you that you may not see in yourself, and I would like to create an opportunity for you to use those strengths and to develop this potential." Engagement can be the simple act of showing interest in and supporting staff to develop their passion and strengths while finding ways to use them to bring value to the organization. This kind of simple, sincere input can be powerful and can make a huge positive impact. So many people have no idea what engagement is about or what gets them excited until someone takes them under their wing and becomes a mentor to them. It can make all of the difference as to whether a person takes a higher road to their authentic self or a lower road where they are swallowed up by the priorities and voices of others.

5. **Combat interruptions.** Flow has been tied to both engagement and performance by improving concentration and motivation. But when you're constantly interrupted it's hard to find a state of flow. One manager in my leadership development program told me about an assignment he had in a time management course. He tracked how many times a day he allowed himself to be interrupted—with emails, phone calls, text messages, and people knocking on his door. He quit counting after he got to fifty—before noon! It is estimated that with every interruption, it takes more than twenty minutes to get back into the flow. If interruptions are disrupting your flow, allow people to switch off email, hold fewer meetings, schedule "open office hours" rather than having an "open door policy," and focus on smaller chunks of work. When you can create an environment where employees love the experience and feel fulfilled in their jobs, engagement, retention, and performance will follow.

6. **Distinguish between "good" tired and "bad" tired.** If you have ever brought out a vacuum cleaner with a two-year-old in your house, you know that you likely won't have to get them motivated to engage their help. You will probably have to *manage* them, but you won't have to *motivate* them. In fact, you probably won't *want* them to be engaged. We come to the world with an innate desire to contribute, even though we have to learn how not to break vacuum cleaners and get in our parents' way. We are hard-wired to help, to want to make a difference, to want to do our part. But there's a difference, my children have taught me, between *contribution* and *chores.* Chores, kids will tell you, are the necessary "joe jobs," but contribution makes a difference. Chores are vital to the family, while contribution is vital to the soul.

No matter where you go around the world, people really want just a few simple things: They want to contribute, they want to know they make a difference, they want to be a part of something beyond themselves, and they want to go home and have a satisfying personal life. We may all have chores to do, but we need to know that our talents make an impact. Checking off the to-do list or emptying our inbox simply doesn't cut it. In the midst of the chores that are assigned to your employees, do they know they make a difference? Is the tiredness at the end of the week, a "good" tired that comes from a fulfilling job that made a meaningful contribution? Or was it merely a "to-do" list of chores that resulted in depleting exhaustion, rather than a fulfilling tiredness that you will recover from on the weekend.

7. **Fit people; don't fix people.** This winter, I traveled to Inuvik in Canada's Northwest Territories to facilitate a leadership development program. I flew up a day early as they had arranged for me to go dog sledding. It was an amazing experience to guide a team of huskies through the frozen terrain of the Arctic. The remarkable animals that pulled my sled were absolutely born to pull. It was in their blood. The minute they were harnessed in you had to anchor them down to keep them

from taking off. Mushing with these teams was an experience in the true meaning of flow. Like people, some dogs had it within them to lead, while others were born to follow, but they were all born to pull. The worst thing you could do to any of these magnificent animals would be to send them to a work/life balance workshop. Rest would kill them or drive them to insanity.

Like these dogs, people need to be doing what they are bred for. To stay engaged and healthy and vibrant, we need to align with our reason for being. When we connect and align with our genius, when we discover our passion, and when we contribute to the world, engagement is born. In the minds of great leaders, disengagement is not a matter of weakness, stupidity, disobedience, or disrespect; it is a matter of miscasting. Work to fit people, not fix people. "Burnout," said Rabbi Ira Eisenstein, "comes not from hard work but from heartache."

A Call to Action: Seven Decisions That Will Change Your Level of Engagement

Simple decisions can build and sustain an engaged culture, as well as an engaged, wholehearted life. Because these actions depend only on you to change, you can apply them to any culture you work or live in, including your team, your division, your entire organization, or your family.

1. **Decide to take responsibility for your own engagement.** As with most things in life, waiting isn't a very effective strategy. *Bring* engagement to your organization instead of waiting for your organization to give it to you.

2. **Decide to *give* what you expect.** To counter the frustration of not getting what you expect, clarify what you expect, and then give that. Employee engagement starts with you. Whatever you want from others, get busy giving it. If you want to be appreciated, get so busy appreciating others that you don't have time to feel sorry for yourself. If you want good service, give good service.

3. **Decide to be engaged.** It's that simple. We have the ability to choose our attitudes and our responses. One of the great revelations of our time is the awareness that changing the inner attitudes of our minds can change the outer aspects of our lives. As Abraham Lincoln said, "Folks are usually about as happy as they make their minds up to be." Happiness, like engagement, is a decision. It's not a destination; it's a method of travel.

4. **Decide on a vision.** Be a purpose-driven-person. Create a compelling vision that gets you up early, keeps you up late, and inspires you to go the extra mile. It's a lot easier to be engaged when you have a reason to be. A vision doesn't have to be profound. You don't have to show it to the world. You can quietly go about your day, serving others, and bringing a generous spirit to everything you do.

5. **Decide to be a contributor rather than a consumer.** Consume means to "destroy, squander, use up," whereas *contribute* means to "build, serve, make better." Look for ways that you can make life a little better for every person you meet today. A smile, a word of encouragement, a little patience. These simple acts of caring go a long way. Make a point to create value everywhere you go. Be a problem solver rather than a problem maker.

6. **Decide to try something new.** Break out of the box. Do something uncharacteristic for you. Take up Aikido. Skydive. Sign up for a ballroom dance class. Do something where you are a beginner and take risks. There's nothing like an adventure to get your adrenaline going, your energy moving, and your heart open. It doesn't have to be big. Maybe it means taking a trip somewhere you've never been. Take up art or yoga or photography. Engaged people make it a habit of doing things regularly that get them out of their comfort zone. A bit of advice is given to a young Native American at the time of his initiation:

    As you go the way of life, you will see a great chasm.
    Jump.
    It is not as wide as you think.

7. **Decide to be grateful.**

This year will be the best year of my life.
It will be a return to enjoying the simple things like family &
friends.
It will be the year of less complaining & more appreciating.
This year I will dance more, laugh more, & love more.
And be healthier than ever because of it.
I will live more consciously, deliberately, joyfully.
This year is my best year because I choose it to be.

Excerpted from the poem "This Year"
by Steward St. John

Kier Barker cited this poem when we spoke together at a conference a few years ago. Kier was born with spina bifida. His parents were told that there was no point in taking him home as he would live less than a week. Kier is now in his 60's and doing well. He has faced and conquered immense challenges in his life, and he is an inspiration to all who know him. A note on Kier's website says: *"Life isn't about waiting for the storms to pass; it's about learning to dance in the rain."*

Tips for Employee Engagement

Effective CEOs and executive teams understand that taking care of your talent asset is one of the best high-return investments. They understand that saying "our employees are our most important assets" is simply not enough. Engaged employees are far less likely to leave, and even if they do, they'll leave a positive legacy. The investment to get people engaged always gives a better return than investing in replacing them.

Your best people can get a job anywhere, but if they trust you to have their best interests at heart, they will be committed to the organization. People want to belong and contribute to something that is lasting. It is inspiring when people want to step up rather than step out.

- **Conduct exit interviews.** Listen to what people have to say when they leave your organization. Are the right people leaving and are they leaving for the right reasons? When people have nothing to lose, you can learn a lot from them.

- **Commit to talent development.** Identify your stars, people that show initiative to go beyond mediocrity and focus on developing them. Find out what they need to move from frustration to engagement. Listen carefully to their ideas for making this a better place. Support your best employees to determine their future goals and highest aspirations and provide action plans to help them reach those goals. Help them take on responsibilities that are aligned with their talents and passions.
- **Reconsider rewards.** Negotiate with your stars for positive consequences. Look for creative ways to reward them that are respectful of the organization's reality and tailored to the requests of the employee. Remember: if you want your employees to stretch, the organization needs to stretch as well. If your company was forced to implement pay cuts or a wage freeze that you can't afford to reinstate, find other ways to compensate staff: days off, flexible working hours, or even product discounts. Find what motivates your people and do what you can to show your commitment to them.
- **Work to fit your underachievers.** Sometimes people are lazy. Sometimes the wrong person was hired. Sometimes people just don't care. While it's tempting to ignore these energy consumers or write them off, put some effort into helping them achieve alignment with their values. Maybe their poor attitude is a symptom of a poor fit. Work to see if there is a fit—either in their current job, in another position with your organization, or in their next job.
- **Reward well for actions that go beyond mediocrity.** My daughter had a summer job working at a coffee shop where all the tips were put into a pot and divided up equally among the staff at the end of the month. Laziness was rewarded the same as excellence. While the system might seem "fair," it created no incentive for engagement and superior performance.
- **Compensate your best employees with an incentive plan that inspires them to stay *and* to stay engaged.** One of my clients offers an attractive compensation plan for their

employees. After three years, they match one percent of their employee's salary for every year of employment toward a registered retirement plan. This moves up to fifteen percent with 15 years of employment, to the maximum allowed contribution by the government. In short, if you work for this company for thirty years, the company would have invested enough in your retirement savings fund to make you a millionaire. The plan does wonders for loyalty, engagement, morale, and a highly productive workplace.

- **Align with people's values.** While generous compensation plans for your best employees *rewards* your stars, you cannot *buy* employee engagement with attractive incentive programs and rewards. The heart of engagement is in people's values. You have to know what matters to them and find a way to align their interests and goals with the organizations. Like the rewards for outstanding employees, engagement is not a "one size fits all." It takes conversation. It takes negotiation. It takes commitment. Above all, it takes time. It starts with understanding and extending trust. You have to invest *in* your people if you want investment *from* your people. You have to give *to* others what you expect *from* others. You have to be loyal if you *expect* loyalty in return.

- **Focus energy on building people's strengths.** We have spent far too much time in the leadership development world finding people's weaknesses and trying to fix them. We have found, and research confirms, you will get a much better return on your engagement when you discover and build on people's strengths rather than their weaknesses. Find areas where people can discover and express their strengths, talents, and unique gifts. Then negotiate to see if they can continue to grow these areas.

- **Care.** As you show your commitment and care to both their lives and their work, employees will become more honest with you. Trust, openness, and honesty are muscles that are developed over time. The bottom line for engagement is care. People really don't care how much you know until they know how much you care. People know you care when you invest time in them, listen carefully for their input, are committed to bringing value to them, and genuinely attempt to give them the resources to do their jobs.

- **Ask for feedback—and take action on what you learn.** One manager had her direct reports rate their current level of engagement to develop a benchmark; then she negotiated an action plan for increasing their engagement in the coming six months. Within that plan were accountabilities for both herself and the individual. New habits were established, and as her team became more engaged, their respective teams also became more engaged. With better engagement came better teamwork, morale, and subsequently, a division that outproduced the rest of the company.

Driving Continual Improvement

Taking care of your talent asset is like taking care of your health. If you aren't intentional with consistent habits and don't make a reliable effort, it simply won't happen. Know what engagement looks like in your organization and what it needs to look like. Be continually working on assessing and closing the gap.

Once you have a vision and a strategy of where you are going as an organization, get clear about what kind of culture you are creating, what kinds of employees you need and what kinds of leaders it will take to build the culture to get you where you want to go. Then you have to make the connection, continuing to add value to the lives of your best people. Get out of your office. Ask yourself regularly what you are doing to connect with your employees, particularly the employees you are committed to keeping. Remember, you don't earn respect from the sidelines.

Finally, you have to get full engagement. Don't keep people who aren't meaningfully engaged in their work and the organization. Treat people like people. Give what you expect. Model engagement. Be engaged yourself. When you find something that inspires you every day you will naturally encourage greatness in others.

Embrace Change

"In times of change, learners inherit the earth, while the learned find themselves beautifully equipped to deal with a world that no longer exists."

Eric Hoffer, Philosopher

In a world of relentless and incessant change, leaders understand that to survive—and thrive—you have to embrace change and learn to adapt. You have to be able to take people from chaos to confidence. You also have to deal effectively with resistance, the natural human reaction to change. Resistance is an indication of life. If you poke something that is alive, it's going to squirm or fight back or withdraw. It's going to protect itself. While certainty is an elusive expectation during continual change, as a leader, you have to be able to create a degree of stability and security. You have to learn what and when *not* to change.

When you have made a decision to be a leader, you become an agent of change. But where is your roadmap? Where are your tools? There are eight stages of change. The first is chaos; the eighth is

NAVIGATING TRANSFORMATION - A ROAD MAP

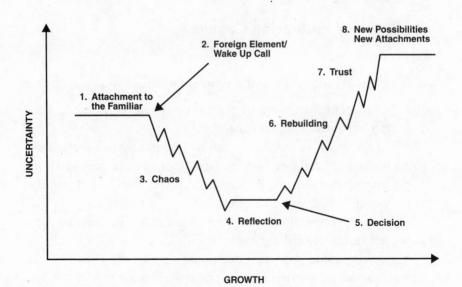

possibility. Once you lead yourself and others to embrace possibility, transforming fear into confidence, you have done your job. When you have mastered the art of embracing change, you will not only build a transformed organization, you will build a transformed life.

Strategies for Navigating the Wilderness

The graph above illustrates the eight stages of change and subsequent transition that takes you from status quo to a transformed reality, from disaster to opportunity, from chaos to confidence. Going through these steps is like taking a journey through the wilderness. You may have heard that "when one door closes, another one opens." While this is true, what you don't often hear is that it's *hell in the corridor*. While *change* happens on the outside of a person—such as a move, an illness, a layoff, a new boss, a restructuring, a new title or role, a death, a birth, or a new technology—transition occurs on the inside of a person. Transition is the reorientation that people go through when they come to terms with change. Let's outline each of these stages of transition and explore specific strategies in each stage that you can use to guide yourself and those you serve through the wilderness of the transformational journey.

Playbook for Embracing Change

Part I: Assessment

All change starts with an honest assessment of where you are. Are you:

- In the comfort zone of the familiar and in need of some growth and subsequent change?
- In the midst of a wake-up call or responding to a foreign element that has thrown you into uncertainty, instability, and grief?
- Immersed in chaos, having entered the world of ambiguity, unfamiliarity, and discomfort?
- In the process of reflecting, seeking a new awareness of yourself and the world around you?
- Making some important decisions?
- Rebuilding, moving forward, renewing yourself?

- Discovering new resources, new connections, new awareness, new levels of trust?
- Uncovering new possibilities and new attachments?

Part II: Appropriate Action

Depending on where you and your team are in the transformational process, there are strategies for navigating the journey.

- **"Attachment to the familiar."** Attachments to familiar patterns and habits need to be continued but are viewed as both a blessing and a curse. Becoming accustomed to the way things are, whether patterns in a relationship, income level, job security, or the route to the office, can become both easy *and* can block your growth. Regularly challenge "the way things are done around here." Take an inventory of your habits, patterns, attachments to what is "secure" and familiar. Ask yourself which of these patterns are serving you and which are hindering you.
- **Foreign elements and wake-up calls:** There's not much you can do to prepare for foreign elements. Foreign elements hit you by surprise. But you can be prepared mentally by knowing that all metaphoric or literal "whacks on the side of the head" eventually are opportunities for new growth. If you keep that in mind you will be able to face grief, suffering, loss, or crisis in your life with a degree of perspective.

In terms of wake-up calls, it's important to stay proactive so that you reduce the tendency to be blindsided by unexpected calls to growth. It's always better to initiate your own wake-up calls, so you have a semblance of control over your own growth.

If you are initiating change in an organization, it's important to give people a rationale for the change and a vision of where you are taking them. You may not have pristine clarity for how you are going to get your team through the chaos, but you need to be able to inspire them with a compelling vision and clear basis upon which you can justify making the change.

Part III: Strategies for Dealing with Chaos

It's been said that circumstances don't determine a person, they *reveal* them. A good marriage, put through the chaos of illness or the birth of a child, will use the experience to become stronger. A bad marriage, when exposed to chaos, will likely become worse. Chaos creates a leadership opportunity to strengthen the system and the people in it. But there are ways to make the most of chaos.

- **Take time.** Chaos presents an opportunity for connecting— by reaching to support and to be supported. It's a time to listen to and value people, to tune in and assess how people are impacted. While chaos isn't necessarily going to be your most productive time, it's a time to build community. It's a time for empathy, connection, and caring. Resist the tendency to hide and withdraw. The key is not just walking around; it is *opening up*, *paying attention*, and *being in touch*.
- **Take accountability.** No one but you can ultimately take you through the wilderness of change. Take accountability for getting yourself through the chaos without blame, a sense of entitlement, or complaints. Take accountability to learn from the experience and to "build a bridge and get over it."

Part IV: Strategies for Reflection

The Reflection Stage is an opportunity to learn from the experience of going through the chaos. While chaos requires support and community, reflection is about new awareness, so you can move forward with new insights and direction. It's when you realize that the chaos, as painful as it was, actually was *necessary* to deepen your connection to your authentic self, reset the compass, and move forward. When you are tired of the emotions associated with chaos, when you are weary of being around the complaining crowd, when you are ready to start moving forward, you are ready for Stage IV.

- **Take stock.** Be aware of indicators of having been in chaos too long, so that chaos becomes the "new familiar." While grief, uncertainty, anger, fear, insecurity, and loss of control are all part of normal chaos, you know you have stayed there too long when these healthy emotions turn to resentment, cynicism, anxiety, low morale, resignation, bitterness, incessant complaining, or indifference. Four assumptions underlie this approach to change:

✓ Change is the only constant in life and is necessary.
✓ Not all change is good.
✓ You won't change if you don't let go.
✓ Change, whether it is thrust upon you or you choose it, is a call to personal and organizational growth.

Given these assumptions, another aspect of taking stock is to assess very carefully your responses to three fundamental questions:

✓ What are you committed to *preserve* in the change?
✓ What must you be willing to *let go* of?
✓ What are you committed to *learn*?

The Reflection stage, after chaos, is also a great time to take stock of your alignment with your authentic self:

✓ Are you still on track with your purpose, vision, and goals?
✓ Are you seeking the right skill sets to accomplish what you desire?
✓ Are your resources adequate to complete the process?
✓ Is your new organizational culture going to support or distract?
✓ Are you on the right wall with the right ladder?

Reflection that emerges in the later stages of chaos is a good time to s-l-o-w d-o-w-n and sort out the urgent/important aspects of your life. While it, like early chaos, may not be your most productive time, it is a prime time for creativity, innovation, originality, and community. It's a great time to bring people together to think outside the box and be inventive and pioneering, both at a personal and collective level.

• **Take a good compass with you on the journey**. There are not adequate maps to guide you through the changes of today's world. What you need for this journey is a reliable compass, a set of clear and uncompromising principles on which you live your life. You need to be clear about what you value and be willing to hold true to what matters most. This kind of integrity is the self-respect necessary to take you on the arduous journey of personal and organizational transformation. A compass is about clear values, separating the urgent from the important, a clear vision, and a clear why—a purpose-driven life. Reflection allows you to go inside and clarify your north star.

Part V: Decisions

There is power in a decision, the power to change the course of your life. Decisions put an alcoholic onto the path of recovery, an employee on the path of a new future with a new attitude, or turn a failing student into a high school graduate. Decisions turn pain into possibilities, fear into faith, despair into delight, chaos into confidence.

Once you have been through chaos and have taken time to reflect and connect with your authentic self, it's a decision that will set you on the road to rebuilding.

Part V starts with a decision to:

- Change your attitude; be a builder rather than a destroyer, be a "we" person instead of a "me" person.
- Exit. Walk away from an organization or a relationship that is not aligned with your values and vision.
- Stay in an organization or relationship because it's the right thing to do, even if it isn't comfortable.
- Change careers.
- Get some coaching, therapy, or mentoring.
- Be honorable, even in the face of dishonor.
- Stop complaining; decide once and for all, that all blame is a waste of time.

Part VI: Strategies for Rebuilding

Once you have turned the decision corner, it is time to define or redefine success and build accountability processes to keep you on track. As a leader, you want to be a step ahead of the crowd who may still be in chaos. Rebuilding can inspire those who may still be struggling in chaos, as long as you stay in contact and maintain their respect and trust. Here are a few strategies to help you in this stage.

- **Become clear about the decisions necessary to move you and your organization forward.** Make the tough decisions that will advance yourself and your organization.
- **Take the necessary time for reflection and refocusing of your intentions.** Learn to get in touch with the silence within yourself and know that everything in life has a purpose.
- **Have a clear and explicit accountability process to keep yourself and others on track.** Stay focused on results. Clarify your purpose, your agreed upon promises, your support requirements, your goals, and the consequences for achieving your accountabilities.
- **Stay connected to people you serve and are accountable to, who still may be in chaos.** Continue to earn the trust of those you serve and give them support. Be honest and tell them what you know and don't know. Affirm emotions that are expressed in constructive ways. Keep moving them toward their own decisions that will help turn the rebuilding corner. If at all possible, resist the inclination to throw more changes on them when they are still coming to terms with the original change.
- **Develop a clear method to assess when you have reached a new status quo, so you know when the cycle is complete.** While many demands and new expectations beyond your control may be throwing you back into chaos, you want to be sure there is at least one project at work and one project in your personal life that you have some measurable control over and can bring to fruition. For example, in the midst of change at work, you may find it very therapeutic to spend time on the weekends gardening, climbing a mountain, or cleaning your garage.
- **Support the emerging leadership.** In the aftermath of the horrific 911 tragedy, Fred Rogers was asked how to help

children through the awfulness of it all. At the time he told the story about when he was a boy and would see scary things on the news. "My mother would say to me, 'Look for the helpers; you will always find people who are helping.'" He then went on to explain that in times of crisis and disaster, he is comforted by realizing that there will always be so many helpers that emerge. The surge of goodness that emanates from humans in times of calamity becomes the type of leadership that binds societies and organizations together. Responding to a crisis and rebuilding always presents an opportunity to step into leadership. In times of change and upheaval, leaders are those who find clarity and compassion in the chaos, who make decisions when others are indecisive, who take action when others are immobilized, who persevere when others abandon ship. Recognize and support those who can be counted on in times of change and expand their roles when the new reality emerges.

Part VII: Building Trust

Trust always takes a hit in times of organizational change. Oftentimes positional leaders take the rap for this, and while this may be justified, trust also takes a hit because trust in yourself can be eroded during times of change.

Eleanor Roosevelt once said that "… every time you meet a situation, though you think at the time it is an impossibility, and you go through the tortures of the damned, once you have met it and lived through it, you find that forever after you are freer than you were before." Every time you resist the tendency to go back to the familiar, every time you face chaos in your life courageously and compassionately, trust—both within and around you—is strengthened as resources materialize.

It's been said that a bird sitting on a tree is never afraid of the branch breaking. It's because her trust is not in the branch but in her wings.

Trust is not built in a day. It is built daily. It's built with consistent action. It's built with care and compassion, empathy and integrity, attentiveness and thoughtfulness. It's built with honesty, stability, and the strength of a promise kept. Trust is built through paying unwavering attention to the small things and listening carefully to what's important to people. Trust is built with bone-deep belief in the value of others, a generous spirit, and a can-do attitude. This is true whether you are rebuilding trust with your teams or rebuilding trust in yourself.

Part VIII: Strategies for New Possibilities

In summary, when going through the corridor of change and subsequent transition, you have both an opportunity as well as accountability to ensure that change management initiatives incorporate some of the following strategies:

- **Give people a clear rationale for the change.** As noted earlier, Friedrich Nietzsche, the German philosopher in the nineteenth century, said that "He who has a *why* to live for can bear almost any *how*." Leaders inspire and make clear the why. Why are we changing? How will we be better off because of the change? While change is necessary, not all change is good. If you have no solid reason for changing, it's best not to be initiating change.

- **Give people a vision.** Asking people to step into the corridor of uncertainty is a part of leading people through the transition to a new reality. If you are always certain, you aren't changing. Uncertainty is an essential ingredient to growth. A vision is a powerful and stabilizing force to help take people through the wilderness of ambiguity.

- **Give people dignity and respect.** In order to build a strong and civil high-performance culture, every right must be accompanied by a subsequent responsibility. As leaders, you have a right to make changes, but you have an accompanying responsibility to initiate change in a respectful, honest way. Give people the dignity and respect they deserve to understand and come to terms with the change.

- **Give people compassion.** It takes time to adjust to change. People often need to bitch before they build. Get out of your

office. Be connected. Listen to people's concerns. Allow people
to grieve. Give them time to let go. Leadership through transitions is about caring for people, not manipulating them. While
you may be able to control things, you can't control people.

- **Give people information.** In times of intense crisis, whether it's
  layoffs or a diagnosed illness or an organizational change initiative
  or a rumor of a new boss, there is a high need for information.
  People need to know what is happening and what to expect. While
  you can never create perfect clarity, what you can do is at least tell
  people what you know. Tell them what you don't know. Be honest. Be transparent. Be real. Do this constantly, even if nothing has
  changed recently. Information rarely makes things worse.

- **Give people boundaries.** People need some structure to get
  through the corridor of change. They need to know that there
  are both accountable and unaccountable ways to handle emotions. It's okay to grieve, to vent, to express resistance in constructive, contained places and respectful ways. It's not okay to
  complain incessantly, tear down others, to gossip, or to undermine the change initiatives. There's a difference between constructive venting and destructive complaining.

- **Give people a decision point.** Similar to boundaries, people need to know when it's time to move on. They need to
  know that while venting, grieving, and expressing concerns are
  all valid emotional responses, eventually, you have to build a
  bridge and get over it.

- **Give people a compass.** If you've ever been lost in the wilderness, you know that roadmaps don't always work. What
  you need when you are lost is a compass, a set of values and
  guiding principles that remain constant and reliable during
  uncertainty and upheaval. By taking an active and ongoing
  collective inventory of what you are committed to preserving amid the change, you connect people to their values and
  establish a foundation in the midst of the storm.

- **Give people your trust.** Change creates all kinds of opportunities. The most important of these is the opportunity to trust that
  people will come to terms with change in their own way and

in their own time. Whenever you can extend trust, you foster trust. Trust that with a clear vision, you will get there together. While you care about people, you don't have to carry people.

- **Give people your courage.** With every change comes potential new resources. After all, this is one of the primary purposes of the human experience: to grow and learn. Courage tends to emerge in those you serve when you have the courage to face and come to grips with change in your own life. Change is the courage to step off the cliff and grow wings on the way down.

Ensure Results

"Everyone on a team knows who is and who is not performing, and they are looking to you as the leader to see what you are going to do about it."

Colin Powell, Former U.S. Secretary of State

How to Hold People Accountable

Far too often, tasks are assigned to employees in a haphazard way, hoping that the worker will "figure it out" and deliver an adequate, even superior, performance. If this is your accountability process, you will soon realize that "hope" is not a very effective strategy. There is another way—a practical process for holding people accountable—in a way that fosters trust, respect, engagement, passion, ability, open communication, *and* gets a grip on results that matter.

There are three reasons why managers don't do a great job of holding people accountable.

- **It's too hard.** Let's face it; it's tough holding people accountable. It takes clarity, courage, and commitment. When you get a promotion, you don't get more power, you get more accountability. And having the courage to have the tough conversations is part of the accountability of every positional leader.

- **They don't want to be the bad guy.** A recent Harvard study showed that many managers, hoping to get promoted, refrain from holding their people accountable because they want to get good performance feedback and stay in line for promotions.
- **They aren't clear about how to do it.** We are all told, as positional leaders, that it is the job of a manager to hold our employees accountable, yet very few are actually shown how.

It's vital to understand that you don't build accountability by increasing rules and procedures and bureaucratizing organizations. If an employee cheats on expenses by padding his travel costs, you don't make people accountable by making more rules. While there certainly are some systemic issues that contribute to greater accountability, accountability is not built with more bureaucracy. It is fostered through better conversations and courageous action.

For those who wish to go deeper in this area, check out the accompanying *Workbook: The Other Everest* for additional exercises and examples.

Playbook for Accountability: The Ten-Step Process for Holding People Accountable

Step 1. Take a Good Look in the Mirror. Positional leaders set the tone for the culture of an organization. If you are leading a culture that lacks accountability, or even if you have an employee who is not achieving the results required, the first place to look for a cure is in the mirror.

Looking in the mirror means taking a careful inventory of your own attitudes and actions. In order to get an accurate picture of how accountable you are, ask yourself as well as those who depend on you (your boss, your staff, your colleagues, your external stakeholders), how you are perceived in the following areas.

- Are you oriented toward results rather than activities? Accountable leaders understand that "working hard," while necessary, is not good enough. Accountable leaders have a bone-deep commitment to bringing measurable value to their relationships. They don't just get there on time. They finish well. They do *whatever* it takes. They are self-motivated. Accountable people understand that if it's their area, function, or project, they are accountable.

- Do you take ownership for your area? Accountable leaders take ownership. Everyone in an organization, from the chief executive officer to the janitor, has some piece of the business and a corresponding set of results that are theirs to achieve. It's about taking ownership for your contribution to the organization and achieving results that drive the business forward.
- Do you honor the promises you make? Do you have a firm resolve that you will never make a promise you don't intend to keep? Do you do what you say you will do? Are you seen as a person who is accountable, who can be counted on?
- Do you take 100% responsibility for your actions? Have you made a decision, once and for all, that all blame is a waste of time? Have you stopped hiding behind such statements as, "They need to listen better?" and replaced it with, "No, *they* don't have to listen better; *you* need to communicate better."
- Are you accountable in the way you respond to stressful situations? Do people perceive you as composed and poised under pressure? Are you considerate of how your reactions impact others when you are under stress? Are you seen as being emotionally mature and stable? Do people feel safe around you?
- Have you given up being an excuse maker? Remember: no one but you cares about the reason you let someone down.
- Are you loyal to others in their absence? Do you refuse to be part of the gossip crowd? Are you known as a person who represents people well when they aren't in the room?
- Are you intentional about living the values you espouse? Are you committed to "walk the talk?"
- Are you open to feedback? Accountability doesn't mean you have to be perfect. It does mean that you have to be seen by others as caring enough to be willing to grow in these areas.

- Is your orientation towards servant leader or controlling leader? Are you committed to removing barriers and providing resources to your staff to help them, in any way you can, to get their job done? Do your staff know that you have their back? If your staff don't trust you or your motives, you will get compliance at best, not accountability.

Step 2. Build Trust. Trust is a belief in, and reliance upon, someone or something. It is the experience of being comfortable and unguarded around another person or situation. While being accountable undoubtedly builds trust, before you can expect to hold someone accountable, there has to be a degree of trust in the relationship. In order to make the shift from compliance to commitment, people have to know you care about something beyond your own self-interest or about the results you produce. In the words of John Maxwell, "You have to get to people's heart before you ask them for a hand."

Ensure that you are doing all you can to earn the trust of people before you start to work at holding them accountable. Accountability without trust is compliance. Accountability is about *ownership*, not obedience.

- Do people see you as invested in your relationship with them? Are you seen as being committed to more than "merely getting the job done?" Do your employees believe you're committed to helping them grow and develop as a person?
- Do you sincerely care about the well-being of those you depend on and those who depend on you?
- Are you open and honest with people?
- Do you honestly *care* about the people you are helping hold accountable? What is your motive? Are you on a power trip, motivated to catch them doing things wrong and punishing them, or are you committed to helping your people be the best they can be?

Before you start trying to hold people accountable, you need to take a close look at *why* you want to hold people accountable. It is important to be honest about your motives. Why do you want to hold people accountable? Is this about building your ego or is it about building your people? Does getting results mean that you look better as a boss? Are you using people for your own gain? Do you honestly care? Are you here to *serve* people or are you here to *use* people? If you are committed to building an accountable culture, people have to believe that you have their best interests in your heart.

Step 3. Discover a Reason—the Why of Accountability.

Accountability without purpose is drudgery. If someone lacks accountability in their work, it usually means they haven't found a *reason* to be accountable. They don't have a *why*. It is easier to hold someone accountable when their heart is in the game. Before you talk about results, help your employees discover a fit between what they are passionate about and skilled at, and what is expected of them. Even if you find out that their primary passion lies outside of work, at least you are supporting them. While not every aspect of a job might be inspiring to an employee, they have to know that you are committed to helping them find a fit, rather than just trying to get them to do a job. Remember, *fit people; don't fix people.*

- Ask people what they love about their job or what aspect of the organization they are passionate about and do the best you can to create an opportunity for them to do more of what gives them energy.
- Ask people what is important to them and do all you can to help them realize their values. Whether you are supporting what matters to them outside of work or bringing their values to their work, alignment with personal values gets people engaged in what they do. Engaged employees are much more likely to be accountable.
- Assess the employee's "fit" and work with them to find alignment between their interests and values and those of the organization by helping discover their strengths. Everyone is good at something. You discover your strengths when you know what comes easily to you. When you can help your employees align their job with their strengths, you are far more likely to get accountability from them.

- Help people know they make a difference. People need to know when they come to work that they make a meaningful contribution beyond the assignment of tasks. People will be far more accountable when they know they are needed and make an impact. Every employee needs a clear, direct line of sight between their job and the success of the organization as a whole. They need to understand how critically important their function is to the overall strategy and culture. When people are fully engaged in a purpose that is both compelling and personally rewarding, they demand much more of themselves and each other.

Step 4. Get Clear. Ambiguity, in the right context, can breed creativity. When clarity is required, however, ambiguity breeds mediocrity. It can create frustration and unnecessary, destructive pressure. Few things are as stressful and de-motivating as working in a place where you are not sure if you are meeting the expectations of the people who rely on you.

Far too often we put an overload of ambiguous demands on people and then wonder why they aren't accountable. While the mindset of ownership is paramount to accountability, if people are too afraid to push back, or if there isn't a safe, open, respectful environment to negotiate priorities or request ways to support each other, people end up being merely polite rather than genuine—a less than ideal environment for accountability.

To be accountable, people need to have clarity in at least five areas. A lack of clarity in these areas will result in unmotivated, frustrated, and stressed employees:

1. **Results:** People need to be clear about expected outcomes and how success is defined within their specific role. What will the outcome of my work look like? How is achievement defined in my role here?
2. **Abilities:** The current level of capability to achieve the required result needs to be specified. What skills, abilities, competencies are needed to be successful in this job?

3. **Resources:** The financial and human resources to achieve success must be spelled out. How realistic is the expected outcome given the existing resources?

4. **Process:** Be clear about the method required to achieve the results you promise. What specific steps are required to achieve success? For example, if you are a salesperson and success is defined as a minimum of 20 sales/month, do you know the precise steps needed to achieve this result? Results without clarity of the process will result in destructive pressure, not motivation.

5. **Willingness:** What level of motivation will ensure delivery on your promise? Just how committed are you? Everyone suffers when people are afraid to be honest. If the willingness isn't there, bringing it out into the open could result in a plan to increase your willingness, create a possibility for a move to another area within the organization, or a move to another job.

There are two fundamental areas of accountabilities where clarity is critical.

- **Operational accountabilities.** Operational accountabilities are brief, clear statements of the operational results that are expected in a particular role. They describe what gets accomplished. Operational accountabilities should challenge you to exert your influence and impact upon the organization. They should be identified in terms of the outcomes that will be achieved through your best efforts. Be as specific as possible when you are helping an employee clarify what is expected. Articulate your role as you want it to be, not necessarily as it is at the present moment.

- **Leadership accountabilities.** Leadership accountabilities, expressed in outcomes or behavioral terms, describe the kind of work environment and attitude expected that will enable exceptional performance. While operational accountabilities deal with *competence*, leadership accountabilities point to the level of *character* required in a particular role.

One of the most difficult areas when it comes to accountability is dealing with a "poor attitude," or an attitude that is not conducive to the kind of culture you want to create. Establishing the work climate is an essential part of the leader's role. You set the tone for the entire culture. In a positive work environment with constructive norms, even the most reluctant employee will feel compelled to get on board. For this reason, leadership accountabilities focus on the "people side" of your role. They describe how you want others to work with each other in the organization, what you expect from yourself as a leader, and the type of culture or work environment you want people to co-create with you.

Your values as a leader should be clearly visible as they challenge and compel you to bring your best self to work. They set the tone for leadership and introduce the notion that "it starts with me."

You can't hold someone accountable for an "attitude." You can only hold them accountable for behaving in specific ways. Indicators of appropriate behaviors that accompany values like respect, accountability, supportive, collaborative, integrity, include:

- People feel safe and are uplifted and feel better about themselves by being around you.
- No gossiping—speak well of people in their absence.
- No blaming or complaining without proposed solutions, recommendations, and personal responsibility.
- No excuses—only ownership for your part of any mistake.
- You never make a promise you don't intend to keep; you do what you say you are going to do.
- Replacing unearned entitlement (you deserve something just because you want it) with *gratitude.*
- Bring a generous spirit to everything you do, giving more than you get.
- Act ethically; any action taken could be shared with the entire team.
- Honesty in your dealings with people.

A good way to develop a set of leadership accountabilities on a team is to have the team brainstorm and narrow down five or six of the most important expectations that people have of each other. This list could then be translated into a "Team Charter" that everyone would agree to. Along with this agreement would also be the agreement to talk with each other when there is a perceived violation.

It is always more powerful when the boss has their skin in the game, meaning they agree to the expectations and discuss their own operational accountabilities with the team.

As with both operational and leadership/attitudinal accountabilities, it is always best to clarify your expectations as early as possible in the relationship. If you clarify expectations before a problem arises, the tough conversations will be much easier to deal with downstream.

Step 5. Hire for Character. Not long ago, I was in a Marriott Hotel in San Francisco where I experienced great customer service. When I was checking out, I asked the clerk what training she was given to give such good service and if everyone got the same superb, consistent customer service.

After thinking about it for a few moments, she replied, *"You can't train someone to be nice. What we do here is hire nice people and train them how to use the computer."*

While we often inherit employees with an ill-suited temperament, if you want a particular attitude, it is much easier to *hire* a person's attitude than it is to *change* a person's attitude.

Far too often people are hired for skills and fired for their attitude. You'll have a much greater chance of getting the right people on the bus if you know, very clearly, what the expected values and behaviors are in your culture and hire only people who live these values. Ask potential employees such questions as what they value and how they learned to live a specific value that is important in the area where they would be working.

Take your time to be sure to hire the right person for the job. It's been estimated that firing a person will cost you—in time and money—up to 200 percent of their annual salary. Just because they look good on a resume doesn't mean they work well in your office.

As the management guru, Peter Drucker, once said, *"Hire slowly; fire quickly."*

Note: If you "inherited" employees with the wrong attitude, or if you didn't do an adequate job to ensure the right attitude in the hiring process, it makes leadership more difficult, but there is still hope. It means working through the rest of the steps.

Step 6. Get a Clear Agreement. Remember, accountability is defined as the *ability to be counted on*. Accountable people don't make promises they can't keep. But we need to get better at making promises. A request is not an agreement. Just because you ask someone to do something, or express a wish, doesn't make it an agreement. Agreement is a two-way street. Before you can hold anyone accountable, they have to be clear about what is expected and have made an agreement to do something. Make it a habit to finish every conversation where there are expectations with an agreement. Without an agreement, there can be no accountability.

Clarifying your agreement means clarifying your expectations of each other. Mutually understood expectations are necessary to live accountably and with less strain. Remember to watch carefully for "vague" responses that lead to misinterpretation and misunderstanding, such as "I'll get at it as soon as possible," "I'll try ...," "I'm pretty swamped right now, but I'll get to it as soon as I can," "ASAP," "I don't know why they didn't get it. I sent them all an email with clear instructions."

These responses are not enough of an agreement to hold someone accountable. You have to be very clear when you are asking people for an agreement. A verbal agreement, followed up with a written understanding of the agreement, is recommended whenever possible.

- My request is ... by [state time].
- What I want from you is ... by [state time].
- What I am asking you to do is ... by [state time].
- The action I need from you is ... by [state time].
- Sink the nail. Be direct by asking clearly: *"Can I count on you to do this?"*

For example, when your request is to have someone complete a proposal by a particular day or to demonstrate a particular behavior in the office, be sure to get an agreement that they are willing to do it. If they explicitly say they aren't willing to do it, then go directly to consequences.

This process may seem superficial while you are practicing it with your team, but over time it will become a habit and integrated into your relationships. And there is power in following a conversation with an email that confirms an understanding of the agreements that were made to each other.

Step 7. Clarify Support Requirements. To be committed, engaged, and ultimately accountable, people need to feel that they can talk openly about the support they require in order to deliver on their accountabilities. Support requirements outline how others are accountable to support you. They list the resources and support required to fulfill an agreement. Accountabilities are what you expect from others. Support requirements are the negotiated accountabilities people can expect from you. A support requirement will become your promise to the people you have expectations of. An agreement without clearly defined support requirements to help fulfill that agreement will soon lead to a gap in accountability. A reciprocated agreement to provide the support required to deliver on the promise is essential. This turns a one-way, "parental," top-down relationship into a *partnership*.

Support requirements can be such things as:

- Involve me early in the discussions that impact my actions.
- Continue to negotiate priorities and assess resources before assigning projects to me. Spend time coaching me in this area.
- Step back and trust me to do the job without so much micro-management.
- Be clear about your expectations.

To ensure a high degree of motivation, the agreement should be based on promises aligned with both personal and organizational values that make a difference to the overall objectives of the organization.

This needs to be negotiated and fully understood before any agreements are made.

Step 8. Discuss Consequences. Accountability without consequences is merely a wish—accompanied by frustration. Three important principles are vital to understanding and applying consequences.

First, talk about consequences at the time you are negotiating agreements, so people are clear up front. Don't wait for a lack of accountability before you start talking about punishment. Second, recognize that it's easier and more effective to start with positive consequences. Positive consequences are the rewards for keeping your promises and fulfilling your accountabilities. They are meant to inspire you to achieve your accountabilities. If these don't do the job, then go to negative consequences. Third, focus on both short and long-term consequences.

We find that most managers struggle the most with consequences. In the companion *Workbook: The Other Everest* you will find an in-depth process for negotiating short and long-term consequences with your staff.

Step 9. Acknowledge the Breakdown—with a Personal Responsibility Approach. This step focuses on two possible areas of breakdown in accountability. The first is when circumstances prevent you from keeping a promise *you* made to someone.

What happens when conditions thwart you from honoring an agreement? We are, after all, human, and as such, we are going to fall short or over-commit. Computers break down. Traffic happens. Other people we depend on don't keep their promises.

Accountable people, as soon as they realize that an agreement is in jeopardy, either because of circumstances beyond their control or because of poor choices or ill-thought-out promises that prevent them from keeping the agreement, have a recovery process.

As previously described in the section about relational integrity, I recommend a three-step recovery process when you are, for any reason, unable to deliver on a promise.

1. Let the creditor—the person you have made a promise to—know *as soon as you know* if the commitment is jeopardized *by taking full ownership for the breakdown.* These are reasons, not excuses, a simple acknowledgment that you were wrong. A reason is a brief explanation of what happened so your creditor understands. An excuse, on the other hand, is a rationalization for the outcome. Accountability has no place for rationalization.

2. Negotiate with your creditor to minimize damages and re-commit to a new promise. Be open to negotiate how you can repair the relationship.

3. Learn from the experience so it doesn't happen again.

The *second* breakdown centers on how you handle it when someone fails to keep their promise to *you.* Just as an individual needs a recovery process to be accountable when their own agreements are in jeopardy, a relationship also needs a process when one of the parties do not honor a perceived promise.

Here is a four-step process for dealing with someone who doesn't keep their promise.

1. Acknowledge the breakdown and accept accountability immediately after the agreement is not kept. It's advised to start with an acknowledgment of your own possible contribution to the breakdown.

2. Make a new agreement.

3. After a maximum of three breaches (it usually takes only two) acknowledge, after each breakdown, that the agreement was not kept—again. After a very brief acknowledgment of your possible part of the failure, you move to focusing on following through on the negative consequences.

4. Discuss and follow through on how the consequences will be applied.

Step 10. Follow-Up. Always assume the best. If trust is extended and the process is clear, most people will step up and learn to deliver on their agreements. Expect that people want to succeed. You aren't, after all, out to nail people. You are out to build them. If they don't succeed, there must be willingness, with the support of your organization, to follow through on the consequences. Without consequences, there can be no accountability.

Take time to ask the following questions to help build the relationship and continue to learn:

- What have we learned?
- What are we going to do differently?
- What positive impact will this have on our relationship?

Follow up means a clear plan for follow-through, including understanding what is required for follow-up and how often we need to meet and with whom in order to ensure that we hold each other accountable for honoring the promises we have made to each other.

If the employee continues to be unaccountable, you will need to follow through on negative consequences which means *you* must now be accountable to follow through on the consequences that were put forward to your employee.

Integrating Accountability in All Parts of Your Life

You might have noticed that the fundamental principles that form the roots of an effective accountability process with others are also the principles that underlie accountability agreements with yourself. You will also find that you can apply these principles and steps to any environment: your family, a volunteer organization, or your workplace. Accountability ensures the roots for sustaining a great culture and a great life. In the words of Henry Ford, "No one can build a reputation on what you're going to do."

Build a High-Performance Culture

"The key to building a great culture is to recognize that ordinary people want to do extraordinary things. Your job as a leader is to create an environment that supports this to happen."

Sean Durfy, "Durf,"
Former President and CEO, WestJet

Our youngest daughter, Chandra, has always had a passion for soccer. When she turned eight, after playing in recreation league for four seasons, she asked to be on a more competitive team. At that time there was no U8 (under 8 years old) team in the local club, so she joined together with some of her friends with a similar interest in taking their skills and talents to another level. Their first season was a bit of a disaster from a win/loss perspective. Not only did they not win a game all year, but they scored only one—that's right—one single goal the entire year. It happened in one of the last games. Their team had performed so poorly that scoring one goal resulted in so much cheering you'd have thought they just won the championship!

Two parents, Andy and DeeDee Cook, had experience playing and coaching the game and had two daughters on that team, so they volunteered to take over the helm. They ended up devoting themselves to coaching this core group of girls for the next twenty seasons (ten indoor and ten outdoor), eventually building this team into a group of young women who competed at the highest level.

Three values formed the implicit fabric of this team:

- Fun—in everything they did.
- Friendships—among every player.
- Fundamentals—of both soccer and of character.

In the seasons that followed, these values remained constant as the friendships grew and the skill levels developed. It was always more important to be a good person on this team than a good soccer player. It wasn't so much about winning in the early days. Win or lose; they were more interested in where they were going to go for ice cream after the game.

Bonding with each other on and off the field, hard work, and discipline, plus strategic coaching and technical sessions for skill development, the team soon became a fascination to soccer players and coaches around the province. The team was attractive, not just because they were winning, but because they were connecting. They were also attractive because of the power of their leadership presence as a team: respect for themselves and others, a commitment to put the team above their self-interest, a positive attitude in everything they did, and a bone-deep commitment to excellence and integrity in how they conducted themselves. Through their presence, the team set a platinum standard across the league for enjoyment of the game, mastery of the skills, and exemplary living.

The coaches relentlessly modeled this strength of character and had this expectation of everyone. They knew how to assess and build on the strengths of every player, creating an environment where every girl knew they belonged and contributed to the success of the team in their own unique way.

Over the years this core group of girls stuck together and grew into a team of young ladies that was absolutely magical to watch. DeeDee and Andy frequently got calls from girls who were willing to drive a great distance just for a chance to play on this team. When they got to high school, a subgroup played together on a team that never lost a single game in four years.

The team has long since dispersed, and the young ladies have pursued other passions in college and beyond. But the habits of character and connections formed in those ten years together will last a lifetime.

The sustained success of this team had less to do with capability than with chemistry, less to do with talent than with the magic that existed between the girls, and less to do with competition than with team values. What they intentionally and deliberately built, through leadership and passion, was a distinctive culture.

Like a great sports team, any successful company that is a recognized leader in its industry has a readily identifiable organizational culture. The most successful companies you know today, such as Google, Zappos, Facebook, REI, Disney, or Southwest Airlines have developed a distinctive culture that is clearly identifiable by its employees.

David Packard, one of the co-founders of Hewlett Packard and creator of the "HP Way" said, *"It has always been important to create an environment in which people have a chance to be their best, to realize their potential, and to be recognized for their achievements."* He and his business partner, Bill Hewlett, understood the importance of culture when they built a company with the intent to have culture be a competitive advantage. They knew that if you are committed to attracting and keeping the best people, providing the best possible service to customers, getting a grip on results, and staying profitable long-term, then you better be committed to building an aligned culture.

Whether created by the initial founder or built through intentional leadership practices, successful organizations that last have developed something special that supersedes corporate strategy, market presence, and technical advantages. While all undoubtedly important, organizations that succeed and last, capitalize on the power that resides in developing and leading a unique corporate culture.

Twelve Guiding Principles Toward the Right Approach

The passion and promise in my work is to build cultures of trust that attract, inspire, and unleash greatness, the capacity to be all you can be. Working to help companies build a great culture for more than a quarter-century, I've learned the following lessons over the years.

1. **While goals give you direction, culture gives you the energy to get there.** While your business is about *what* you do, culture is about the *way* you do it.
2. **Even though you may not be aware of it or able to clearly articulate it, your workplace has a culture.** You can either

create your culture by *default* or *design*. If you are committed to create your culture by design, somebody has to make the decision about the kind of culture you are going to build, and everybody needs to understand the process you are using to build it.

3. **Culture is to an organization what health is to a person.** A person who considers themselves healthy became so by *design*, not by *default*. Healthy people get there with a clear intention, with some rigorous disciplines, and through consistent action. The same is true with an organization's culture. If you aren't intentional and disciplined, your culture will defer to default.

4. **Culture isn't what you *say*; culture is how you *act*.** If you want to know what your culture is, don't just read the value statements on the wall. Ask: "Who gets hired? Who gets promoted? Who gets recognized and rewarded?" The answers to these questions will tell you more about your culture than what you read on your website. Actions always speak louder than words.

5. **Culture answers some fundamental questions:** "What is my experience of being here?" "What makes us special?" "What is our way of doing things around here?" "What do people talk about when the boss isn't in the room?" "What do we value?" "What is it that we do that makes a difference in people's lives?"

6. **If you are committed to attract and retain the best talent, culture will be the most important investment of your time and resources.** This is because your best people have a low tolerance for compliance and insist on engagement. The talent pool is not only shrinking, but those within it are educated, connected, and grounded in the idea of personal choice. They want opportunity. They want to work with friends. They want to work in a place where they can be engaged and be themselves. They want to work in a place where they are trusted and recognized for their contributions. A tall order but that's the new reality.

7. **There is a difference between *values* and value *statements*, just as there is between a *mission* and a mission *statement*.** We've all been in places that had a fancy mission statement on the wall, but when you talked to the employees, you wondered if he even read the statement behind him. While value statements might describe the culture you want to achieve, you need a disciplined process of accountability to get the value statements off the wall and into every employee's actions.

8. **Don't mistake *climate* for *culture*.** Climate is how people feel about the organization and their work (employee satisfaction, engagement, etc.). Culture is what *causes* them to feel that way.

9. **While positional leaders define the culture and set the tone, *every* employee, working together, makes the culture.** Because leadership is about *presence*, not position, every employee can help lift and lead the culture when they are given the clarity, the resources, and the tools to make it happen. Like everything worthwhile in life, from marriage to personal happiness, waiting is not a very effective strategy.

10. **Pleasing everyone is not realistic.** It's reasonable to expect that the positional leaders make an effort to "walk the talk" that they espouse. But they will rarely meet every employee's expectation for living and working congruently to what they claim. This is not because they are necessarily unethical or unaccountable. It means that they are human. What's even more important than "walking the talk," is the ability and willingness to talk about the misalignment when you see it. Most of the time when leaders don't "walk the talk," it's more about perception than it is about intention. Talk about it and respectfully hold each other accountable. Only when you are aware of your blind spots can you have any hope to change.

11. **Like everything else in life, when it comes to culture, personal responsibility is the one thing that changes everything.** Before you criticize others for not "walking the talk," look in the mirror. Ask yourself, "Am I doing everything I can to live in accord with what we claim to be?" "Do I feel a sense of ownership in this culture?" It's always easier to see a lack

of accountability in others than it is in yourself. The day you decide that all blame and unearned entitlement are a waste of time will be the day that your life will change forever.

12. **It's always easier to *build* than it is to *change* a culture.** But changing a culture is always possible—and worth the investment if you do it right.

Capturing Opportunities: What to Expect

Many benefits come with a clearly articulated and well-designed culture, a vision of what you are building together and what you expect from everyone in the culture.

- **Better hiring:** You know how to interview so you get the right kind of people on the bus.
- **Better promotions:** You get the right people in leadership positions.
- **Better "internal fit:"** People enjoy coming to work because their values are aligned with the values of the organization.
- **Better engagement: people are authentic.** They can be who they are. There is more energy, passion, and desire to come to work and to contribute. Commitment results when organizational interests and values align with employee interests and values.
- **Better retention:** When there is values alignment, and when you work with friends, you stay in an organization a lot longer.

Fundamentals of Building Culture through Character

Your culture is defined by your organization's character. The character of an organization, like the character of an individual, is the enduring root that upholds and sustains you. The enduring character of an organization is, in the words of Jim Collins and Jerry Porras in their Harvard Business Review article, *Building Your Company's Vision*, the "core ideology" of an organization is "a consistent identity that transcends product or market life cycles, technological breakthroughs, management fads, and individual leaders."

Organizational character provides the glue that holds an organization together as it grows, reorganizes, and diversifies over time. Like personal character, it consists of two distinct elements: core *purpose*—the organization's most fundamental reason for existence, and core *values*—a system of guiding principles and tenets.

Core Purpose. Core purpose, the first component of an organization's character, is the organization's reason for being. An effective purpose reflects people's idealistic motivations for doing the company's work. It doesn't just describe the organization's output or target customers; it captures the soul of the organization. Both DeeDee and Andy understood, as coaches of Chandra's soccer team, that the core purpose of this team was not about winning games and provincial championships, or even about producing great soccer players. The purpose of the team was ultimately about building strong character in these young ladies. Soccer was merely the tool.

The purpose of an organization has to get at the fundamental reasons for an organization's existence beyond just making money. It has to get to the fundamental reason that it exists in the first place. In other words, why are we here? I think many people incorrectly assume that a company exists simply to make money. While profit is an important result of a company's existence, we have to go deeper and find the real reasons for our being. In this way, business becomes a tool to create what really matters to the people inside that business.

As organizations investigate this, they inevitably come to the conclusion that a group of people converge so they are able to accomplish something collectively that they could not accomplish separately. In short, they make a contribution to society, a phrase which sounds trite but is fundamental. In the business community, you can see people who are interested in money and nothing else, but the underlying drive comes largely from a desire to make a difference, to bring some value to others, to offer a service that makes this world a better place. Listen to people in truly great organizations talk about their achievements, and you will hear little about profit and earnings to shareholders.

For more than half a century, Farm Credit Canada has been Canada's leading agriculture lender and has intentionally built an amazing culture. When a Relationship Manager Associate succeeds at loaning a farmer money, she doesn't say, "I put my heart and soul into this relationship because it will add 35 cents to our earnings per share." No, she will tell you that she helped a family live their dream. She passionately talks about how her work supports, strengthens, and celebrates the agriculture industry, and the pride she feels to be a part of this industry. When the best companies talk about their organizations, they will tell you about the contributions they are making, the impact of their products and services on the world, and the difference they make in the lives of those they serve. When people know their *why*, it inspires their *way*.

Jim Collins reminds us to not confuse purpose with goals or business strategies. Where you might achieve a goal or complete a strategy, you cannot ultimately fulfill a purpose; purpose is like a guiding star on the horizon—forever pursued but never reached. Yet although purpose itself does not change, it inspires change. The very fact that purpose can never be fully realized means that an organization can never stop fueling change and progress.

Core Values. Core values are the essential and enduring guiding principles of an organization. They have intrinsic value and importance to those inside the organization. Disney's core values of imagination and wholesomeness stem not from a strategy, but from the founder's inner belief that these values should be cherished and fostered for their own sake. A great organization decides for itself what values it holds to be core, largely independent of the current economic environment, competitive requirements, or management fads. The organization, like an individual, then succeeds not in their attempt to be popular, but on their clarity and commitment to stand for lasting core principles that matter.

Remember that values are more than a description. They don't just describe a culture. They should *inspire* a culture. Don't confuse core values with value statements. Value statements don't make a culture. How many companies have the value "safety" written eloquently on their website and the posters on the walls of their offices, but in reality, have a deplorable safety rating? How many times do you see "respect" espoused on the top of a list of value statements, while disrespectful relationships abound?

Value statements are what we claim to be. Values are what we actually do. Your culture is not your statements. Your culture is your *actions*. An organization can have a very strong set of core values without a formal statement, just as a company can have a fancy set of value statements without any degree of aligned understanding and commitment to a set of values. The purpose of having the statements is the inspiring and engaging journey it took to get there, and the clear reminder of what we stand for, what we strive for, what we celebrate, and the importance of having the courageous conversations to ensure accountability.

Playbook for Success: Creating an Aligned, Engaged Culture

Building an aligned culture in an organization is complex. There is no formula or cookie cutter path. However, I have observed principles and strategies that you may find useful on your journey. Adapt these to make them meaningful to you and to any organization that you lead and influence.

Start with articulating the parameters of your culture. Are you a CEO building an entire corporate culture? A manager responsible for a division or a plant? A supervisor with five employees? A board chair? The president of a community association? A coach for a sports team? A pastor in a church? A parent who wants more alignment and engagement as a family? You'll find that these strategies can be applied to any culture. Consider what is within your sphere of influence before you get started and be sure you have clearly defined the scope of the culture you are committed to build.

1. **Make building trust your number one leadership priority.** Before embarking on any kind of culture initiative, ensure that your stakeholders see you as committed to adding value. Be certain that you have earned credibility and trust with your significant stakeholders. Any culture effort will fall short if people have any doubt about whether you actually care.

2. **Define and ensure a cohesive leadership team.** A high trust, aligned, cohesive organizational culture starts with a high trust, aligned, cohesive executive team. Identify your key leaders—the allies—who have the positional power, the capacity, the passion, and the commitment to make it happen. Then work to ensure cohesiveness at this level. An organization simply cannot be healthy if the people entrusted to run it are not cohesive. In any organization a lack of cohesion at the top breeds misalignment throughout. Be sure you have taken the time to build a unified leadership team. You lead the way by your actions. You can't fake culture. It's got to be real, and it's got to start with you.

3. **Clarify your purpose.** A primary role of core purpose is to guide and inspire. One powerful method for getting at purpose is called the "Five Whys" as outlined by Geoff Bellman in his book, *Your Signature Path: Gaining New Perspective in Life and Work*. Start with the descriptive statement of what you do: "We make X products" or "We deliver X services," then ask, "Why is that important?" five times. After a few whys, you'll find that you're getting down to the fundamental purpose of the organization. "The Five Whys" can help companies in any industry steer their work in a more meaningful way. Spend time as a leadership team excavating, clarifying, and articulating the core purpose—your *why*—as an organization.

4. **Define the kind of culture you are committed to create.** You define your culture by clarifying your values—the core principles you stand for as an organization that will be a framework to guide all of your decisions and actions. You don't "create" these per se; you *excavate* them. Values have to be authentic. Don't ask, "What core values *should* we hold?" Instead ask, "What core values *do we truly and passionately hold*?" Don't confuse values that you think the organization "ought" to have but does not, with *authentic* guiding principles. This is what creates cynicism in an organization. Your values, like your purpose, should inspire you. Core values are the inspiration that comes from telling the stories and sharing the passion. Also

vital in the process of clarifying your values are *behaviors* that describe the espoused values—behaviors that people expect from their managers, and behaviors that managers expect from their staff.

5. **Create a "culture statement."** As a leadership team create your "culture statement"—a document that declares the kind of culture you are committed to build. This document should ideally fit on one page and should consist of your purpose, your core values, and the guiding principles that you stand for. It should reflect where your organization aspires to go, the way that you expect every employee to behave, the kind of employee you want in your organization, and the kind of leader you expect in every leadership position. Often this will take months to develop. Expect your organization to generate a variety of statements over time to describe your core. In Hewlett-Packard's archives, there are more than half a dozen distinct versions of the HP Way, drafted by David Packard between 1956 and 1972. Your culture statement is an evolving document that doesn't have to be perfect. The purpose of a culture statement is to inspire clarity, conversation, and commitment.

6. **Take time to get your culture document right.** Once your leadership team composes a draft of your culture statement, be careful not to "roll" it out too quickly. Consider the original document developed by your leadership team as just that: a *draft*. Take your time. When it comes to culture, it's the same as your health: *direction* is more important than *velocity*. Get input on this draft document from a variety of levels in the organization, right down to the front lines. Talk about it with each other and with your organization for a few months. Be sure that as many people as possible feel a sense of ownership in the document. Appoint a small group of people who are passionate about this document and your culture to wordsmith the draft over a period of a few months until as many people as reasonably possible become passionate about it.

7. **Develop a "Team Charter" with your leadership.** Once the leadership team has clarity about the kind of culture required, they develop a Team Charter or what some refer to as a Code of Conduct. This is a statement that describes what you, as an executive team, expect of each other and how you will hold each other accountable for *living* the values. A Team Charter also includes a clear process for dealing respectfully and honestly with anyone who knowingly or unknowingly violates these agreements without rejection, guilt, or diminished self-respect. An aligned culture starts with a cohesive leadership team. They develop a plan for how they will stand united as a group and make a promise to the organization that they can be counted on to live the values. To ensure a tight leadership team and to prepare you to define the culture you are committed to build, an off-site meeting is recommended to discuss the expectations you have of each other and how to communicate your commitment to live these values with each other and with the entire organization, as well as an expectation of what the senior leadership team has of every positional leader and every employee to follow suit.

8. **Create a "Culture Team."** Ultimately, someone in your culture has to be given the authority and the support to be accountable for culture. This is a culture champion, someone so passionate about culture that they are a "monomaniac on a mission." The culture champion establishes a "Culture Team" to lead the culture initiative and be accountable to develop culture strategies, keep culture relevant, meaningful, and on every employee's radar, and follow the culture initiative through to fruition. This team, consisting of five to seven people, should represent a cross-section of employees who are passionate about the culture, have a pulse at every employee level, and will be held accountable and given the resources to build a strategy and process to make the culture document living and fluid. This team would be tasked with the responsibilities of finding as many creative ways as possible to get the culture message to every positional leader to ensure

they: a) understand the expectations of the culture; b) understand how to inspire and make these expectations real with their direct reports; c) understand how to hold themselves and their direct reports accountable for living the espoused values; d) understand how to assess when there is both alignment and misalignment in the culture; e) ensure that the senior leaders stay connected to the front-line supervisors and workers; and f) understand how to keep employees at every level meaningfully engaged in the process. They would also be charged with the responsibility of ensuring that the systems and processes in the organization are aligned with the culture document. For example, are our hiring practices aligned with our values? How about our practices for promotions, our performance management processes, our HR practices? How about our onboarding processes and our processes for rewards and recognition? Where is there alignment? Where are the discrepancies? What actions are needed?

9. **Turn your values and principles into behaviors—through the power of conversations.** While the culture document will contain some rather generic expected behaviors, the only way to get the document off the wall and into people's hearts is through courageous conversations. You can't hold people accountable for living the espoused values and guiding principles until you turn them into concrete, specific, measurable actions, specific to each individual role within the organization. While you can attempt to outline some of the expected actions in the one-page document, the power will come in the conversations—at every level of the organization. The culture document needs to be translated into the world where each employee lives and works. This happens only through commitment conversations, where accountabilities and support requirements are owned and agreed upon within specific roles. Turn conversations about values into mutually agreed upon actions and promises.

10. **"Roll out" your culture document with your entire organization.** Once you are clear about the current alignment,

meet with your entire organization in a serious of "town hall" meetings. With your leadership team at the front of the room, outline your culture document. Explain its purpose. Outline how it was developed. Clarify why you have invested in creating this document, along with your expectations of the positional leaders, of every employee, and most importantly, of yourselves as senior leaders. Encourage people to make noise about the document. Here are a few specifics that will be important in turning this declaration into a living, breathing, life-giving compass that will guide you, inspire you, and help keep you on track by reinforcing the message:

- **Be honest and real.** Tell people that in the beginning, as you begin new habits, this culture journey may feel artificial. Until it gets integrated into your way of being, it's going to feel insincere. Keep hanging in there and trust that, in time, it will become a meaningful way that we work together.
- **Tell the story.** Celebrate success. Shine a light on employees that live the values. Start your operational meetings with a success story. Catch people doing it right. Watch for reasons to celebrate and acknowledge when there are sincere actions that are aligned with those on your culture document.
- **Use the document as a teaching tool.** Tell your employees that if you haven't found contradictions in the document, you haven't gone far enough into it. Practice talking about the values at every opportunity. Coach each other in pointing out when there are unintended misalignments, success stories, and teaching opportunities.
- **Embrace the negative.** In every culture initiative you have your espoused values, and then you have reality. No person lives in complete alignment with their advocated personal values, and the same is true in organizations. We are all human, and as such, we will get off course. If the intention isn't there to live the values, then the employee

needs to move on. But assuming good intentions, we need to encourage people to respectfully bring you the bad news, the discrepancies, the contradictions, the misalignments. Model the way by being honest about your own unintended discrepancies. Make it safe for people to bring you the bad news, making it right through conversations and new agreements. If people are perceived as "not walking the talk," let's talk about it. While you want to focus on success, embracing the negative is integral to making culture real.

- **Repeat the message.** Inspire dialogue by modeling it at the front of the room. Invite and encourage honesty about the document and about the culture. Take time to ask questions. Over-communicate the document and your expectations of yourself and each other. Use as many creative ways that you can come up with to communicate the document, including videos, online programs, Q & A sessions, focus groups, etc. Keep it alive through conversations at every level of the organization. Get ownership by talking about how the culture document is *relevant* to each employee. Begin and sustain the process and build trust through the power of dialogue.

Pro Tip: Be the Message You Want to Convey

When I started teaching this process of culture alignment and engagement I took my then sixteen-year daughter with me on a speaking engagement to Eastern Canada. On the way home, I asked for her feedback on my presentation.

"You are sure passionate about what you talk about, Dad. You are a good presenter. But I think you should practice what you preach."

In keeping with my premise that we need to "embrace the negative," I resisted the natural inclination to get defensive. I thanked her for her honesty and asked her to explain what she meant.

"Well, you told these executives that we, as a family, have a culture. If that is the case, what are our values?"

I responded by saying that while we may not have "value state-ments," we still have family values, and I promoted Hayley to be the culture champion in our home. Over the coming months, we crafted a list of core values and came up with a "culture document" for the Irvine family. Every three months, my teenagers gave me a report card, complete with a grade and a list of recommended actions that I, as a father, should stop doing, start doing, and continue doing. The culture document became a living document that helped us take the cultural alignment and engagement in our home to a new level.

Changing an organization's culture is a challenging endeavor at best. It requires enormous commitment and dedication on the part of any leadership team to make it work. Perseverance to make your pur-pose and values real, aligning your employees, and sustaining engage-ment are all required. The investment you make is great, and the return on this investment is worth it. The real work of culture change lies in relentless implementation and follow-through. Plan on a multi-year effort, and plan on returning to these steps over and over again. The same can be said if you are applying these principles to a family, a community association, a church, or a team. It takes a focused and dedicated intention. A designed, aligned, engaged culture gives you an opportunity to experience increased personal growth, fulfillment, and a meaningful connection to the people you care about. If work, community, and family life don't provide this, then we're spending far too much of our lives on it. After all, you're going to have a culture anyway. Why not have a great one?

I have learned that with culture, as it integrates into authentic leadership, presence, not perfection, is what's important. Be the mes-sage you are committed to convey. Be the leader you most desire in your culture. If you are clear about your own purpose, about your values, and about your own design for your leadership and life, then preparation is not about information or processes or strategies. Preparation is about being in the right state of being.

Optimizing Alignment: Greatest Depth to Greatest Heights

Great leaders consistently convey authenticity as they craft cultures that attract, retain, and unleash success.

The journey of *The Other Everest* is about developing and maximizing your ability to do this through the power of authentic leadership.

It's a journey that focuses strongly on looking inward and sharpening your internal compass and the key to success is ultimately about alignment—linking your core authentic identity and values with the leadership and vision you project to the world.

By diving to our greatest depths to better understand and draw strength from who we are, we are better able to align our authentic leadership approach to help us and those influenced by our leadership to reach our greatest heights.

The pathway toward your destination becomes more clear, and your footing and energy become stronger as you move along it.

You gain clarity and focus when you know what you value and live in accordance with those values in both organizations and in life.

You are able to make consistent decisions and take committed, concentrated, productive action.

Ultimately, you are able to improve the results you get in those areas that are truly most important to you and to the organizations and companies that you serve.

Field Notes

1. *Trust is the glue of life. Where are your connections strong and where are they weak? How can you better build trust in the weak areas?*
2. *Creating clarity requires developing vision. Where is your vision of direction strong and where is it weak? How can you better create clarity in the weak areas?*
3. *Engaging talent is about the power of authentic alignment. "Your vibe becomes your tribe." Think hard about the identity you are projecting—does it align with the identity of the talent you are trying to project? How can you improve this?*
4. *Embracing change requires strategies for "navigating the wilderness." How would you assess your openness to change and confidence in navigating? What are the gaps where improvement would help you remove fear and embrace possibility?*
5. *Ensuring results hinges on accountability. How would you assess your approach to holding people accountable and how can this improve?*
6. *Think about the team culture of your company or organization. What are the top three shared values that hold it together? Are they the right values (i.e., support the True North of the direction you want to target)?*
7. *What are the top three "notes to self" you can take away from this section of The Other Everest?*

Those using the companion Workbook: The Other Everest can find additional teachings and exercises in the workbook to help absorb and utilize the information from Part III.

Epilogue: Embracing Shadows Toward New Light

The privilege of a lifetime is being who you are. The privilege of authentic leadership is supporting people to be who they are.

Over the course of our lives, my brother and I spent much time hiking and climbing mountains together. However, as I walked with him through his brain cancer journey and eventual passing, the cancer journey together was an experience of the *"Other Everest,"* the journey down.

Hal was a rural physician who practiced medicine in the hospital across the street from where he lived for more than three decades. Between visits to the cancer center and caring for him in his home, I would push him in his wheelchair around the neighborhood and the hospital grounds that were so much a part of his life for so many years. On our strolls, we inevitably would run into one of Hal's patients or a patient's family member or a colleague or a staff member who would stop, hug him, and weep with him. Hal was a beloved doctor. He wasn't just admired. He wasn't just respected and revered and well-liked. Hal was *loved.*

In meeting the myriad of people that Hal impacted in his career, I would sometimes ask those who were touched so deeply by his presence, *"What made Hal such a great physician?"* The answer was the same as what makes a person a great leader, a great parent, a great citizen, a great human being. The answer inevitably came down to,

"Hal was loved because he cared. He cared about his patients. He cared about his colleagues. He cared about his profession and his work. He cared."

These conversations and the time I spent caring for Hal and seeing a caring community surround him inspired me to write a book about caring entitled *"Caring Is Everything: Getting to The Heart of Humanity, Leadership, and Life."* Since the book's release and Hal's subsequent passing, I have been setting aside time to refine my focus, clarify my personal mission and vision, and re-examine my life's work, my calling, and my commitments. The compass of my life is being reset. Death, as painful as it is, can be strangely and amazingly healing, as it magnifies what truly matters in your life.

I am now resolved to be more present in the present moment. Life is lived now. Not tomorrow or yesterday. We simply never know when our time is up. Facing death squarely and honestly helps us see what is fully around us now. Paradoxically, the realization that the life we have today won't last forever enables us to appreciate it and experience it more deeply. The realization of your own mortality brings into focus important insights. It is the impermanence of life that makes it possible to realize its incredibly precious value.

I have also never been more committed to guide leaders in all walks of life to their authentic self and bring the message of caring to those I teach.

My message is clear: Everyone is a leader, and through your personal journey, you can have an important impact on others, not with a title or techniques but by who you *are* as a person. Leadership is a universal expression of the human experience, a desire to do your part to evolve the world and make a difference. Leadership is about caring and connecting and courage and authenticity. It's about *presence*, not position. My approach to leadership development is that leadership can't really be taught, but it can be learned.

In my observation and research with leaders over the past three decades, a very small percentage cite formal training as the outstanding development experiences of their lives. The vast majority of peak learning experiences occur on the job and in life—through mentoring, conversations, and observing and learning from others. Leadership and personal development come far more from serendipity than they do from planning. You don't "teach" people a different way of being. As has been stated so often in this book, leadership is not a basket of tricks or techniques; it is the quality and character and courage of the leader. It's a matter of ethics and a moral compass, the willingness to remain vulnerable. Rather than a set of skills, leadership development is more about creating the conditions so one can discover where their natural leadership comes from.

At its most fundamental roots leadership is about having the courage and clarity to be who you are in the service of others. There is an old Gnostic tradition that believes we don't invent things, we just remember. That's what the authentic journey is—remembering who we are meant to be and bringing that to life. It's about being authentic rather than spending energy managing the impression you are making on others.

At the University of North Carolina at Charlotte, there stands a magnificent sculpture of a man sculpting himself. The effigy is hunched over his knees, with a chisel in hand, carving himself. The Greeks understood the internal work needed to sculpt ourselves. The eyes in their statues have no iris. The eyes were chiseled looking inward, focusing on the back of their eyes, demonstrating the essence of leadership as a journey from within, a kind of consciousness that is creating a world out of what is inside of you.

The core of leadership, it turns out, is reaching within ourselves and bringing the full spectrum of ourselves to our life and our work.

Although I have had many experiences that were painful and often traumatic at the time, they were actually necessary and profound teaching moments providing a passage to a deeper connection to my authentic self. At the time they seemed to be random occurrences that I coped with the best way I could, not knowing that they were leading me to my destiny. Below the surface of my "traumas," there was the power of a sculptor, calling me to connect with a deeper essence that addressed the fundamental questions, "What is it, in my heart, in my soul, that I must do and be? Who am I, really?"

Learning from Your Life Story

All of us have a spark of leadership in us, whether it is in business, in the public or community service, nonprofit volunteerism, or our family. The challenge is to understand and appreciate ourselves well enough to discover where and how we can use our leadership gifts to serve others and make the world a better place. Like musicians, artists, and athletes, leadership development is about dedicating yourself to a lifetime of realizing your potential, developing self-awareness and new choices from your experiences.

The journey to authentic leadership begins with understanding your life story, significant defining moments, factors that led you to be the person you are now. These range from the positive impact of parents, athletic coaches, teachers or mentors, to the awareness that emerges from trauma, betrayal, death, or facing addictions, to conveying ourselves artistically. Discovering your authentic leadership requires the time and effort to understand how your life story is shaping your life's work, and the courage to live in alignment with the passion and gifts that emerge from that awareness. On the path of trying to establish yourself in the world, authentic leadership requires that you make room for self-exploration.

The work of the authentic journey is not without its pain. It's not neat or linear, and it can be messy. Far too many people decide it's just not worth the journey and fall asleep, living lives, described by Henry David Thoreau, of "quiet desperation." However, at some point in our lives, the desperation can no longer be quieted, and our authentic presence must come forth in the service of the world.

When National Hockey League (NHL) player Theo Fleury announced publicly that his former junior hockey coach had sexually abused him, it helped release him from the internal trauma he had been suffering. Over the years, that trauma had driven him to drugs, alcohol, and promiscuity. He'd managed to hold the secret inside himself throughout his impressive sixteen-year NHL career, but it was steadily destroying him. Through a concerted and courageous desire to look inside and heal himself, Theo is now helping to heal others. By speaking out and becoming an advocate for sexual abuse victims, he has brought healing and recovery to thousands of hurt and struggling individuals who have experienced similar trauma. Looking within and having the courage to serve others is not just good for the soul; it's good for the world. This is the work of authentic leadership.

Reaching the Summit: How Will You Measure Your Life?

It would be devastating to reach the end of your life and realize you have never lived. In my leadership development programs, I ask participants to carefully assess how they will measure the value of their life. Over many years, three themes have emerged:

1. Planting Your Flag at the Top: *The Dimension of Success*

A 23-year-old real estate agent who leads a team of realtors shared that his measurement of a successful life is to own a Jaguar. When this came out in the group, I congratulated him. Many leaders are reluctant to admit, with such honesty, that they are propelled to achieve by measuring their success against the outside world's parameters, to enjoy the recognition and status that come from promotions and financial rewards. I also applauded him because, particularly at this stage in life, he was determined and focused. Like a young athlete who is clear about their goal, determined to achieve that goal, and committed to doing whatever it takes, this kind of initiative can catapult us out of the dependency of childhood and into the emerging realization of our fullest individual potential.

Whether it is in the field of athletics, art, business, music, or drama, the pursuit of success is required to live authentically. The ability to plant your own flag, raise it high, and follow a path of challenge is integral to the authentic life.

2. Lessons from the Journey: *The Dimension of Significance*

Within each of us lies a desire to matter. We want our lives and our stories to make a difference. The day we become intentional about going beyond success on the world's terms and find and follow a path of significance is the day we step into the journey of authentic leadership.

If a person senses an internal "call" for a cause beyond themselves and doesn't follow it, they may well find themselves at the top of the ladder and discover that it is leaning against the wrong wall. One day they wake up with the realization that the life they are living is not the same as the life that wants to live in them. If my real estate friend is as driven for another Jaguar at the age of forty as he was at the age of twenty, he may find himself wondering whose life he is actually living.

Moving away from the measurement of external validation of personal achievement to the internal validation of contribution and significance isn't always easy. Achievement oriented leaders grow accustomed to successive accomplishments throughout their early years, and it takes courage to follow internal pursuits. They also realize that success and significance are not mutually exclusive. You don't have to be poor to live a life of significance. Instead, it is about being *guided* by a well-developed conscience rather than *driven* by the culture around you. If you don't feel secure and at peace with yourself, you may well discover that the world is incapable of giving you enough.

In the classic movie *It's a Wonderful Life*, George Bailey dreams of traveling the world and building great things but instead stays home in Bedford Falls because he repeatedly chooses to do what he believes is for the betterment of others. A turning point in the movie occurs when George experiences a moment of crisis, and he comes to the erroneous conclusion that everyone around him would be better off if he had never been born.

An important development unfolds in the story when, with the help of an angel, George gets a chance to see what his town and the lives of others would look like if he had not existed. Without him, it would have been a dark and lonely place. George comes to recognize the positive impact he had on others by doing what was right as he learns that each person's life is an opportunity to touch so many others—in small ways that make a difference.

My definition of leadership has evolved with my own development. I currently define leadership as a serving relationship with others that inspires their growth and makes the world a better place. The servant-leader knows that others yearn to be heard and engaged— not in debate but in genuine, heart-to-heart dialogue that springs from a caring intent.

3. Synergy with the World Around You: *The Dimension of Connection*

Not long ago a client came to see me for coaching. When I asked him to define success in our time together, the room got very still as he fought back moistened eyes.

"Last week we buried my father, who died suddenly of a heart attack. My father was a successful entrepreneur who mentored many people. He was a generous philanthropist. He sat on many boards. He was part of many associations, did extensive volunteer work, and gave selflessly of his time. Over a thousand people came to my father's funeral. Many sent cards and spoke to me privately about the difference he made in their life."

There was another pause in the conversation.

"You know, I admired my father. I respected my father. I looked up to him. I loved him. I value deeply the impact he had on the world and the contribution he made to the lives of so many ..."

Then a long pause prevailed.

"*And my father was very hard to get close to ...* and I don't want my children to say that about me after I'm gone. That's what I am here for."

Authentic leadership, to fully come to fruition, must start with success, evolve into significance and along the way, foster connections with the most important people in our lives. It's about living an integrated life, being loved by and connected to the people you are closest to as well as by the people you impact.

The Peak of Authentic Understanding: Being at Peace with Who You Are

Authentic leadership is the realization that you can't be a good leader until you are good with yourself. What does "good with yourself" look and feel like?

First, it means having the courage to be open to an *awareness* of yourself, and how your life impacts those around you. It's about knowing what drives you and what blocks you while understanding and appreciating your blind spots. It's about facing the darker sides of your nature, to acknowledge the traumas, inadequacies, self-doubts, insecurities, and fears, and having the willingness to work with and heal these aspects of yourself.

Second, being "good with yourself" means having a degree of self-*acceptance*. Rather than judging, acceptance means realizing that all behavior stems from a positive intent, and healing begins with learning to be friendly with all parts of yourself. It means appreciating that each aspect of yourself can be both a blessing and a potential curse, a strength and a weakness. Acceptance means finding empathy for others by being gentle with yourself.

Third, being "good with yourself" means taking *action*, having an orientation toward results. *Action* means a life-long commitment to continually change, to learn, to grow, to evolve. Growth is a combination of self-awareness and risk-taking. Action means not trying to do everything that everyone expects of you in the way they expect it but to feel comfortable enough with yourself to take the necessary risks that move you out of your comfort zone. You no longer have to create an illusion that you are any further along than you are. Being "good with yourself" means being comfortable enough to be who you are and keep growing. Being "good with yourself" means remembering what *enough* actually feels like.

Remember Humility: From Your Greatest Depth to Greatest Heights

Humility is an honest evaluation of conditions as they are. You can only be humble if you are at peace with yourself and honest with yourself. When you see people acting in an abusive, arrogant, or disrespectful, demeaning way toward others, their behavior is a symptom of their own lack of self-confidence. People who have been hurt, hurt others. They need to put someone else down in order to feel good about themselves.

Authenticity is a steady, confident presence, a sense of self, being an integrated person by attending to work, family, personal relationships, and your health. Humility means you feel good enough about yourself, that you don't care who gets the credit. Humility is about making a decision that all blame is not only a waste of time; it's also a defense against taking personal responsibility to do something about your situation. In order to honestly evaluate conditions as they are, you have to be open to learning, to know that you never accomplish anything alone, that everyone has something to teach you and every experience is a learning opportunity.

So why all of the emphasis on identity and authenticity and the inner work when you may just want to be a better leader? If you have ever been to a banking convention, you will have inevitably heard the "Willie Sutton Quote." The story goes that Willie Sutton, the infamous bank robber in the early 1900s, was finally captured. In his trial, the judge allegedly asked him, "So, Willie Sutton, before I send you to jail I have one question for you. Why did you rob banks?"

Without much hesitation, Willie responded, "Because that's where the money is."

So why investigate the nature of your identity in relation to your leadership capacity? Because that's where the money is. Investigating identity—understanding, discovering, and strengthening your authentic presence—gets to the very heart, the source of leadership, of impacting others.

Authentic leadership, or values-aligned-leading that emerges from a strong identity—with *presence* rather than *pressure*—is and was well understood by all the great leaders of our time—Mahatma Gandhi, Nelson Mandela, Eleanor Roosevelt. These kinds of leaders teach us that a leader's most persuasive leadership tool is who we *are*. Each of these leaders—and others that preceded and followed them—had their own personal journeys to prepare them to step into their leadership work. In this way, leadership emerges from within. It's not an act; it is your life, a way of being, a life-long process. Leadership behavior develops naturally once this internal foundation of authentic presence has been laid. If it isn't, mere technique can never compensate.

That's leadership: Authentic leaders give you the confidence and the permission to be true to yourself. They create an environment where being true to yourself is not inconsistent with being true to the organization, to the boss, or the positional leader. As a leader, the more I am willing to acknowledge and accept that I am an authentic person, just like you, then I can admit and own up to my frailties, my inexperience, and my mistakes. I am not expecting myself to be perfect, so I am certainly not going to be expecting you to be perfect either. We are in this thing called the human journey together.

Reside in Your Own True Nature

From the Sufi tradition comes a story about a pregnant tigress who comes upon a flock of goats, and, being hungry, chases after them in search of a meal. She pounces upon them and with all the energy that she expended, brings on the birth of her little one—as well as her own death.

The goats, meanwhile, scattered, and after returning to their grazing place found the just-born little tiger and his dead mother. With very strong parental instincts, they adopted the little guy, who grew up amid the flock. Surrounded by goats as his only models, he began to believe he was one. He learned to bleat, and he learned to eat grass, even if the grass, with all its cellulose, turned out to be very hard on his digestive system. As a vegetarian tiger with only the capacity to say *Maaaaa*, he was a pretty miserable specimen of his species.

One day a male tiger came upon the flock, and as he chased them, they scattered, leaving only the young tiger to stand helplessly and bleat.

"What are you doing living with these goats?" the elder tiger asked this skinny little feline.

The little tiger responded with, *Maaaaa,* and started nibbling grass in a kind of embarrassed way. The big fellow was mortified and swatted him back and forth a few times as the little tiger continued to bleat and eat grass. Then he took him by the neck and carried him to a pond. There was no wind blowing. In the stillness, the young tiger was told to look into the pond. And for the first time in his young life, he saw his face.

As the young tiger looked into the water, the big fellow gave a roar. In response to the elder's request to roar, the young tiger only blurted out, *Maaaaa*. And the older tiger responded, "No, you have to roar like a true tiger!" as he again showed him how.

After several attempts, the young fellow was able to open his throat and roar fully with the sound of a tiger. That deep, dark roar, is what the Sufis would say is equal to one human being who discovers his true nature.

As leaders, we have a basic decision in life. Do we want to live like goats or do we want to live the lives we are destined for? The decision to live like a tiger involves the deepening of consciousness, the transcending of all denial to find out who is it that we really are. Then, through the strength and courage of this presence, gently guide those you serve to the water where their true nature is reflected and remembered. This is the real work of authentic leadership.

Acknowledgments

I owe a great deal of gratitude to the authentic leaders I have learned from in the past thirty plus years. Were it not for these principled and courageous men and women, there would be no book, and more importantly, my vision for authentic leadership presence and practices would not exist. These remarkable leaders remind us that individuals with a vision and a commitment to make a difference can be an incredible force for good in the world.

You, the reader, have also inspired me on this life-long authentic leadership journey.

Many friends and colleagues have helped shape my thinking and the writing of this book. Their wisdom, perspective, and caring, authentic presence are felt in my work and in the pages in this book. I'm a better person for having these people in my life. I would like to thank Marg Barr, Geoff Bellman, Pat Copping, Vincent Deberry, Rick Elliott, Jim Fries, Larry Malazdrewicz, Tim O'Connor, Corey Olynik, Chris Saciuk, Mark Szabo, and Julianna Veldtman.

Jim Reger, thank you for the impact of your presence in my life. It was your original inspiration and encouragement that set me on this path of integrating authenticity into my leadership development programs many years ago.

Ashis Gupta at Gondolier, thank you for believing in this project.

Thank you to my editor, Brad Brinkworth, for helping me define the vision for this book, and for spending countless hours helping to craft and shape it to make it what it is.

George Masselam, thank you for your rare and precious friendship. Your support in my life and in this project is valued and appreciated beyond words.

Jeff Lichty, thanks for your friendship and support of this project. Your guidance in the integration of the physical practice of yoga in the work of strengthening authentic presence has been pivotal.

Mellissa, Hayley, and Chandra, you continue to be a source of inspiration in my life. You will always be my teachers.

And of course, thank you to my absolutely amazing wife, Val. Were it not for your healing, ever-patient, unconditional loving presence in my life, I would not be the person I am today, much less completed this book.

About the Author

David Irvine, The Leader's Navigator™, is one of the world's most respected thought leaders, speakers, mentors, and executive coaches on the topic of authentic leadership. He resides with his wife in Cochrane, Alberta, in the foothills of the Rocky Mountains.

Contact us for a list of David Irvine' keynote presentations, workshops, retreats, coaching opportunities, books, podcasts, and audio programs.

Phone: 1-866-621-7008
Email: info@davidirvine.com
Website: www.davidirvine.com
Twitter: @DavidJIrvine
Facebook: David Irvine & Associates
LinkedIn: David Irvine